THE HOGAN GUIDE

Interpretation and Use of Hogan Inventories

Robert Hogan

Joyce Hogan

Rodney Warrenfeltz

CONTENTS

ACKNOWLEDGMENTS

It is difficult to describe the challenge of putting together a guide that effectively covers the interpretive information related to the Hogan inventories. The accumulated knowledge that went into this effort spans four decades and includes countless assessments, discussions with colleagues, and feedback sessions with our customers. We should begin by thanking all of those people who have willingly given of their time to help us build an interpretive knowledge base that is specific, behavioral, and most importantly, the most accurate in the personality assessment arena.

Five groups that we would like to specifically acknowledge for their contribution to this guide include the Hogan Consulting Team, our international affiliates, our customers, our consulting partners, and our colleagues.

The Hogan Consulting Team played a key role in creating this guide. Each of our consultants made specific contributions to various chapters and they all provided critical feedback and recommendations throughout the editing process.

Our international affiliates have been a constant source of interpretive information and ideas regarding our inventories. They have caused us to think more globally and helped us better understand the use and interpretation of inventory results throughout the world. Because of their efforts, our inventories are becoming the global standard for personality assessment.

Our customers and consulting partners deserve a large part of the credit for the accuracy we have been able to achieve with our inventory interpretations. Over the years, they have participated in hundreds of validation studies and helped us collect the criteria data necessary to develop industry leading interpretive reports. They have been loyal, dedicated advocates of personality assessment and have given us the means to build a world-class organization.

We also would like to thank our colleagues for their willingness to review this guide and provide us with their thoughts and ideas. Their contributions helped us make significant improvements to the final version of this guide.

Finally, we would like to thank Kelly Thomas for her dedication, drive, and energy in helping us make this guide a reality.

Many thanks to those who helped!

Robert Hogan   Joyce Hogan   Rodney Warrenfeltz

August 2007

THE AUTHORS

Robert T. Hogan, Ph.D.
President, Hogan Assessment Systems

Robert Hogan, Ph.D., President of Hogan Assessment Systems, is an international authority on personality assessment, leadership, and organizational effectiveness.

Dr. Hogan received his Ph.D. from the University of California, Berkeley, specializing in personality assessment. He was McFarlin Professor and Chair of the Department of Psychology at The University of Tulsa for 17 years. Prior to that, Dr. Hogan was Professor of Psychology and Social Relations at The Johns Hopkins University. He received a number of research and teaching awards.

Dr. Hogan is the author of more than 300 journal articles, chapters, and books. His book *Personality and the Fate of Organizations* was published by Lawrence Erlbaum Associates in June 2006. The 167-page book offers a systematic account of the nature of personality, showing how to use personality to understand organizations, to staff teams, and to evaluate, select, deselect, and train people. He is the coeditor of the *Handbook of Personality Psychology* and author of the Hogan Personality Inventory.

He is widely credited with demonstrating how personality factors influence organizational effectiveness in a variety of areas—ranging from organizational climate and leadership to selection and effective team performance. Dr. Hogan is a fellow of the American Psychological Association and the Society for Industrial/Organizational Psychology.

Joyce C. Hogan, Ph.D.
Vice President, Hogan Assessment Systems

Joyce Hogan, Ph.D., specializes in employment test development and validation as well as human performance. Dr. Hogan is responsible for the development of assessment products and directs research projects to validate customized employment testing programs.

Dr. Hogan received her Ph.D. from the University of Maryland. From 1975 to 1982, Dr. Hogan taught and was Senior Research Scientist at The Johns Hopkins University. From 1982 to 1997, Dr. Hogan served in many capacities at The University of Tulsa. From 1982 to 1985, she was Assistant Professor in the

Department of Research, and in 1984 was promoted to Chair of the Department of Research, a position she held through 1985. For the next 10 years, Dr. Hogan served as Associate Professor in the Department of Psychology, and in 1995 was promoted to Professor of Psychology, a position she held until 1997. Since 1997, Dr. Hogan has dedicated herself to assessment development and research for Hogan Assessment Systems, the firm she and her husband, Dr. Robert Hogan, cofounded.

Dr. Hogan has performed pioneering research on problems in the development of job profiles, job families, and test transportability for various occupations. She is an international authority on personnel selection and serves as a consultant and expert witness regarding employment discrimination for the U.S. Department of Justice. She is recognized nationally as an expert in human performance and served as editor of the *Human Performance* journal from 1994 to 2000. In 1991, Dr. Hogan was named fellow of the American Psychological Association.

Dr. Hogan has authored more than 100 published research articles, chapters, and books. She serves on the editorial boards of *Journal of Applied Psychology*, *Human Performance*, *Human Factors*, and *International Journal of Selection and Assessment*.

Rodney B. Warrenfeltz, Ph.D.
Managing Partner, Hogan Assessment Systems

Rodney Warrenfeltz, Ph.D., is a Managing Partner with Hogan Assessment Systems.

Dr. Warrenfeltz has more than 20 years of experience in executive assessment and development. He was most recently Executive Vice President and National Practice Leader for coaching and consulting services at Manchester, Inc.

Prior to working for Manchester, Dr. Warrenfeltz was Vice President at Development Dimensions International (DDI), responsible for establishing a consulting business focused on the assessment and development of executives. In this role, Dr. Warrenfeltz developed a worldwide consulting team that included 45 professionals working throughout Europe, Asia, Australia, and the United States. He designed and implemented a wide range of consulting projects, including General Motors' global leadership development program, Whirlpool's succession management system (Protégé), and PPG's high-potential development process.

Dr. Warrenfeltz has more than 100 publications and technical reports to his credit. He received his M.S. in psychology from Vanderbilt University and his Ph.D. in industrial/organizational psychology from Colorado State University.

USING THE HOGAN GUIDE

We wrote this guide to organize the vast amount of interpretive information that we have gained using our inventories over the years. It is clear to us that experience is the best teacher when it comes to interpreting Hogan inventory results, but the foundation for interpreting and using these results tends to generalize across many applications. This guide reflects the fundamentals necessary for accurate and insightful interpretations. We did not intend for this guide to be a cover-to-cover read. Rather, we intended for it to be more of a desk reference for those using our inventories.

In Part 1, we describe the origins of each inventory and the fundamentals of scale-by-scale interpretation. For those that have been through a Hogan Assessment Certification Workshop, this information will be very familiar. Scale-by-scale interpretation is the starting point for learning about our inventories. We believe that the chapters in this part of the guide will be valuable to those needing a quick way to look at specific scale interpretations or locate some effective descriptive information regarding an inventory.

In Part 2, we take a more advanced look at interpretation. We review the fundamentals of configural interpretation within and across inventories. We also have included some new ideas regarding conflict interpretation. Although most people who are skilled at interpreting our inventories have dealt with results that, on the surface, appear to conflict, this is the first time we have put into print the fundamentals for interpreting so-called conflicts. This part of the guide also includes extensive information on competency interpretation. This is perhaps the most requested area of information at Hogan Assessment Systems. Our customers want to be able to use their company's competencies while incorporating our assessments. We believe the chapters addressing the Hogan Performance Model and competency interpretation go a long way toward addressing this need.

The final part of the guide concerns the fundamentals of feedback and development. Over the past 10 years, we have seen enormous growth in the use of inventories for identifying and developing leaders. This section provides a detailed description of the best practices we have learned about development and personality. It also contains prescriptive information for those considering the use of our inventories for development.

In conclusion, this guide represents the comprehensive source for interpretive information about the Hogan inventories. We hope that it will meet a growing need among our customers for a reliable desk reference that can be called upon to augment their knowledge and solidify their confidence with our inventories. For those interested in going beyond the guide, we have provided a closing chapter on additional resources and support available through Hogan Assessment Systems. Welcome to our world of interpreting Hogan inventories.

PART 1

UNDERSTANDING HOGAN INVENTORIES

CHAPTER 1

INTRODUCTION

*According to the political scientists, the fundamental question in human affairs is, "Who **shall** rule?" As psychologists—who are less infused with the spirit of realpolitik—we believe the question is, "Who **should** rule?"*

– Robert Hogan

OVERVIEW

The key to success in business is money and people. Personality psychology is about people—it is about the nature of human nature. Some understanding of human nature and the ability to measure its key components would seem to offer a huge advantage to applied psychologists. Despite its practical significance, personality has lived a troubled existence in academic psychology. The topic was popular after WWII; however, the 1960s brought the response set (or faking) controversy, which challenged the foundation of personality assessment. Then the 1970s and 1980s brought Walter Mischel's revolution, which taught us that we cannot measure personality because it does not exist—people's actions are not determined by their personalities, but by "situational factors." Situational factors are like dark matter in physics—they are strange, undefined, invisible forces that exist "out there," which capture us and then make us do their bidding.

In the 1990s, personality made a comeback in industrial psychology. The comeback was fueled by the news that well-constructed measures of personality predict job performance almost as well as measures of cognitive ability, but with no adverse impact. The critics went silent for about 10 years, but now they are back (c.f. Schmitt, 2004). They argue that claims for the validity of personality measures have been vastly overstated and that the data reveal only trivial relationships between these measures and occupational performance.

Despite persistent attacks on the efficacy of measuring personality as a means of predicting job performance, the empirical data clearly demonstrate the value of such measures when they are properly constructed and implemented in organizational settings. Hogan and Holland (2003) conducted the most definitive study to date supporting this position. Their findings, based on an exhaustive meta-analytic evaluation of 43 studies addressing the validity of personality measures in predicting job performance outcomes, offer three important conclusions:

1. Well-constructed measures of personality do indeed predict important aspects of job performance.
2. The relationships between personality measures and job performance were found to be robust across a wide range of industries and jobs.
3. The relationships improved as the quality of the predictor and criterion measures improved.

These findings, in conjunction with a plethora of research conducted by Hogan Assessment Systems (HAS) over the past 25 years, serve as a backdrop for this guide. Our purpose here is to provide users of Hogan inventories with a definitive guide for interpreting the results of our inventories. We will begin with a brief overview of our concept of personality and its role in predicting job performance outcomes. We will then systematically cover interpretative information derived from our three primary inventories:

- Hogan Personality Inventory (HPI) – A state-of-the-art measure of normal personality, based on the Five-Factor Model (FFM)
- Hogan Development Survey (HDS) – An inventory designed to measure career-derailing tendencies including 11 patterns of behavior that impede work relationships, hinder productivity, or limit overall career potential
- Motives, Values, Preferences Inventory (MVPI) – A measure based on 80 years of research regarding motivational constructs that reveals a person's core values, which are key to work and life satisfaction

We will conclude with a discussion of various methods to arrive at configural interpretations (or interpretations involving combinations of scales across inventories) and techniques for conveying interpretive information during an assessment feedback session.

PERSONALITY PSYCHOLOGY

Personality psychology concerns the nature of human nature. It answers three general questions: (1) How and in what ways are we all alike? (2) How and in what ways are we all different? (3) Why do we (as individuals) do what we do?

Why should anyone be interested in personality psychology? There are three reasons. First, because other people are the most consequential, helpful, and also dangerous parts of the environment in which we live, it seems sensible to have some understanding of these (often) dark forces. Second, without a theory of some sort, it is difficult to make sense out of the world. All of us have more or less well-articulated theories of human nature, but these theories are almost surely in need of some maintenance and even repair. We need to understand personality in order to make sense of the personal, business, and political worlds in which we live. And third, true change depends on understanding how the world works. If we want to improve our lives, relationships, careers, business organizations, or societies, we need as accurate a view of human nature as we can devise.

What Is Personality?

In everyday language, the word *personality* has two meanings, and these meanings serve very different purposes. For the sake of rational conversation, it is important to keep the two meanings distinct. On the one hand, there is the

(1) identity

"actor's view" of personality; this is personality "from the inside" and it concerns *the you that you know*—the person you think you are, your hopes, dreams, aspirations, values, fears, and theories about how to get along, get ahead, and find meaning (McAdams, 1993). On the other hand, there is "the observer's view" of personality; this is personality "from the outside" and it concerns *the you that we know*—the person we think you are, based on your overt behavior. *(2)*

reputation

There are several points to be noted about these two aspects of personality. First, we refer to the actor's view of personality as your **identity**, whereas we refer to the observer's view of personality as your **reputation**. Your identity is the story you tell yourself and others about you; it is the generic part that you play during social interaction. Your reputation is the summary evaluation of your past performances during interaction as shared by the members of your community. Second, the concepts of identity and reputation serve very different functions in everyday language. We use reputation to describe your past performances or to predict your future performance—reputations are used to describe or predict behavior. We use identity to explain your behavior. Reputation concerns what you do, and identity concerns why you do it.

Thoughtful nonpsychologists have always understood the point of distinguishing between personality from the inside and from the outside. For example, Richard Jenkyns (2003), Professor of Classics at Oxford University, makes the following observation in a review of Janet Browne's (2002) magnificent biography of Charles Darwin: "So, after a thousand pages, do we know the man? Browne speculates very little about [Darwin's] interior life. There are few cases, probably, in which we can know much about a person's inner being—biographers who purport to know about such matters are usually impertinent or fanciful or both. Still, Browne gives us a vivid sense of what can be legitimately described: how he appeared to his family, his friends, and the public at large" (p. 31). The point is that we can talk knowledgably about reputation, but our observations about another person's identity are typically speculative at best.

A third point to remember about identity and reputation concerns their relative degrees of verifiability or truth value. Identity, once again, concerns the you that you know. Sigmund Freud, the Viennese psychiatrist and founder of psychoanalysis, would say that the you that you know is hardly worth knowing. This is because we invent ourselves; our identity is a story that we made up in *(1)* order to give us a part to play in social interaction. It is empirically well-established that peoples' self-stories are only tangentially related to their past performances and, in many cases, are radically discrepant with them. Identities are quite hard to study in a rigorous fashion, largely because they are so subjective and even fanciful. In contrast, reputation is easy to study—we

(2)

simply ask the peer community to describe an actor using a standardized reporting format. Such descriptions typically show a high degree of agreement across the persons who provide them, and such descriptions tend to be very stable over long periods of time. Moreover, because the best predictor of future behavior is past behavior, and because reputations reflect past behavior, reputations are the best single predictors of a person's future behavior.

Extensive research conducted over the past 100 years shows there is a very stable and even universal structure to reputations. Regardless of the culture in which a person lives, or the language that his/her peer community speaks, all reputations can be characterized in terms of five broad themes— Self-confidence, Extraversion, Agreeableness, Conscientiousness, and Curiosity. Personality psychologists refer to this finding as the FFM (Wiggins, 1996). The development of the FFM has had a profound effect on personality research since about 1990. We will discuss the FFM in more detail in Chapter 2.

Finally, no matter how fanciful or contrived a person's identity may be, it is the core and bedrock of each person's psychological being and the primary means by which each person guides and interprets his/her life. And this fact leads to an interesting paradox. Although actors are primarily concerned about their identities, observers are more concerned about the actors' reputations. Affection and status are granted on the basis of reputation—people hire us, fire us, marry us, loan us money, and otherwise support us based on our reputations.

Why Is Personality Important?

Personality is important for many reasons. Here we discuss the importance of personality for performance in a job or organization. A couple of simple questions clarify why personality is important with respect to performance. Before hiring someone, would you like to know if that person is easy to manage, hardworking, cooperative, good with customers, thorough, innovative, and quick to learn your business? Before investing in the development of someone, would you like to know more about his/her strengths, weaknesses, preferred learning methods, and even core values and motivations? Personality is central to answering these questions.

Let us begin by considering the concept of "fit." The degree to which an individual is a fit with the requirements of a job or an organization will largely dictate success or failure. A person who is successful in a sales job will typically possess an outgoing, relationship-building, interpersonal style. He or she may also be driven and willing to take risks—all characteristics found in a personality profile. In contrast, a successful air traffic controller should be even-tempered, conscientious, and avoid being distracted by social interactions. The contrast between these different jobs illustrates the concept of "job fit" and why personality determines a person's fit to one of these jobs. Would you want the landing of your next flight directed by someone with the personality of a great salesperson?

Similarly, "organizational fit" can be critical in determining a person's success. Some organizations need individuals who are creative, willing to take risks, and careless about following routine, well-structured processes—an advertising firm might be one example. Other organizations live and breathe practicality, process adherence, and consistent execution of the details—a freight transportation company would be a good example. The components of personality related to satisfaction in specific work environments would be quite different for these two organizational examples. That is not to say that one needs to be a perfect organizational fit; however, as the degree of fit increases, so does the probability of success.

The field of leadership is another arena for understanding why personality is important. Estimates for the rate of management derailment or leadership failure range as high as 7 in 10, and that ratio shows no signs of declining. The following are some of the reasons why leaders fail:

- Inability to adapt to the demands of a new position
- Inability to think strategically
- Inability to develop good working relationships with key stakeholders
- Inability to build and maintain a team
- Inability to execute plans and drive change
- Inability to get results

All of these reasons for failure are rooted in personality. For example, the "inability to develop good working relationships with key stakeholders" begins with poor interpersonal skills. McGovern et al. (2001), in a study of 100 executives who participated in formal coaching, found that 35% of the challenges these executives had were interpersonal, which reduced their ability to build and maintain relationships. Interpersonal skills are found in the Surgency and Agreeableness factors of the FFM.

The only conclusion that can be drawn from data such as these is that personality plays a central role in determining successful performance in a job or organization. It shapes a person's ability to be successful in specific jobs. It highlights the reasons why a person might enjoy one type of work environment over another. It even sets the stage for a person to build and maintain a high-performing team, which is at the heart of leadership. The remainder of this guide moves beyond the importance of personality—we believe that question has been put to rest. We focus the remaining chapters on exploring

Hogan assessment tools. The information that is covered provides insights into the ways these tools solve practical problems associated with enhancing successful performance in a job or organization.

CHAPTER 2

HOGAN PERSONALITY INVENTORY

For every manager learning how to be a better leader, there are 10 employees trying to figure out how to make it stop.

– Scott Adams

The Hogan Personality Inventory (HPI) is a measure of normal personality. It is designed for use in personnel selection, individualized assessment, and career-related decision making. It provides detailed information regarding what we call the "bright side" of personality: characteristics that facilitate or inhibit a person's ability to get along with others and to achieve his/her educational and occupational goals.

FOUNDATION FOR THE HPI

Before considering the interpretation of the HPI, it is important to understand two areas of work that provided a foundation for its development—the Five-Factor Model (FFM) and the California Psychological Inventory (CPI). The development of the FFM (c.f. Digman, 1990; Goldberg, 1992; John, 1990, p. 72; McCrae & Costa, 1987), based on 50 years of factor analytic research on the structure of peer ratings (c.f. Thurstone, 1934; Tupes & Christal, 1961; Norman, 1963), suggests that we think about and describe one another in terms of five broad themes (see Table 1). This structure is a useful starting point for inventory construction. It is useful not because it reflects underlying psychic truth, but because it is a systematic method for classifying individual differences in social behavior. In fact, the evidence suggests that all existing multidimensional personality inventories can be described, with little difficulty, in terms of these five dimensions (Wiggins & Pincus, 1992). Consequently, the FFM has become, in a sense, the paradigm for modern research in personality assessment.

Table 1: Five-Factor Model

Factor	Description
I. Surgency *extraversion*	The degree to which a person needs social attention and social interaction
II. Agreeableness	The degree to which a person needs pleasant and harmonious relations with others
III. Conscientiousness	The degree to which a person is willing to comply with conventional rules, norms, and standards
IV. Emotional Stability *self confidence*	The degree to which a person experiences the world as threatening and beyond his/her control
V. Openness to Experience *curiosity*	The degree to which a person needs intellectual stimulation, change, and variety

Although the FFM is a logical starting point for inventory construction, the model also has some important limitations. For example, some significant dimensions of personality (i.e., masculinity-femininity) are not included in the FFM (e.g., Hough, 1992; Kamp & Hough, 1986). In addition, the FFM concerns the structure of observer ratings; the structure of self-ratings is necessarily more complex (J. Hogan & R. Hogan, 1991). Moreover, modern research on social cognition suggests that when we first meet another person, we automatically categorize that person in terms of his/her gender, age, ethnicity, and status. It is only after we know the person somewhat better, that is, after talking for a minute or two, that we begin to make the distinctions implied by the FFM. Finally, although people can describe themselves in terms of the FFM, they probably do not normally think of themselves in these terms. Rather, they tend to think about themselves in terms of their values, goals, aspirations, and fears.

The original model for the HPI is the CPI (Gough, 1975). We worked with the CPI for more than 25 years because we agree with its measurement goals. In brief, the CPI is designed to assess folk concepts—aspects of social behavior that are cross-culturally significant and that nonpsychologists intuitively understand. In addition, the CPI is not designed to measure traits. The most important feature of the CPI, we believe, is that it was designed to predict important social outcomes. Consequently, in the development of the CPI (and in the development of the HPI), formal psychometric considerations were used to facilitate prediction; they were not ends in themselves.

Both the FFM and the CPI were important influences in the development of the HPI. The FFM provided a useful framework for considering what should be measured. The CPI provided a perspective on measurement goals that was rooted in predicting important social outcomes. Predicting performance outcomes has been an overarching goal for everything we have done in the development of the HPI.

INITIAL DEVELOPMENT

The HPI began in the late 1970s as a project in a graduate class in personality assessment. The two fundamental questions in personality assessment concern what to measure and how to measure it. We believed the literature on the FFM provided an answer to the first question. With regard to the second question, we believed that Hase and Goldberg (1967) were correct when they argued that there is little to choose among the various methods of scale construction as long as the end product is evaluated in terms of empirical validity. We suggested to our graduate class that if the FFM is correct, and if the Hase and Goldberg argument is correct, then we have solid guidelines for constructing an inventory of normal personality, that is, we know what to measure and how to measure it. As for the inventory items themselves, socioanalytic theory provided a guide for item writing: taking each of the major dimensions of reputation in turn, one should ask what sorts of self-presentational behaviors might lead to high or low standing on that dimension as evaluated by others.

Consider Factor V of the FFM, Openness to Experience. Persons with high scores on this factor seem bright, sophisticated, and aesthetically oriented. This suggests that an Openness scale should contain items about the degree to which a person enjoys chess, opera, and trendy cuisine. From a socioanalytic perspective, we wrote items to reflect the standard FFM dimensions (c.f. Goldberg, 1992) using the foregoing algorithm. In the process, we made three discoveries. First, the standard FFM dimension called Surgency has two components that are conceptually unrelated. One component is Sociability, which concerns impulsivity and the need for social interaction or a lack of shyness. The other component is Ambition, which concerns a desire for status, upward mobility, power, recognition, and achievement. Clearly there are shy people who are ambitious—Richard Nixon—and sociable people who are lazy—Falstaff. Second, we found that the FFM dimension called Openness to Experience has two components: one component concerns an interest in culture and ideas, and the other concerns academic performance. Our third discovery was that each of the primary scales we created for the HPI breaks down into a group of related subthemes. For example, the Adjustment scale contains themes about anxiety, guilt, complaints, moodiness, and irritability. Because the items in these subthemes clustered together, we called them Homogenous Item Composites (Zonderman, 1980) or HICs.

We wrote items for HICs within each of the scales and pilot tested the items using undergraduate samples. We retained items that correlated highly with the other items on a HIC and discarded items that did not. We continued this process until we arrived at a reasonably coherent set of 45 HICs containing 420 items distributed across six scales.

Between 1979 and 1984, we assessed more than 1,700 people, including students, hospital workers, U.S. Navy enlisted personnel, clerical workers, truck drivers, sales representatives, police officers, hourly and professional staff in a large insurance corporation, school administrators, and incarcerated felons. The ages in these samples ranged from 18 to 60. There were 470 women and 1,159 men, 726 Whites and 232 Blacks. Some demographic data were missing. About 20% of the participants were college educated. It is important to point out that the initial development work focused on adult workers. To date, the HPI is still one of the only measures of normal personality that was developed on working adults.

LATER DEVELOPMENT

HIC = homogeneous item composites.

In the spring of 1984, we carefully refined the internal consistency of each HIC. In the process, we shortened the inventory to 225 items on 43 HICs; we retained 85 unscored items for research purposes, so that the HPI test booklet contained 310 items. Between 1984 and 1992, we tested more than 11,000 people, primarily employed adults in organizations around the country. In this sample, the ages ranged from 18 to 67 years. There were 7,061 men and 3,465 women, 5,610 Whites, 1,036 Blacks, 348 Hispanics, 231 Asians, and 253 Native Americans. Some demographic data were missing. About 20% of the participants in this sample were college educated. We conducted more than 50 validity studies in various organizations, and we gathered matched sets of data with other tests, inventories, and observer descriptions.

In 1990, we developed a scale called Unlikely Virtues. This scale was designed to identify individuals who try to create an excessively favorable impression on the HPI by manipulating their responses. After working with this scale for two years, we decided to delete it; three reasons prompted this decision. First, the scale rarely disqualified a profile because the base rate for faking in the general population is low. Second, in those cases where a score on Unlikely Virtues raised a question about faking, the respondent was found to be the kind of person who in fact would get a high score on Unlikely Virtues—he/she was cautious, conforming, and moralistic. Finally, our customers, the persons in organizations who use the test to make personnel decisions, never understood the point of the scale. As a result, it created more problems in individualized assessment than it solved. The core of the Unlikely Virtues scale now appears on the Prudence scale in the form of a HIC called Virtuous.

In the spring of 1992, using all our archival data, we conducted a number of factor analyses of the HIC correlation matrix. We concluded that there are about eight factors underlying the matrix. These eight factors formed the basis of the present HPI scales. A few HICs had substantial loadings on two factors. We used this information to balance the number of items on each scale; that is, if a HIC had nearly the same loading on two factors, and one scale was defined by fewer HICs than the other, we assigned the HIC to the smaller factor so as to balance the scale length. The 1992 HPI (revised edition) contains seven primary scales and a validity scale. These scales contain a total of 206 items arranged in 41 HICs. No items overlap on HICs, and no HICs overlap on scales.

KAIZEN PSYCHOMETRICS

Throughout the 1990s, we conducted a steady stream of validation studies and implemented the HPI across a wide range of organizations in both employee selection and development situations. During this period, we began to formulate an approach to inventory development that we labeled Kaizen Psychometrics. This approach was largely in response to what we felt was a critical business need if an inventory was going to withstand the test of time. Kaizen Psychometrics refers to continuously improving an inventory to ensure its psychometric properties remain stable over time and to ensure that it reflects the prevailing research-based evidence. This approach to inventory development is illustrated by our efforts to improve the HPI over the past few years and the work we have planned for the future.

In 2002, we began a systematic review of the psychometric properties of the HPI. We had three major concerns. First, over time, the average scores on several HPI scales had begun to creep up so that average scores on certain scales in 2002 were somewhat higher than average scores on those scales in 1992. We were certain that the same was true for our competitors' tests, but also realized it was a problem that needed fixing. Second, two HPI scales (Ambition and Interpersonal Sensitivity) were badly skewed. For example, a person who missed one item on the Interpersonal Sensitivity scale would be in the 83rd percentile, a person who missed four items would be in the 20th percentile, and so on. This meant the scales were doing a very poor job discriminating among people at the high end and a good job discriminating among people at the low end. Because we do a lot of work with high-level managers and executives, it is essential that the HPI be able to discriminate well in the upper score ranges. And third, as a result of a government contract, very large numbers of people were completing the HPI, and it was only a matter of time before the items themselves were memorized and then sold by test takers.

The solution to these three problems involved extensive item analyses to determine the source of the problem. Using item analytic methods and our extensive archival databases, we have been able to refine the HPI in two important ways. First, we fine-tuned the inventory so that HPI norms now closely approximate norms from the late 1980s. Second, we fixed the skew problem so that the score distributions on all scales closely approximate normal distributions. Subsequent simulations indicate that we have resolved these issues with no impact on test validity or test discrimination vis-à-vis minorities.

Meanwhile, our competitors' tests use the items and scoring procedures they developed 30 to 60 years ago.

SUMMARY OF THE CURRENT STRUCTURE OF THE HPI

As we have developed the HPI over the last 30 years, we have attended to the structural integrity of the inventory. In the next version of the HPI technical manual, we will outline the latest research concerning the HPI since the 1996 version. Although we have a number of updates planned (see Future Development Planned for the HPI), much of the new data closely resemble those presented in the 1996 version of the technical manual. This suggests that the underlying structure of the HPI has remained the same, despite the item-level changes.

FUTURE DEVELOPMENT PLANNED FOR THE HPI

We have carefully reviewed the existing HPI validity data and the new literature on the structure of personality. This literature confirms the current seven scale structure of the HPI, but suggests two changes. First, the Inquisitive and Learning Approach scales probably should be combined into one general measure of cognitive style. Second, there seems to be an additional dimension somewhere between the Prudence and Interpersonal Sensitivity scales. These two scales have their particular content (rule following and perceptiveness, respectively), but share a common component of social appropriateness. The data suggest this theme of social appropriateness should be a stand-alone scale.

Therefore, the next version of the HPI will also have seven scales: Resilience (Adjustment), Ambition, Sociability, Interpersonal Sensitivity, Prudence, Openness, and Restraint (the social appropriateness dimension). There will be the same number of HICs on each scale, and each HIC will contain the same number of items, bringing a nice degree of symmetry to the structure of the inventory (some reviewers have complained about the "knobbly" structure of the current HPI).

GENERAL INTERPRETATION GUIDELINES FOR THE HPI

- Interpretation of HPI results is job specific. Scores that are more successful in one job may be detrimental in another job. As such, there is no such thing as a "good" personality.

- Because HPI interpretation is job specific, higher (or lower) scores are not necessarily better. There are positive and negative characteristics associated with both higher and lower scores.

- Scores above the 65th percentile are considered High, between the 36th and 64th percentile Average, and below the 35th percentile Low.

- Extremely high (>90%) or low scores (<10%) can hinder performance.

- Multiple scales and HICs are used to make interpretations.

- The validity scale detects careless or erratic responding. When the validity score is less than 10, the HPI profile is invalid and cannot be interpreted. Ninety-eight percent of the people who take the HPI have a score of 10 or greater.

HPI FACTS

- The initial version of the HPI was developed in 1976. The test has gone through a number of revisions since that time.

- The latest version of the HPI consists of seven major scales, 41 HICs, and 206 items.

- Millions of people have taken the HPI, and the inventory has been validated in more than 400 jobs ranging from janitor to CEO.

- There are no practical gender or ethnic differences in scale scores.

- There are three major types of reports: Suitability or Selection reports, Career Management Series reports, and Leadership Forecast Series reports. The Career Management Series reports and Leadership Forecast Series reports are some of the best feedback reports in the testing industry.

- The HPI provides percentile scores for the seven major scales. These scores can be based on general population, manager, or executive norms.

- The HPI is a Level B assessment.

HPI GLOBAL PORTABILITY

Research has consistently demonstrated that the FFM effectively describes personality regardless of a person's nationality or culture. In fact, a significant portion of norm differences that have been reported with respect to cross-cultural differences in personality can be directly attributed to translation or sampling issues. We decided early in the development of the HPI that we wanted to create the global standard for assessing the FFM of personality throughout the world. We have been pursuing this objective for more than a decade now and have one of the most widely translated personality inventories in the industry. At the time of this printing, the HPI is available online in the following languages:

- Bahasa (BM)
- Brazilian Portuguese (BP)
- Castilian Spanish (CA)
- Czech (CS)
- Danish (DA)
- Dutch (NL)
- Finnish (FI)
- French Canadian (FC)
- French Parisian (FR)
- German (GR)
- Icelandic (IS)
- Italian (IT)
- Japanese (JA)
- Kenyan (KE)
- Korean (KO)
- Norwegian (NO)
- Polish (PL)
- Romanian (RO)
- Russian (RU)
- Simplified Chinese (ZH)
- Slovak (SK)
- South African (AE)
- Spanish (ES)
- Swedish (SV)
- Traditional Chinese (ZC)
- Turkish (TR)
- UK English (UK)
- US English (US)

In conjunction with our international partners, we are also rapidly expanding our norm data and validation research throughout the global marketplace. We want to offer our customers the best global research archive available in the industry that will allow the HPI to be used with confidence regardless of cultural boundaries.

CHAPTER 3

HOGAN PERSONALITY INVENTORY SCALES

Adjustment	*Confidence is contagious. So is lack of confidence.*	– Vince Lombardi
Ambition	*I am a member of a team, and I rely on the team, I defer to it and sacrifice for it, because the team, not the individual, is the ultimate champion.*	– Mia Hamm
Sociability	*The best thinking has been done in solitude.*	– Thomas Edison
Interpersonal Sensitivity	*Diplomacy is the art of saying "nice doggie" until you can find a rock.*	– Will Rogers
Prudence	*The trouble with organizing a thing is that pretty soon folks get to paying more attention to the organization than to what they're organized for.*	– Laura Ingalls
Inquisitive	*I not only use all the brains I have, but all I can borrow.*	– Woodrow Wilson
Learning Approach	*Education's purpose is to replace an empty mind with an open one.*	– Malcolm Forbes

SCALE 1 – ADJUSTMENT

Adjustment measures the degree to which a person appears calm and self-accepting, or conversely, self-critical and tense. Important areas of concern include composure, optimism, and stable moods.

Performance Implications of High Scores (65%–100%)

Positive Performance Implications: High-scoring individuals adjust to fast-paced environments and/or heavy workloads, stay calm under pressure, avoid overreacting, and do not react negatively to stress. They are even-tempered and confident in their abilities, and others will value their resiliency in urgent, stressful times. These individuals are trusting of others and tend to see the glass as half full rather than half empty.

Negative Performance Implications: Because high-scoring individuals are so calm, they may not realize when others are stressed, they may continue to pile work onto others, and they may not be empathic. They tend to view positive feedback as a means of "patting themselves on the back," and because of their high level of self-confidence, they tend to discount, or even ignore, negative feedback. High-scoring individuals also tend to ignore their mistakes and overestimate their workplace contributions.

Performance Implications of Average Scores (36%–64%)

Positive Performance Implications: Average-scoring individuals are seen as balanced and stable, and they remain calm under stress and pressure. They will also listen to others' suggestions and apply feedback from others.

Negative Performance Implications: Average-scoring individuals may tend to appear nonchalant in their approach to work tasks and priority assignments. Others may perceive them as not being truly aware of their circumstances.

Performance Implications of Low Scores (0%–35%)

Positive Performance Implications: Low-scoring individuals will be introspective, vigilant, and concerned about their work products, and will use feedback as a means to improve performance. These individuals should be responsive to coaching and feedback.

Negative Performance Implications: Low-scoring individuals are overly self-critical, tend to be their own worst enemy, and are inclined to take criticism personally. They are perceived as remorseful, unhappy, intense, edgy, stress prone, tense under pressure, anxious, and self-derogatory. Setbacks and inconveniences will annoy them and cause stress for these individuals.

Table 2 contains the behavioral implications and Homogenous Item Composites (HICs) for Adjustment.

Homogeneous item composites → (handwritten)

Table 2: Behavioral Implications and HICs for Adjustment

	Low Adjustment Score		High Adjustment Score	
	Positive Behaviors	**Negative Behaviors**	**Positive Behaviors**	**Negative Behaviors**
	• Emotionally expressive • Candid and honest • Self-aware • Open to feedback • Shows a sense of urgency	• Tense and self-critical • Moody and temperamental • Worrisome and stress prone • Easily irritated with others • Defensive about work • Takes criticism personally	• Calm and consistent • Handles stress/pressure well • Self-confident • Even-tempered and upbeat • Patient with others • Does not personalize criticism • Adapts well to changes	• Unwilling to be self-critical • Ignores negative feedback • Will not take advice • Acts indifferent to deadlines • Seems arrogant • Does not ask for input

HIC	Items	Definition	Low Score	High Score	Sample Item
Empathy	5	Absence of irritability	Irritated by the faults of others	Seems empathic	I would rather not criticize people, even when they need it
Not Anxious	4	Absence of anxiety	Anxious or tense	Seems relaxed	I am seldom tense or anxious
No Guilt	6	Absence of regret	Prone to worry about past mistakes	Does not worry about past mistakes	I rarely feel guilty about some of the things I have done
Calmness	4	Lack of emotionality	Gets emotional at times	Is calm	I keep calm in a crisis
Even-tempered	5	Not moody or irritable	Is temperamental or moody	Is even-tempered	I rarely lose my temper
No Complaints	5	Positive attitude toward performance	Complains about many issues	Does not complain	I rarely complain about anything
Trusting	3	Not suspicious of others	Questions others' intentions	Trusts others	People really care about one another
Good Attachment	5	Good family relationships	Hostile toward authority	Has positive attitude toward authority	No matter what happened I felt my parents loved me

SCALE 2 – AMBITION

Ambition measures the degree to which a person seems socially self-confident, leaderlike, competitive, and energetic. Important areas of concern include taking initiative, being competitive, and seeking leadership roles.

Performance Implications of High Scores (65%–100%)

Positive Performance Implications: High-scoring individuals tend to be leaderlike, energetic, driven, competitive, and focused on achieving results and success. They will also take initiative, be persistent when completing a task, and are eager to advance in the organization. These individuals are self-confident, comfortable when presenting their ideas in front of groups, and will lead others to focus on major business goals.

Negative Performance Implications: High-scoring individuals may tend to compete with their peers or subordinates to facilitate their own advancement. They may assume they have all the answers and may not seek others' input when strategizing or generating ideas. These individuals will become restless in dead-end jobs.

Performance Implications of Average Scores (36%–64%)

Positive Performance Implications: Average-scoring individuals are seen as relatively ambitious, reasonably hardworking, and good team players. Although they are not driven by status concerns, they normally do not mind moving into positions of authority, and they will be supportive of team efforts to complete projects.

Negative Performance Implications: Average-scoring individuals may be seen as indifferent and not very strategic in their decision making; consequently, others may have difficulty maintaining confidence in these individuals' leadership potential. Because of their tendency to not seek out challenges, they may be seen as lacking both the skill and desire to achieve high-impact results.

Performance Implications of Low Scores (0%–35%)

Positive Performance Implications: Low-scoring individuals will prefer to have tasks assigned to them and will be more comfortable following others than leading. They tend not to engage in "political behavior" and will work well in team and subordinate roles.

Negative Performance Implications: Low-scoring individuals will be perceived as unassertive, indecisive, uninterested in advancement, satisfied with the status quo, and lacking focus or a clear vision. They tend to not take initiative or action unless asked to do so and may reject offers of leadership or advancement.

Table 3 contains the behavioral implications and HICs for Ambition.

Table 3: Behavioral Implications and HICs for Ambition

Low Ambition Score		High Ambition Score	
Positive Behaviors	**Negative Behaviors**	**Positive Behaviors**	**Negative Behaviors**
• Content with position in life • Good team player • Willing to follow others • Avoids office politics	• Lacks focus or vision • Does not appear energetic • Will not take charge • Uncomfortable making public presentations	• Energetic/competitive • Self-assured and assertive • Leaderlike and mature • Effective communicator • Takes initiative • Sets high expectations • Goal- and results-oriented	• Too involved in office politics • Poor listener • Competes with others • Ruthless • Restless and forceful • Overly dominant

HIC	Items	Definition	Low Score	High Score	Sample Item
Competitive	5	Being competitive, ambitious, and persistent	Laid back	Enjoys competition and works to get ahead	I am an ambitious person
Self-confident	3	Confidence in oneself	Lacks confidence	Confident	I am a very self-confident person
Accomplishment	6	Goal attainment	Unhappy with accomplishments	Enjoys self and work	I am known as someone who gets things done
Leadership	6	Capacity for leadership	Reluctant to assume leadership roles	Willing to assume authority positions	In a group I like to take charge of things
Identity	3	Satisfaction with one's life tasks	Lacks career direction	Focused career direction	I know what I want to be
No Social Anxiety	6	Social self-confidence	Socially retiring	Confident in social settings	I do not mind talking in front of a group of people

SCALE 3 – SOCIABILITY

Sociability measures the degree to which a person seems to need and/or enjoy interactions with others. Important areas of concern include seeming talkative, socially bold, and entertaining.

Performance Implications of High Scores (65%–100%)

Positive Performance Implications: High-scoring individuals tend to be described as approachable, gregarious, outgoing, talkative, entertaining, and dynamic. They will make a positive first impression and be comfortable in high-profile positions—especially if they can be the center of attention. These individuals meet strangers well, enjoy interacting with others, and are seen as socially skilled by both peers and customers.

Negative Performance Implications: High-scoring individuals may have difficulty engaging in active listening and may frequently interrupt others. They tend to compete for center stage instead of understanding their role in the bigger picture. Over time, more reserved coworkers may see these individuals as loud and overbearing, which will reduce their effectiveness. They may be impulsive and fail to think through the consequences of their actions, risking hasty, poor decisions (check for low Prudence).

Performance Implications of Average Scores (36%–64%)

Positive Performance Implications: Average-scoring individuals are neither extroverted nor socially retiring. They will be seen by others as friendly and congenial, but not overly attention seeking. Customers and coworkers will see them as approachable, accessible, and willing to listen to their needs before offering suggestions.

Negative Performance Implications: Average-scoring individuals tend not to seek recognition for their performance; consequently, they may be viewed as lacking involvement or dedication. They tend to not voice their ideas and opinions to avoid drawing too much attention to themselves.

Performance Implications of Low Scores (0%–35%)

Positive Performance Implications: Low-scoring individuals tend not to engage in small talk, and consequently will be more business focused and task-oriented. They will enjoy and excel at solitary tasks, will be good listeners, and will not need continuous social interaction to keep them interested and satisfied with their job.

Negative Performance Implications: Low-scoring individuals tend to be described as reserved, quiet, and somewhat shy. They may also be described as cold, socially aloof, and may use their shyness as a manipulation technique. As managers, they may hold back during discussions, not give enough feedback to their staff, and seem unapproachable.

Table 4 contains the behavioral implications and HICs for Sociability.

Table 4: Behavioral Implications and HICs for Sociability

	Low Sociability Score	
Positive Behaviors	**Negative Behaviors**	
• Understanding • Independent • Able to work on his/her own • Effective listener • Strong individual relations	• Does not interact with strangers • Does not give others feedback • Does not network well • Social interactions are difficult and draining	

	High Sociability Score	
Positive Behaviors	**Negative Behaviors**	
• Outgoing and gregarious • Colorful • Talkative • Optimistic (check Ambition) • Enjoys the center of attention • Easily approachable • Enjoys working with others	• Does not enjoy working alone • Attention seeking • Loud and boisterous • May not listen well • Interruptive • Socializes unnecessarily • Demanding and outspoken (check Interpersonal Sensitivity)	

HIC	Items	Definition	Low Score	High Score	Sample Item
Likes Parties	5	Enjoys parties	Does not enjoy social gatherings	Enjoys social gatherings	I would go to a party every night if I could
Likes Crowds	4	Finds large crowds exciting	Prefers smaller groups	Enjoys large groups	Being part of a large crowd is exciting
Experience Seeking	6	Preference for variety and challenge	Unadventurous and prefers little variety	Adventurous, actively seeks out experiences	I like a lot of variety in my life
Exhibitionistic	5	Exhibitionistic tendencies	Avoids the limelight	Wants attention	I like to be the center of attention
Entertaining	4	Is witty and entertaining	Not particularly entertaining	Charming, amusing, good sense of humor	I am often the life of the party

SCALE 4 – INTERPERSONAL SENSITIVITY

Interpersonal Sensitivity measures the degree to which a person seems perceptive, tactful, and socially sensitive. Important areas of concern include being agreeable, considerate, and skilled at maintaining relationships.

Performance Implications of High Scores (65%–100%)

Positive Performance Implications: High-scoring individuals will be seen as diplomatic, trustworthy, friendly, warm, considerate, and nurturing in relationships. They tend to be perceptive, thoughtful, and cooperative team members who try to build and maintain coalitions with others. They encourage cooperation and teamwork, and foster trust and respect from their peers and staff.

Negative Performance Implications: High-scoring individuals have a propensity to avoid confrontation. They tend to be focused on getting along with others; consequently, they may not address poor performance issues in a timely manner, which can create perceptions of favoritism. Others may take advantage of this person.

Performance Implications of Average Scores (36%–64%)

Positive Performance Implications: Average-scoring individuals are seen as cooperative and friendly, but are still able to voice their opinions. These individuals will be comfortable confronting conflict and tend to do so in a tactful way.

Negative Performance Implications: Average-scoring individuals may become impatient with others' shortcomings and avoid interacting with them at a professional level.

Performance Implications of Low Scores (0%–35%)

Positive Performance Implications: Low-scoring individuals will confront nonperformance issues promptly, using a frank and direct manner. They will not be swayed easily by others' emotions or personal concerns and will be comfortable enforcing tough rules and procedures.

Negative Performance Implications: Low-scoring individuals will be seen as direct, blunt, tough, and possibly insensitive. They may be harsh, unconcerned with staff morale, and indifferent to others' feelings; consequently, others will not turn to them in times of need. These individuals tend to be socially imperceptive and say things without realizing the consequences of their words and actions (e.g., they may give orders instead of making suggestions). They may also be seen as becoming easily impatient with others' shortcomings (check for low Adjustment).

Table 5 contains the behavioral implications and HICs for Interpersonal Sensitivity.

Table 5: Behavioral Implications and HICs for Interpersonal Sensitivity

Low Interpersonal Sensitivity Score		High Interpersonal Sensitivity Score	
Positive Behaviors	Negative Behaviors	Positive Behaviors	Negative Behaviors
• Task-oriented • Will give negative feedback • Can speak his/her mind • Forthright and independent • Challenges assumptions • Will confront others	• Appears cold and tough • Critical and skeptical • Tells rather than suggests • May be argumentative • Does not build a sense of teamwork	• Friendly and engaging • Warm and agreeable • Encourages cooperation • Encourages teamwork • Earns others' trust • Gathers opinions • Builds and maintains trust	• Thin-skinned • Dependent on others' opinions • Does not handle conflict well • Slows down decision making • Does not confront performance problems

HIC	Items	Definition	Low Score	High Score	Sample Item
Easy To Live With	5	Tolerant and easygoing nature	Not always tolerant and kind-hearted	Perceived as easygoing by others	I work well with other people
Sensitive	4	Tends to be kind and considerate	Not very tactful	Tactful	I always try to see the other person's point of view
Caring	4	Interpersonal sensitivity	Does not appreciate others' needs	Perceptive and understanding	I am sensitive to other people's moods
Likes People	6	Enjoys social interaction	Socially withdrawn	Enjoys others' company	I enjoy just being with other people
No Hostility	3	Lack of hostility	Critical of others	Generally accepting	I would rather not criticize people, even when they need it

SCALE 5 – PRUDENCE

Prudence measures the degree to which a person seems conscientious, conforming, and dependable. Important areas of concern include detail orientation, being organized and planful, and following rules.

Performance Implications of High Scores (65%–100%)

Positive Performance Implications: High-scoring individuals are seen as orderly, dependable, planful, organized, reliable, and responsible. They will hold high standards for their own and others' performance and will be described as procedurally driven and attentive to details. These individuals tend to be good organizational citizens who are attentive to the rules, procedures, and details of the organization. They will gather all information necessary to make an informed decision.

Negative Performance Implications: High-scoring individuals may be overly controlling and have difficulty managing change. They will be described by others as micromanaging the details of projects and being somewhat unable to delegate tasks to others. These individuals tend to not be visionary or "big picture" oriented (check for low Inquisitive), which may reduce their overall effectiveness. Individuals with very high scores (90th percentile and above) tend to be seen as rigid and inflexible.

Performance Implications of Average Scores (36%–64%)

Positive Performance Implications: Average-scoring individuals will be seen as responsible employees who are planful, mindful of details, and able to tolerate close supervision. They are open to new experiences, ideas, and initiatives and will look beyond standard procedures to solve problems.

Negative Performance Implications: Average-scoring individuals may have difficulty prioritizing work, being flexible in uncertain situations, and knowing when they have enough information to make a decision.

Performance Implications of Low Scores (0%–35%)

Positive Performance Implications: Low-scoring individuals will be quick to act and make things happen within the organization. They will be flexible, open, and comfortable with change, innovation, and new initiatives.

Negative Performance Implications: Low-scoring individuals tend to be impulsive and careless with respect to rules, policies, and procedures. They tend to be inattentive to details, resist supervision, ignore small process steps, do not plan ahead, and rarely think through the consequences of their actions.

Table 6 contains the behavioral implications and HICs for Prudence.

Table 6: Behavioral Implications and HICs for Prudence

	Low Prudence Score		High Prudence Score	
	Positive Behaviors	**Negative Behaviors**	**Positive Behaviors**	**Negative Behaviors**
	• Flexible • Open-minded • Open to change • Nonconforming • Can be innovative and original	• Poor planner • Disorganized and careless • Easily bored • Impulsive • Impatient with details and supervision	• Dependable and reliable • Organized and thorough • Rule compliant • Conscientious and hardworking • Good organizational citizen • Plans work and anticipates changes in workload	• Resistant to change • Formal and overconforming • Micromanages others • Does not delegate well • Cannot see the "big picture" • Rigid and inflexible about rules and procedures

HIC	Items	Definition	Low Score	High Score	Sample Item
Moralistic*	5	Adhering strictly to conventional values	Prefers to set his/her own rules	Willing to follow rules	I always practice what I preach
Mastery*	4	Being hardworking	Relaxed attitude about his/her work	Concerned with doing a good job	I do my job as well as I possibly can
Virtuous*	5	Being perfectionistic	Willing to admit minor faults	Diligent and precise	I strive for perfection in everything I do
Not Autonomous	3	Concern about others' opinion of oneself	Seems independent and feedback resistant	Concerned about how others view him/her	Other people's opinions of me are important
Not Spontaneous	4	Preference for predictability	Spontaneous	Planful in his/her approach	I always know what I will do tomorrow
Impulse Control	5	Lack of impulsivity	Enjoys being impulsive	Likes to "play it safe"	I rarely do things on impulse
Avoids Trouble	5	Professed troublemaker	Takes unnecessary and negative risks	Considers actions and their consequences	When I was in school I rarely gave teachers any trouble

* Endorsement of 13 or more items across Moralistic, Mastery, and Virtuous may suggest faking positive or socially desirable responding.

SCALE 6 – INQUISITIVE

Inquisitive measures the degree to which a person is perceived as bright, creative, and interested in intellectual matters. Important areas of concern include being curious, imaginative, visionary, and easily bored.

Performance Implications of High Scores (65%–100%)

Positive Performance Implications: High-scoring individuals tend to be imaginative, have many ideas, and are resourceful problem solvers. They are often creative (check for low Prudence), adventurous, curious, open-minded, and focused on the bigger picture. These individuals are usually strategic "outside the box" thinkers who can bring a variety of ideas and solutions to the table.

Negative Performance Implications: High-scoring individuals may become easily bored without new and stimulating activities. They may have difficulty diagnosing the practicality of ideas and concepts, downplay operational or process matters, and prefer conceptualizing over implementation. Individuals with very high scores (above 90%) are often perceived as easily distractible (especially when performing tedious tasks), unpredictable, and overly passionate about topics of personal interest.

Performance Implications of Average Scores (36%–64%)

Positive Performance Implications: Average-scoring individuals will seem somewhat imaginative and have varying degrees of interest in creativity or conceptual thinking. While they will contribute to the strategic planning of the organization, they will tend to stay in the background and evaluate ideas rather than generating their own. These individuals often enjoy taking visionary ideas and translating them into workable solutions.

Negative Performance Implications: Average-scoring individuals may lose sight of the big picture and lack enthusiasm for strategic planning. Others may see them as lacking ideas and being indifferent to change and advancement in technology or operating procedures.

Performance Implications of Low Scores (0%–35%)

Positive Performance Implications: Low-scoring individuals will be seen as practical, levelheaded, process-focused, and tolerant of repetitive tasks. They tend to have a practical, hands-on approach to problem solving and are good with application and implementation.

Negative Performance Implications: Low-scoring individuals will be cautious in their acceptance of new ideas and experiences, making them uncomfortable in ambiguous situations. They tend to focus on details and operational matters and ignore the big picture.

Table 7 contains the behavioral implications and HICs for Inquisitive.

Table 7: Behavioral Implications and HICs for Inquisitive

Low Inquisitive Score		High Inquisitive Score	
Positive Behaviors	**Negative Behaviors**	**Positive Behaviors**	**Negative Behaviors**
• Follows rules and procedures • Very focused interests • Tolerates routine tasks • Not easily bored • Can focus on the details of the business	• Lacks imagination • Resists innovation • Has a narrow perspective • Ignores the big picture • Uncomfortable with ambiguity • Prefers to use familiar, instead of creative, ways to solve problems	• Imaginative and creative • Bright and inventive • Quick-witted • Understands the big picture • Open to change • Interested in new ideas • Thinks strategically about business	• Overanalyzes problems • Difficulty in making decisions • Impractical • Can become easily bored • Impatient with details • Poor implementer • Lack of tolerance for routine

HIC	Items	Definition	Low Score	High Score	Sample Item
Science Ability	5	Interest in science	Shows little interest in why things happen	Takes an interest in why things happen	I am interested in science
Curiosity	3	Curiosity about the world	Low degree of curiosity	High degree of curiosity	I have taken things apart just to see how they work
Thrill Seeking	5	Enjoyment of adventure and excitement	Not interested in stimulation/excitement	Wants challenge, stimulation, and excitement	I would like to be a race car driver
Intellectual Games	3	Enjoys intellectual games	Not interested in intellectual games	Interested in riddles and puzzles	I enjoy solving riddles
Generates Ideas	5	Ideational fluency	Does not see himself/herself as an idea generator	Good at generating new ideas	I am a quick-witted person
Culture	4	Interest in culture	Narrow interests	Wide variety of activities	I like classical music

47

SCALE 7 – LEARNING APPROACH

Learning Approach measures the degree to which a person seems to enjoy academic activities and value educational achievement for its own sake. Important areas of concern include enjoying formal education and actively staying up-to-date on business and technical issues.

Performance Implications of High Scores (65%–100%)

Positive Performance Implications: High-scoring individuals value education and view learning as an end unto itself. They tend to remain up-to-date with current trends and developments in their profession, and they will push for learning and training opportunities for themselves and their staff. They are achievement-oriented and enjoy applying their knowledge to situations.

Negative Performance Implications: High-scoring individuals may tend to focus more on learning rather than doing uninteresting, yet required, tasks. They may tend to jump on new technology crazes without verifying the organizational usefulness and may overwhelm others with their zeal for training opportunities. These individuals may also be perceived as dogmatic about the value of knowledge; consequently, they may be seen as a "know-it-all," causing them to lose credibility.

Performance Implications of Average Scores (36%–64%)

Positive Performance Implications: Average-scoring individuals will seek learning opportunities, but not with great urgency. They will encourage others to stay up-to-date on current trends, but will not make it mandatory. Although the prevailing perception is that these individuals are informed of the latest procedures, occasionally they may be caught off guard by those who really pursue new advancements.

Negative Performance Implications: Average-scoring individuals may delay their learning of new information, which can be a detriment to the organization. Further, they may tend to talk about employee development, but rarely provide their staff with the opportunities to do so.

Performance Implications of Low Scores (0%–35%)

Positive Performance Implications: Low-scoring individuals look to hands-on, nontraditional venues of training and learning (e.g., through a mentor, listening to tapes, and on-the-job training) versus traditional educational media. They usually prefer applying skills rather than learning new methodologies.

Negative Performance Implications: Low-scoring individuals tend to view traditional venues of education as something to be endured rather than enjoyed. Consequently, they often seem unconcerned with staff development and may not equip their staff with the necessary skills to carry out their assignments.

Table 8 contains the behavioral implications and HICs for Learning Approach.

Table 8: Behavioral Implications and HICs for Learning Approach

Low Learning Approach Score		High Learning Approach Score	
Positive Behaviors	**Negative Behaviors**	**Positive Behaviors**	**Negative Behaviors**
• Prefers hands-on learning • Prefers practical training • Prefers to apply skills rather than learn new methods or concepts	• Endures education • May have narrow interests • May not set clear goals • Unconcerned with staff development	• Enjoys and values education • Seems insightful • Values training • Stays up-to-date with recent technical and business developments	• Intolerant of the less informed • May overrationalize events • May be a know-t-all • Lacks depth on topics

HIC	Items	Definition	Low Score	High Score	Sample Item
Education	3	Is a good student	Negative experiences with education	Positive attitude about education	As a child, school was easy for me
Math Ability	3	Is good with numbers	Does not work well with numbers	Works well with numbers	I can multiply large numbers quickly
Good Memory	4	Has a good memory	Somewhat forgetful	Can remember things easily	I have a large vocabulary
Reading	4	Enjoys reading	Does not keep up-to-date	Keeps up-to-date	I would rather read than watch TV

CHAPTER 4

HOGAN DEVELOPMENT SURVEY

There are plenty of people who are leadership legends in their own minds who are also charismatically challenged in the eyes of others.

– Gordon Curphy

The Hogan Development Survey (HDS) assesses 11 performance risks that interfere with a person's ability to build relationships with others and create cohesive, goal-oriented teams. The counterproductive behaviors associated with these performance risks negatively influence people's careers, relationships, and life satisfactions. Although the themes of the Hogan Personality Inventory (HPI) can be seen in a person's day-to-day behaviors, the performance risks of the HDS will only be seen in situations where the person is not actively managing his/her public image. These might include situations with high stress or change, multitasking, task saturation or accomplishment, poor person-job fit, or those in which a person feels comfortable enough with those he/she works with that he/she no longer manages his/her public image.

FOUNDATION FOR THE HDS

Some background comments may help the reader better understand the purpose of the HDS. Sigmund Freud, Alfred Adler, Karen Horney, and H.S. Sullivan all studied self-defeating behavior. However, they explained this behavior very differently. Freud was concerned with intrapsychic processes (events occurring inside the mind), whereas the others were concerned with interpersonal processes (events occurring between people). Consequently, the others are known as interpersonal theorists.

Freud thought everyone (who had not been psychoanalyzed) was neurotic; however, the interpersonal theorists thought that the problems most people have were much less severe than a neurosis. Freud thought people could be characterized in terms of how they manage their neuroses; the interpersonal theorists thought people could be characterized in terms of their expectations about how others will treat them. Because some of these expectations are wrong, people tend to behave in ways that others find annoying and that, over time, may interfere with their life goals. Freud's view that everyone is somewhat neurotic is surely incorrect—people who are neurotic are severely impaired and most people are not deeply disturbed. Nonetheless, his view prevailed and inspired the early history of personality measurement that, in turn, led to the development of instruments such as the Minnesota Multiphasic Personality Inventory (MMPI, Hathaway & McKinley, 1943; MMPI 2, Butcher, Dahlstrom, Graham, Tellegen, & Kaemmer, 1989).

Adler, Horney, Sullivan, and the later interpersonal theorists are probably right in their view that, although not everyone is neurotic, the nature of experience in childhood is such that almost everyone feels inadequate about something. That is, childhood is almost inevitably stressful, and most people develop expectations of being criticized in certain situations; they also develop methods for dealing with the criticism. For Freud, all neuroses have a single cause—a failure to resolve the Oedipus complex. For the interpersonal theorists, there are many reasons for feeling inadequate, and almost everyone feels insecure about something—few of us have had a perfect childhood.

The interpersonal theorists have had far less influence on personality assessment than Freud, despite the importance of the problems they analyze. Other than research on the interpersonal circumplex inspired by Leary (1957) and elaborated brilliantly by Wiggins (1979), there has been little systematic effort to classify the key interpersonal processes. In our judgment, the first step in studying these processes is to develop a taxonomy of what we call "performance risks." Horney (1950) identified 10 "neurotic needs" that seem to be the first taxonomy of flawed interpersonal tendencies. She later summarized these needs in terms of three themes:

- Moving away from people – Managing one's feelings of inadequacy by avoiding contact with others.

- Moving against people – Managing one's self-doubts by dominating and intimidating others.

- Moving toward people – Managing one's insecurities by building alliances.

We believe that Horney's taxonomy is a useful first step in classifying performance risks; moreover, it is implicit in the classification of personality disorders contained in DSM-IV (American Psychiatric Association, 1994).

DEVELOPMENT GUIDELINES

In developing the HDS, we were guided by four considerations. The first concerns what to measure. We regard the personality disorders described in the DSM-III-R and DSM-IV as lists designed by committees; as such, they are inevitably somewhat arbitrary and generally not founded in science. However, they do offer a provisional taxonomy of flawed interpersonal strategies that can be reflected in the range of normal personality. Table 9 presents the 11 HDS scales with their performance risks in comparison to the personality disorders they parallel.

The second consideration concerns how to conceptualize the constructs listed in Table 9. Many people define the personality disorders as types. Furthermore, each type refers to a distinctive cluster of behaviors that characterize certain people. For example, a person with a high score on a narcissism scale will manifest more narcissistic behavioral tendencies than a person with a low score. In our view, however, the performance risks measured by the HDS are more dimensional in nature. Each refers to a distinct theme appearing in interpersonal relations. People are normally distributed on these dimensions, and any single person may have high or low scores on any of the dimensions.

The third consideration we used in developing the HDS has to do with how to measure the various personality disorders. The standard approach to constructing these scales is to write items for each personality disorder using the diagnostic criteria listed in the DSM-IV. For example, the criteria for the Avoidant personality include sensitivity to criticism, anxiety proneness, fearfulness, and low self-confidence. To develop an Avoidant scale, therefore, a test author would write items reflecting each of these themes. The problem is that the DSM-IV assigns many of the same attributes to more than one personality disorder. For example, being sensitive to criticism is a criterion for diagnosing 4 of the standard 10 disorders, and items concerning being sensitive to criticism would appear on four of an inventory's scales constructed in this manner. This builds in item overlap and necessarily reduces the power of such inventories to discriminate among people.

To avoid this problem when developing the HDS, we wrote items directed at the heart of each disposition, and then carefully reviewed the item content across scales to eliminate item overlap and enhance the discriminatory power of the entire inventory. Thus, for example, items on the Skeptical scale concern suspiciousness, mistrust, and a heightened readiness to confront persons suspected of giving offense, whereas items on the Reserved scale concern being aloof, insensitive, and indifferent to the problems of others. The content of each scale is independent of the content of the other scales.

The final consideration shaping the development of the HDS concerns the actual content of the items. The HDS is intended to be used in everyday contexts for career development, job placement, promotion, and other "people decisions." This is in stark contrast to inventories designed to measure personality disorders to determine mental health status or inventories used for medical evaluations. Our items reflect themes from the world of work (e.g., how one is perceived at work, how one relates to supervisors, coworkers, and friends, attitudes toward competition and success, etc.). In addition, to further enhance the acceptability of the HDS in everyday applications, the scales have been renamed so persons receiving specific scores on the various dimensions are not stigmatized or labeled. Finally, we are aware of the implications of recent rulings, especially the Americans with Disabilities Act of 1990 (ADA, 1990), as they affect test item content (Hogan, Hogan, & Roberts, 1996). The items on the HDS have been carefully reviewed to ensure they do not contain medical or psychiatric content. Furthermore, as part of our process of Kaizen Psychometrics, we continuously update item content to ensure the HDS complies with all legal requirements.

INITIAL DEVELOPMENT

The original model for the HDS was the PROFILE, developed by Warren Jones (1988) shortly after the appearance of the DSM-III, Axis 2 personality disorders (American Psychiatric Association, 1987). Jones intended to use the PROFILE as a psychometrically defensible alternative to the inventories of personality disorders available to clinical psychologists at the time. Table 9 comprises a listing of the PROFILE scales including a comparison to the HDS and DSM taxonomies. We used the PROFILE for about five years with our clients in business and conducted several validity studies. We began to see associations between PROFILE scores and problem managers and other indications of failure in the achievement of career potential. We concluded that there is a role for the assessment of "performance risks" in the workplace. However, we were concerned about the overt content of the PROFILE and its emphasis on anxiety and depression. With the passage of the Americans with Disabilities Act of 1990 (ADA, 1990), it became clear that scales of the PROFILE would be seen as evaluations of mental disabilities, which are prohibited for preoffer employment inquiries.

We saw a need for a nonclinical inventory that would assess interpersonal behaviors that adversely affect the performance or reputation of people at work. We envisioned a tool to be used primarily for professional development and coaching rather than personnel selection. However, we have observed growing interest in a tool such as this for selection, in light of the high-profile executive derailments over the past few years.

There were three primary sources of information that influenced our thinking about the scales of the HDS. The first was the DSM-IV, Axis 2 personality disorders. The second was the literature on managerial derailment—a literature that became accessible through the technical reports and popular publications from the Center for Creative Leadership. The third source was data from performance appraisals of others at work and, in particular, evaluations of first-line supervisors by their subordinates (Millikin-Davies, 1992). In our view, first-line supervisors probably affect the productivity and satisfaction of more workers than any other element of organizational structure. Therefore, we targeted for assessment the problems that these supervisors display most frequently.

Our strategy for writing the items focused on the distinctive characteristics of each performance risk. We wrote items with work-related and interpersonal content and avoided items referring to clinical or medical themes, religious beliefs, or sexual preferences. Like the HPI, the HDS items are designed to reflect what a person with that particular performance risk might say or do. Finally, we tried to develop scales with nonoverlapping and homogeneous themes and avoid repeating descriptors across scales. This was challenging because symptoms such as anxiety are common to many of the standard personality dispositions. We also tried to minimize intercorrelations between the scales.

We began working on the HDS in the fall of 1992. We wrote items for one scale at a time. We wrote an initial set of items, tested samples of people, computed internal consistency reliabilities and correlations with other well-established measures, reviewed the data, and revised the items so as to (a) enhance internal consistency reliability and (b) sharpen convergent and discriminant validity. We also solicited and received valuable input from many colleagues in the United States and Europe concerning the content of the scales. The HDS is the product of six cycles of item writing, revision, testing, and further revision. The final set of items was defined during the summer of 1995. From 1995 to 1996, we assessed more than 2,000 people, including employed adults, job applicants, prisoners, and graduate students. The ages in these samples ranged from 21 years to 64 years with a mean of 38.5 years. There were 1,532 men and 322 women, 620 Whites and 150 Blacks. We estimate that about 15% of the sample was college educated.

Table 9: Evolution of the Hogan Development Survey

	DSM–IV, Axis 2	PROFILE		HDS	
Labels	**Theme**	**Scale**	**Theme**	**Scale**	**Theme**
Borderline	Inappropriate anger; unstable and intense relationships alternating between idealization and devaluation	Unstable Relationships	Flighty; inconsistent; forms intense albeit sudden enthusiasms and disenchantments for people or projects	Excitable	Moody and hard to please; intense, but short-lived enthusiasm for people, projects, or things
Paranoid	Distrustful and suspicious of others; motives are interpreted as malevolent	Argumentative	Suspicious of others; sensitive to criticism; expects to be mistreated	Skeptical	Cynical, distrustful, and doubting others' true intentions
Avoidant	Social inhibition; feelings of inadequacy and hypersensitivity to criticism or rejection	Fear of Failure	Dread of being criticized or rejected; tends to be excessively cautious; unable to make decisions	Cautious	Reluctant to take risks for fear of being rejected or negatively evaluated
Schizoid	Emotional coldness and detachment from social relationships; indifferent to praise and criticism	Interpersonal Insensitivity	Aloof; cold; imperceptive; ignores social feedback	Reserved	Aloof, detached, and uncommunicative; lacking interest in or awareness of the feelings of others
Passive-Aggressive	Passive resistance to adequate social and occupational performance; irritated when asked to do something he/she does not want to do	Passive-Aggression	Sociable, but resists others through procrastination and stubbornness	Leisurely	Independent; ignoring people's requests and becoming irritated or argumentative if they persist
Narcissistic	Arrogant and haughty behaviors or attitudes; grandiose sense of self-importance and entitlement	Arrogance	Self-absorbed; typically loyal only to himself/herself and his/her own best interests	Bold	Unusually self-confident; feelings of grandiosity and entitlement; overevaluation of one's capabilities
Antisocial	Disregard for the truth; impulsivity and failure to plan ahead; failure to conform with social norms	Untrustworthiness	Impulsive; dishonest; selfish; motivated by pleasure; ignoring the rights of others	Mischievous	Enjoying risk taking and testing limits; needing excitement; manipulative, deceitful, cunning, and exploitative

Table 9 (continued): Evolution of the Hogan Development Survey

	DSM–IV, Axis 2		PROFILE		HDS	
Labels	**Theme**	**Scale**	**Theme**	**Scale**	**Theme**	
Histrionic	Excessive emotionality and attention seeking; self-dramatizing, theatrical, and exaggerated emotional expression	Attention Seeking	Motivated by a need for attention and a desire to be in the spotlight	Colorful	Expressive, animated, and dramatic; wanting to be noticed and needing to be the center of attention	
Schizotypal	Odd beliefs or magical thinking; behavior or speech that is odd, eccentric, or peculiar	No Common Sense	Unusual or eccentric attitudes; exhibits poor judgment relative to education and intelligence	Imaginative	Acting and thinking in creative and sometimes odd or unusual ways	
Obsessive-Compulsive	Preoccupations with orderliness, rules, perfectionism, and control; overconscientious and inflexible	Perfectionism	Methodical; meticulous; attends so closely to details that he/she may have trouble with priorities	Diligent	Meticulous, precise, and perfectionistic; inflexible about rules and procedures; critical of others' performance	
Dependent	Difficulty making everyday decisions without excessive advice and reassurance; difficulty expressing disagreement out of fear of loss of support or approval	Dependency	Demand for constant reassurance, support, and encouragement from others	Dutiful	Eager to please and reliant on others for support and guidance; reluctant to take independent action or go against popular opinion	

LATER DEVELOPMENT

The primary goal of the HDS was to produce a reliable indicator of behavioral tendencies that could interrupt or "derail" a person's career success. We found evidence that these tendencies not only exist among working adults, but are actually commonplace. For example, Bentz (1985) identified leadership styles associated with managerial derailment in the retail industry (e.g., playing politics, exhibiting moodiness, and dishonesty). Researchers at the Center for Creative Leadership and at Personnel Decisions International have concluded that managers who are technically competent, but fail, are variously perceived as arrogant, vindictive, untrustworthy, selfish, emotional, compulsive, overcontrolling, insensitive, abrasive, aloof, too ambitious, or unable to delegate (Hazucha, 1991; Lombardo, Ruderman, & McCauley, 1988; McCall & Lombardo, 1983). It would seem that, like the Five-Factor Model (FFM), performance risks measured by the HDS reflect common themes in the lives of people who are getting by, but perhaps gradually failing, or at least not realizing their potential.

During the decade following the initial development of the HDS, our research showed support for the notion that performance risks are common among working adults. We wanted to establish that, armed with the self-awareness that can be obtained through the HDS, focused development efforts can reduce the career impact of these performance risks.

More than 1,500,000 employed adults have taken the HDS. They represent every sector of the global marketplace, including manufacturing, communications, health care, retail, banking and finance, construction, transportation, security, law enforcement, and many others. The research that has been conducted over this period of time involves more than 100 validation studies covering a wide range of job categories. Most of these studies have linked HDS scores with ratings of managerial/professional incompetence, and demonstrated the ability of the inventory to account for unique variance beyond that obtained with traditional Five-Factor inventories.

A consistent result has been the finding that HDS scores are stable over time, with test-retest reliabilities ranging from .58 to .87 (mean = .75). Nonetheless, we have concluded that a focused development effort can reduce the risk associated with high scores. Put another way, an individual who is aware of a high score on his/her HDS can take action to mitigate the risk of negative behaviors occurring on the job. This is an important distinction between the HDS and traditional Five-Factor inventories. It is the foundation for using the HDS in dozens of development programs. Many of these programs improve the performance of leaders by helping them eliminate or reduce the negative behaviors highlighted by the HDS.

SUMMARY OF THE CURRENT STRUCTURE OF THE HDS

The HDS performance risks are caused by people's distorted beliefs about how others will treat them, and they can be grouped into three broad categories or super factors:

- Moving Away – These risks help individuals manage their anxiety by maintaining their distance and pushing others away.

- Moving Against – Oftentimes, the best defense is a good offense. These risks help people manage their anxiety by manipulating or controlling others.

- Moving Toward – These risks help people manage their anxiety by building alliances with others.

The HPI measures the "bright side" of personality—those behaviors others see on a day-to-day basis. However, extreme scores on the HPI can have some potentially negative consequences. These negative consequences often appear as "dark side" personality traits on the HDS.

FUTURE DEVELOPMENT PLANNED FOR THE HDS

Like the HPI, we have taken a Kaizen Psychometrics approach to the development of the HDS. The most important change planned for the HDS will be in the structure of the scales. Each scale will be composed of a number of facets or Homogenous Item Composites (HICs). In a manner comparable to the HPI, having these HIC data available will substantially facilitate the process of interpreting profiles.

GENERAL INTERPRETATION GUIDELINES FOR THE HDS

- The HDS can be used for selection with appropriate validation support and for individual development (particularly with respect to those in or aspiring to leadership positions).

- Interpretation of HDS results is not necessarily job specific. The counterproductive behaviors associated with performance risks will be exhibited whenever a person is not paying attention to their public image.

- Higher scores on an HDS scale increase the chances that counterproductive behaviors will be more problematic for that performance risk.

- Scores at or above the 90th percentile are considered High Risk.

- Scores between the 70th and 89th percentiles are considered Moderate Risk.

- Scores between the 40th and 69th percentiles are considered Low Risk.

- Scores less than the 39th percentile are considered No Risk.

- Almost everyone has one or two elevations (i.e., scores approaching or in the High range). If an individual has three or more High Risk scores, then his/her behavior is likely to be more problematic. If a person does not have any High scores, then elevated scores become more meaningful.

HDS FACTS

- The initial version of the HDS was known as the PROFILE. The PROFILE was developed in 1988 by Warren Jones at The University of Tulsa.

- Research studies using both the HPI and the PROFILE indicated that traits assessed by the PROFILE were valid predictors of job performance. However, the test items and overall structure of the PROFILE needed substantial revision before it would be ready for commercial publication.

- Several versions of the HDS have been developed. The current version was published in 1997 and consists of 11 primary scales and 168 items.

- More than 1,500,000 people have taken the HDS. Most of these individuals worked in sensitive individual contributor or leadership positions.

- There are no practical gender or ethnic differences in scale scores.

- There are three major types of reports: Suitability, Career Management Series, and Leadership Forecast Series. The Career Management Series reports and Leadership Forecast Series reports are some of the best feedback reports in the testing industry.

- The HDS provides percentile scores for the 11 primary scales. These scores can be based on general population, manager, or executive norms.

- The HDS is a Level C assessment.

HDS GLOBAL PORTABILITY

The HDS continues to gain international support as the inventory for measuring performance risks that significantly impede job performance or career success. Interestingly, the performance risks measured by the HDS resonate as well in the international marketplace as they do domestically. As with the HPI, we have engaged in a large-scale translation effort over the past decade. At the time of this printing, the HDS is available online in the following languages:

- Bahasa (BM)
- Brazilian Portuguese (BP)
- Castilian Spanish (CA)
- Czech (CS)
- Danish (DA)
- Dutch (NL)
- Finnish (FI)
- French Parisian (FR)
- German (GR)
- Icelandic (IS)
- Italian (IT)
- Japanese (JA)
- Kenyan (KE)
- Korean (KO)
- Norwegian (NO)
- Polish (PL)
- Russian (RU)
- Simplified Chinese (ZH)
- Slovak (SK)
- South African (AE)
- Spanish (ES)
- Swedish (SV)
- Traditional Chinese (ZC)
- Turkish (TR)
- UK English (UK)
- US English (US)

As with the HPI, we are also expanding our norm data and validation research throughout the global marketplace for the HDS. The results we have obtained to date regarding norms and validity for the HDS continue to support its global portability.

CHAPTER 5

HOGAN DEVELOPMENT SURVEY SCALES

Excitable	*Give a speech when you're angry, and you'll give the best speech you'll ever regret.*	– Ambrose Bierce
Skeptical	*I told my psychiatrist that everyone hates me. He said I was being ridiculous—everyone hasn't met me yet.*	– Rodney Dangerfield
Cautious	*The truth is that many people set rules to keep from making decisions.*	– Mike Krzyzewski
Reserved	*Indifference and neglect often do much more damage than outright dislike.*	– J.K. Rowling
Leisurely	*"Get out of show business." It's the best advice I ever got, because I'm so stubborn that if someone would tell me that, I would stay in it to the bitter end.*	– Walter Matthau
Bold	*Sometimes a neighbor whom we have disliked a lifetime for his arrogance and conceit lets fall a single commonplace remark that shows us another side, another man, really; a man uncertain, and puzzled, and in the dark like ourselves.*	– Willa Cather
Mischievous	*The most mischievous liars are those who keep sliding on the verge of truth.*	– Augustus Hare
Colorful	*I only wore makeup when I went onstage.*	– Little Richard
Imaginative	*I like nonsense—it wakes up the brain cells. Fantasy is a necessary ingredient in living. It's a way of looking at life through the wrong end of a telescope. Which is what I do, and that enables you to laugh at life's realities.*	– Dr. Seuss
Diligent	*Perfectionism becomes a badge of honor with you playing the part of the suffering hero.*	– David D. Burns
Dutiful	*A "No" uttered from the deepest conviction is better than a "Yes" merely uttered to please, or worse, to avoid trouble.*	– Mohandas Gandhi

SCALE 1 – EXCITABLE

The Excitable scale measures behaviors ranging from emotional calmness to emotional explosiveness. Important areas of concern include being overly enthusiastic about people or projects and then becoming disappointed with them. The perception that may be created by a person with a high score is a lack of persistence.

Potential negative behaviors associated with a Moderate to High score:

- Overreacts to difficult situations
- Unpredictable
- Tense under pressure
- Stressed relationships
- Easily annoyed by others
- Critical
- Moody and inconsistent

Performance Implications of High Scores (90%–100%)

Individuals with High scores are perceived as intense and energetic, but also temperamental and potentially explosive. They tend to be critical, easily irritated, prone to emotional outbursts, and easily upset with people and projects. These individuals tend to develop strong enthusiasms for people, projects, or organizations, and then become disappointed with them. Furthermore, if they become disappointed with people, they may not follow through on commitments, or they may quit in frustration. These individuals tend to become annoyed easily, let little things bother them, and change jobs more frequently than other people. They may be hard to work with because they seem moody, hard to please, and do not handle pressure well.

Performance Implications of Moderate Scores (70%–89%)

Individuals with Moderate scores are perceived as energized and active, but also moody and irritable. They tend to be easily annoyed, critical of others' work, self-doubting, and tense. At times, these individuals may also overreact to difficult situations or give up when projects do not go well. They may be hard to work with because they are perceived as being somewhat unpredictable and critical.

Performance Implications of Low Scores (40%–69%)

Individuals with Low scores are perceived as self-confident, tolerant, and even-tempered. They are not easily upset and tend to stay calm in difficult situations. These individuals rarely need reassurance and are usually tolerant of others' shortcomings.

Performance Implications of No Risk Scores (0%–39%)

Individuals with No Risk scores are perceived as calm, steady, reliable, and emotionally mature. They are usually in a good mood and are not easily disappointed. These individuals seem relaxed, easygoing, and they rarely get excited, even when provoked. They tend to stay focused on the task at hand. They can also be counted on to complete projects in a timely fashion.

SCALE 2 – SKEPTICAL

The Skeptical scale measures behaviors ranging from having confidence in others to expecting to be disappointed. Important areas of concern include being socially insightful, but cynical and overly sensitive to criticism. The perception that may be created by a person with a high score is a lack of trust for others.

Potential negative behaviors associated with a Moderate to High score:

- Sensitive to criticism
- Argumentative
- Critical
- Defensive
- Easily angered
- Suspicious of others' intentions
- Prone to fault-finding

Performance Implications of High Scores (90%–100%)

Individuals with High scores are perceived as bright and perceptive, but critical, fault-finding, and alert for signs of betrayal. They tend to be cynical, easily angered, and mistrustful of others' actions and intentions. These individuals are tense, easily upset, and expect to be mistreated. Although they are shrewd and difficult to fool, others may find them hard to work with because they take criticism personally, tend to feel misused, and are prone to retaliate when they feel wronged. High-scoring individuals are also prone to fault-finding and are willing to bend the rules to defend themselves against perceived mistreatment.

Performance Implications of Moderate Scores (70%–89%)

Individuals with Moderate scores are perceived as insightful about others' motives, but skeptical and critical. They tend to be uncooperative when they do not understand why they should do something. Others tend to see them as defensive, sensitive to criticism, argumentative, and suspicious of authority. These individuals may be hard to work with because they tend to exaggerate grievances, feel readily misused, and are prone to be accusatory when they feel wronged.

Performance Implications of Low Scores (40%–69%)

Individuals with Low scores are perceived as tolerant, open-minded, not defensive, and approachable. They tend to build stable relationships and do not take things personally. These individuals do not hold grudges, can analyze other people and situations, and are easy to coach.

Performance Implications of No Risk Scores (0%–39%)

Individuals with No Risk scores are perceived as optimistic, positive, trusting, and steady. They are open to feedback and do not take criticism personally. These individuals believe in people and are willing to forgive the faults of others; consequently, they tend to form long-term relationships and are seen as trustworthy and reliable.

SCALE 3 – CAUTIOUS

The Cautious scale measures behaviors ranging from a confident willingness to undertake new ventures to a cautious reluctance to try new things. Important areas of concern include being overly worried about being criticized. The perception that may be created by a person with a high score is a resistance to change and reluctance to take chances.

Potential negative behaviors associated with a Moderate to High score:

- Slow to make decisions
- Resistant to change
- Reluctant to take chances
- Motivated not to fail
- Unassertive
- Conservative
- Perceived as holding back others

Performance Implications of High Scores (90%–100%)

Individuals with High scores are perceived as shy, self-doubting, conservative, emotional, and unassertive. They tend to avoid making decisions and are slow to adopt new procedures or technology because of the perceived likelihood of failure, criticism, and embarrassment. Although these individuals tend to follow company policy carefully, they may be hard to work with because they worry about making mistakes, are indecisive, are reluctant to say what they feel and believe, and may give up on difficult assignments.

Performance Implications of Moderate Scores (70%–89%)

Individuals with Moderate scores are perceived as tense, quiet, careful, and indecisive. They are described by others as slow to act or make decisions, reluctant to try new methods, resistant to changes in policies and procedures, and needing encouragement when faced with challenging assignments. Although these individuals are usually good corporate citizens, others may find them hard to work with because of their need to stay within the lines, resistance to innovation or new procedures, and reluctance to state their opinions.

Performance Implications of Low Scores (40%–69%)

Individuals with Low scores are perceived as upbeat, emotionally poised, stable, and composed. They meet the public well, handle disappointments in a mature fashion, and are willing to experiment with new methods. These individuals enjoy the company of others, will speak up at meetings, and review the impact of their actions and decisions. They try to anticipate problems and are careful not to offend.

Performance Implications of No Risk Scores (0%–39%)

Individuals with No Risk scores are perceived as active, confident, rational, and mature. They are decisive, unafraid to make mistakes, open to innovation, and willing to accept challenges. These individuals are relaxed around strangers, are willing to state their views, and express their emotions appropriately.

SCALE 4 – RESERVED

The Reserved scale measures behaviors ranging from caring about the problems of others to seeming indifferent to, or unconcerned about, other people. Important areas of concern include a lack of interest in or awareness of the feelings of others. The perception that may be created by a person with a high score is someone that has a difficult time communicating.

Potential negative behaviors associated with a Moderate to High score:

- Interpersonally insensitive
- Preference for working alone
- Uncomfortable around strangers
- Uncommunicative
- Feedback deficient
- Reserved
- Not a team player

Performance Implications of High Scores (90%–100%)

Individuals with High scores are perceived as socially insensitive, self-absorbed, preoccupied, and tough. They tend to keep to themselves, do not call attention to themselves, prefer to work alone, and dislike working in teams. These individuals are indifferent to the moods and feelings of others and are unconcerned about the impression they make on other people. They are usually poor communicators because they tune out what they do not want to hear. They are also not very insightful or perceptive about social cues or office politics, and they rarely display public support for their employers or coworkers. Although these individuals work well alone, others may find them hard to work with because they are uncommunicative, insensitive, tend to remain at a distance, and do not want to be bothered with matters that do not concern them.

Performance Implications of Moderate Scores (70%–89%)

Individuals with Moderate scores are perceived as independent, tough, reserved, and detached. They tend to be uncomfortable around strangers and prefer to work alone. These individuals distance themselves from others and seem unconcerned about their problems. They tend to misinterpret feedback and ignore social cues. Although they may work well by themselves, others may find them difficult to work with because they stay uninvolved, act without consulting others, have thick skin, and will listen only when they have a special interest in the message.

Performance Implications of Low Scores (40%–69%)

Individuals with Low scores are perceived as socially self-confident, but are still concerned about others. They seem to have the ability to read people quickly and will ask questions in order to better understand the perspective of others. They are polite, considerate, help out when asked, and can weather others' emotional storms.

Performance Implications of No Risk Scores (0%–39%)

Individuals with No Risk scores are perceived as outgoing, friendly, kind, and understanding. They have good social skills and tend to interact well with strangers. Most are kind, considerate, and enjoy working in teams. These individuals are often good listeners, insightful about interpersonal issues, and sympathetic to others' feelings, and they put people around them at ease.

SCALE 5 – LEISURELY

The Leisurely scale measures behaviors ranging from being cooperative, cheerful, and open to feedback to being stubborn, irritable, privately resentful, and hard to coach. Important areas of concern include being independent, ignoring others' requests, and becoming irritable if the requests persist. The perception that may be created by a person with a high score is someone that is stubborn, procrastinates, and is uncooperative.

Potential negative behaviors associated with a Moderate to High score:

- Seems cooperative on the surface
- Unwilling to confront others
- Does not understand others' urgency
- Passive resistance (e.g., forgetful of due dates)
- Works according to own timetable
- Hard to coach
- Stubborn
- Procrastinates when performing uninteresting work

Performance Implications of High Scores (90%–100%)

Individuals with High scores are perceived as overtly cooperative, but edgy, mistrustful, and hard to coach. Although they seem cooperative on the surface, they express their feelings (especially anger) in indirect ways, will prefer to work according to their own timetable, and may put off tasks they do not see as being personally important. These individuals tend to overvalue their independence, feel mistreated and unappreciated when others make demands on them, and covertly question coworkers' competence. Although they can be outwardly pleasant and sociable, others may find them hard to work with because of their procrastination, tardiness, and stubbornness, their reluctance to be part of a team, and their tendency to ignore constructive criticism and not follow through on commitments.

Performance Implications of Moderate Scores (70%–89%)

Individuals with Moderate scores are perceived as sensitive, skeptical, and somewhat stubborn. While they are pleasant, they may not be as cooperative as they seem because they try to achieve influence by failing to cooperate (e.g., procrastinating). Although they seem agreeable and polite, they may be hard to work with because they tend to put off tasks they do not like, question corporate policy, become irritated when their work is interrupted, and are hard to coach.

Performance Implications of Low Scores (40%–69%)

Individuals with Low scores are perceived as friendly, obliging, positive, and coachable. They are patient with interruptions and straightforward in their communications and dealings with others. These individuals tend to be good corporate citizens who display loyalty to their superiors and monitor business goals effectively.

Performance Implications of No Risk Scores (0%–39%)

Individuals with No Risk scores are perceived as outgoing, helpful, upbeat, and open to coaching. They tend to seek constructive feedback and are willing to listen to suggestions on how to improve performance. These individuals are good corporate citizens who will show support for the organization and honor their commitments.

SCALE 6 – BOLD

The Bold scale measures behaviors ranging from modesty and self-restraint to assertive self-promotion and unrealistic expectations of success and power. Important areas of concern include having inflated views of one's competency and self-worth. The perception that may be created by a person with a high score is someone that is unable to admit mistakes or learn from experience.

Potential negative behaviors associated with a Moderate to High score:

- Feedback resistant
- Overestimates talents and accomplishments
- May not seek different opinions
- Demanding and overbearing
- May blame mistakes on others
- Self-promoting
- Strong sense of entitlement
- No sense of team loyalty

Performance Implications of High Scores (90%–100%)

Individuals with High scores are perceived as bold, assertive, and energetic. They tend to be confident, aggressive, ambitious, and visionary. These individuals may be seen as impulsive, self-promoting, unresponsive to negative feedback, competitive, and demanding. They tend to overestimate their talents and accomplishments, ignore shortcomings, and blame their mistakes on others. Although these individuals often make a good first impression, they can be hard to work with because they feel entitled to special treatment, ignore criticism, test the limits, intimidate others (especially subordinates), and have unrealistic career goals. Consequently, they are often unable to foster and develop a sense of loyalty or teamwork among their associates.

Performance Implications of Moderate Scores (70%–89%)

Individuals with Moderate scores are perceived as confident, socially skilled, assertive, and unafraid of failure or rejection. They have clear career goals, are willing to challenge others, will take initiative, and seek leadership positions. Although these individuals are often charismatic and typically make a strong first impression, others may find them hard to work with because they tend to be demanding, opinionated, and self-absorbed.

Performance Implications of Low Scores (40%–69%)

Individuals with Low scores are perceived as understated, unassertive, calm, and laid back. They are confident, energetic, tolerant of others' shortcomings, and remain optimistic when others have lost confidence. These individuals take direction well, are willing to let others lead, and tend to avoid confrontations. They rarely seek public recognition and tend not to speak up in meetings.

Performance Implications of No Risk Scores (0%–39%)

Individuals with No Risk scores are perceived as easygoing, content, modest, and restrained. They seldom interrupt, criticize, test the limits, or challenge others. These individuals tend to have vague agendas for their careers and prefer to follow rather than lead.

SCALE 7 – MISCHIEVOUS

The Mischievous scale measures behaviors ranging from seeming quiet, unassuming, and responsible to seeming bright, charming, impulsive, and limit testing. Important areas of concern include being charming, risk taking, and excitement seeking. The perception that may be created by a person with a high score is someone that has trouble maintaining commitments and learning from experience.

Potential negative behaviors associated with a Moderate to High score:

- Makes intuitive, not fact-based, decisions
- Unwilling to follow others' rules
- May not learn from past mistakes
- Takes ill-advised risks without reviewing consequences
- Pushes the limits
- Ignores commitments
- Motivated by pleasure

Performance Implications of High Scores (90%–100%)

Individuals with High scores are perceived as charming, interesting, daring, and fun. They enjoy testing the limits, need variety and excitement, and are very quick to act. While they are usually strategic about their own agendas, they may make some bad decisions because they are motivated by pleasure and are oblivious to the concerns of others. Although these individuals usually make a favorable first impression, others may find them difficult to work with because they are impulsive, downplay their mistakes and commitments, take ill-advised risks, have no regrets, and do not fully evaluate the consequences of their actions.

Performance Implications of Moderate Scores (70%–89%)

Individuals with Moderate scores are perceived as charming, impulsive, pleasure seeking, and adventurous. They are willing to make quick decisions, are unafraid of risk, and do not dwell on mistakes. These individuals enjoy change and have the energy to bring it about. Although they are fun to be around, others may find them hard to work with because they test the limits, are easily bored, and can be manipulative.

Performance Implications of Low Scores (40%–69%)

Individuals with Low scores are perceived as quiet, dependable, focused, disciplined, and persistent. They are easy to understand, think before they act, make good decisions, rarely take chances, and are persistent about finishing tasks.

Performance Implications of No Risk Scores (0%–39%)

Individuals with No Risk scores are perceived as unassertive, conforming, responsible, and socially appropriate. They are self-controlled, reasonable, communicate well, and make high-quality decisions. These individuals avoid taking unnecessary risks and prefer to follow rather than be in leadership positions. Others usually trust them, in part, because they think about the consequences of their decisions before acting.

SCALE 8 – COLORFUL

The Colorful scale measures behaviors ranging from modesty and quiet self-restraint to dramatic and colorful self-expression. Important areas of concern include being dramatic, engaging, and attention seeking. The perception that may be created by a person with a high score is someone that is preoccupied with being noticed and is lacking in sustained focus.

Potential negative behaviors associated with a Moderate to High score:

- Self-promoting
- Attention seeking
- Poor listening skills
- Easily distracted (e.g., confuses activity with productivity)
- Managing by crisis
- Problems with organization
- May lack follow-through

Performance Implications of High Scores (90%–100%)

Individuals with High scores are perceived as quick, fun, and socially skilled. They seek leadership positions, innovate and challenge the system, and are skilled at influencing others. These individuals enjoy multitasking, but they may have problems with staying organized, strategic decision making, and follow through. They love having a high profile and being recognized for their accomplishments; consequently, they are clever at calling attention to themselves (e.g., making dramatic entrances and exits). While they may be energetic and entertaining, others may find them hard to work with because they tend to be self-promoting, overcommitted, easily angered, and quickly bored.

Performance Implications of Moderate Scores (70%–89%)

Individuals with Moderate scores are perceived as interesting, entertaining, and lively. They make a strong first impression, enjoy leadership positions, and expect others to find them attractive. These individuals are charming, engaging, and enjoy being in the limelight. Although they may be amusing, others may find them hard to work with because they are easily irritated, impulsive, easily distracted, disorganized, and substitute activity for productivity.

Performance Implications of Low Scores (40%–69%)

Individuals with Low scores are perceived as modest, unpretentious, cooperative, and self-controlled. They rarely test the limits, do not seek the limelight, and work well in a structured environment. They prefer nonleadership positions and are good team players who will support the performance of others.

Performance Implications of No Risk Scores (0%–39%)

Individuals with No Risk scores are perceived as retiring, quiet, obliging, and self-restrained. They are responsible, good corporate citizens, and willing to share credit with others. These individuals rarely challenge others and prefer to let others take the lead. They are most comfortable in "behind the scenes" roles and do not like to be the center of attention.

SCALE 9 – IMAGINATIVE

The Imaginative scale measures behaviors ranging from being levelheaded, sensible, and practical to imaginative, unusual, and unpredictable. Important areas of concern include thinking and acting in interesting, unusual, and even eccentric ways. The perception that may be created by a person with a high score is someone that seems creative, but possibly lacking in judgment.

Potential negative behaviors associated with a Moderate to High score:

- Different perspectives and ideas
- Poor influence and persuasion skills
- Whimsical and eccentric
- Potentially creative, but sometimes way off the mark
- Preoccupied
- Unconventional
- Unaware of how their actions affect others

Performance Implications of High Scores (90%–100%)

Individuals with High scores are perceived as unconventional, innovative, and unpredictable. They tend to think and act in ways that are unusual, different, striking, and at times, even odd. These individuals believe that their own opinions matter most, and they take pride in being different and experimental. They are preoccupied, easily bored, distractible, and may lack follow through. They often have trouble getting their ideas adopted because their playfulness, need to show off, and lapses in judgment have compromised their credibility. Although they can be insightful, others may find them hard to work with because they tend to be eccentric, attention seeking, and unaware of how their actions affect others.

Performance Implications of Moderate Scores (70%–89%)

Individuals with Moderate scores are perceived as clever, imaginative, fun-loving, and impulsive. They tend to be original thinkers, curious, interesting, and unconventional. These individuals have a unique way of seeing events and ideas and enjoy expressing their views. While they may understand others' intentions, they can be hard to work with because they make impractical decisions, have ideas that seem to come "out of left field," get lost in thought, and are attention seeking.

Performance Implications of Low Scores (40%–69%)

Individuals with Low scores are perceived as steady, disciplined, sensible, and modest. They are serious about their work, predictable under pressure, and tend to maintain a low profile. These individuals also tend to be restrained, open-minded, and good corporate citizens.

Performance Implications of No Risk Scores (0%–39%)

Individuals with No Risk scores are perceived as quiet, steady, and practical. They are modest, reserved, and prefer to work by themselves. These individuals are very good at staying on task, making practical decisions, and not wasting time or kidding around.

SCALE 10 – DILIGENT

The Diligent scale measures behaviors ranging from being relaxed, tolerant, and willing to delegate to being meticulous, picky, critical, and overly conscientious Important areas of concern include being conscientious, perfectionistic, and hard to please. The perception that may be created by a person with a high score is someone that tends to disempower staff.

Potential negative behaviors associated with a Moderate to High score:

- Perfectionistic
- Nit-picky
- Resistant to change
- May not delegate
- Micromanager
- Place similar priority on all tasks
- Stubborn when under pressure
- Slow decision making

Performance Implications of High Scores (90%–100%)

Individuals with High scores are perceived as polite, detail-oriented, hardworking, inflexible, and uncomfortable with ambiguity. They tend to maintain stringent standards of conduct and performance for themselves and others and take pride in being attentive to detail and conscientious. Consequently, these individuals often try to make everything top priority, overestimate their competence, and find it difficult to delegate. These tendencies create extra pressure for these individuals and deprive their staff of developmental opportunities. Although they are hardworking, attentive to detail, and careful, others may find them difficult to work with because they also tend to be micromanaging, critical, demanding, fussy, and stubborn under pressure.

Performance Implications of Moderate Scores (70%–89%)

Individuals with Moderate scores are perceived as polite, conscientious, hardworking, and good with details. They tend to be planful, well-organized, evenhanded, and careful. These individuals will provide their staff with structure, direction, and feedback, but will find it difficult to let others make their own mistakes, which is in fact how some people learn. Although they are responsible, others may find them hard to work with because they tend to do everything themselves, supervise others closely, and can be inflexible about their methods.

Performance Implications of Low Scores (40%–69%)

Individuals with Low scores are perceived as understanding, responsive, and tolerant. They know how to prioritize, are willing to delegate, and provide their staff with learning opportunities. As coaches and mentors, they will be approachable and available, but may be somewhat reluctant to give others critical feedback. These individuals tend to approach strategic planning with a short time frame, focusing on near-term challenges and opportunities while ignoring long-term issues.

Performance Implications of No Risk Scores (0%–39%)

Individuals with No Risk scores are perceived as friendly, approachable, undemanding, and relaxed about rules. They seek out close relationships and actively try to understand others. These individuals prioritize tasks appropriately, are willing to delegate tasks, and provide their staff with learning opportunities. On the other hand, they may not give others much feedback regarding the negative aspects of performance, leading them to think they are doing better than they actually are.

SCALE 11 – DUTIFUL

The Dutiful scale measures behaviors ranging from being independent and willing to challenge people in authority to being conforming and reluctant to take independent action. Important areas of concern include being eager to please and reluctant to act independently. The perception that may be created by a person with a high score is someone that tends to be pleasant and agreeable, but reluctant to support subordinates.

Potential negative behaviors associated with a Moderate to High score:

- Compliant
- Reluctant to make decisions
- Unwilling to go against the status quo
- Withdraw from politically charged situations
- Conforming
- Strong desire to please others
- May not stick up for subordinates

Performance Implications of High Scores (90%–100%)

Individuals with High scores are perceived as obliging, predictable, unassuming, and likeable. They are comfortable following people in authority, work hard to avoid "rocking the boat," and are eager to please others. They often defer to others' judgment in order to maintain cordial relationships and gain approval, and are reluctant to go against the status quo. These individuals may promise more than they can deliver in an effort to please others, and may not stick up for their subordinates. Although they are pleasant and agreeable, others may find them hard to work with because they can be indecisive, reluctant to act independently, ingratiating, and can rely excessively on others to make decisions.

Performance Implications of Moderate Scores (70%–89%)

Individuals with Moderate scores are perceived as agreeable, pleasant, attentive, and cooperative. They support corporate policy, keep others informed, and are eager to please. They are polite, approachable, and do not like controversy. These individuals prefer to follow the consensus and would rather use persuasion than make demands on others. Although they make positive first impressions, others may find them hard to work with because they are reluctant to make decisions on their own and are excessively careful to please their superiors.

Performance Implications of Low Scores (40%–69%)

Individuals with Low scores are perceived as self-starting, needing little direction, self-sufficient, and loyal to their staff. They are willing to support, encourage, and develop others. These individuals prefer to work in teams when there is a clear, well-defined purpose to the activity. They tend to be autonomous, willing to take initiative, and able to handle controversy and disagreements with poise.

Performance Implications of No Risk Scores (0%–39%)

Individuals with No Risk scores are perceived as independent, self-reliant, and tough-minded. They are willing to challenge people in authority, are not easily discouraged by negative feedback, and will stick up for their subordinates. They can tolerate ambiguity, enjoy challenges, make decisions without prior approval, and will take steps to develop their staff.

CHAPTER 6

MOTIVES, VALUES, PREFERENCES INVENTORY

The indispensable first step to getting the things you want out of life is this: decide what you want.

– Ben Stein

The Motives, Values, Preferences Inventory (MVPI) evaluates the fit between an individual and the organizational culture. It also helps people understand their interests, motives, and drivers. These values and goals are part of a person's identity; consequently, they are what a person desires and will strive to attain. In addition, people prefer to work with others who share their values, dislike those who do not, and are happiest working in environments that are consistent with their values.

FOUNDATION FOR THE MVPI

The MVPI is designed to serve two important goals. First, the MVPI permits an evaluation of the fit between an individual and the organizational culture. This is important because no matter how talented or hardworking a person may be, if his/her values are incompatible with the values of the larger culture—and the culture is usually defined by the values of top management—then he/she will not do well in the organization. Second, the MVPI is unique among currently available inventories in that it allows assessment of a person's motives directly. The standard interest measures allow inference about a person's motives based on his/her expressed occupational choices. Based on MVPI results, one can determine immediately the degree to which, for example, a person is motivated by money, security, or fun. The only alternative to the MVPI for directly assessing a person's motives is to use a projective measure. The scales of the MVPI represent dimensions that have historic presence in the literature on motivation.

We reviewed 80 years of theory and research on motives, values, and interests and developed 10 content scales. We were specifically influenced by the taxonomies of Spranger (1928), Allport (1961), Murray (1938), Allport, Vernon, and Lindzey (1960), and Holland (1966, 1985). Although the labels that these authors use to orient their taxonomies are different, and some of their dimensions are trait-like while others refer to types, there is, nonetheless, considerable overlap in the attitudes, values, needs, interests, goals, and commitments that they regard as important. Gregory (1992) summarizes these motivational constructs (see Table 10) and indicates how their content aligns with the 10 scales of the MVPI. Because the history of each of these constructs is useful for understanding measurement goals for each MVPI scale, we highlight some of the views that have influenced what we believe to be an adequate taxonomy of motives.

Table 10: Logical Taxonomy of Motives, Attitudes, Values, Needs, Interests, Goals, and Commitments

MVPI	Attitudes: Spranger	Values: Allport, Vernon, & Lindzey	Needs: Murray	Interests: Holland	Goals: Richards	Goals: Wicker, Lambert, Richardson & Kahler	Goals: Pervin	Commitments: Novacek & Lazarus
Recognition	Political	Political	Exhibition		Prestige	Competitive, Ambition	Aggression-Power	Power/Achievement
Power	Political	Political	Achievement, Dominance	Enterprising	Prestige	Competitive, Ambition	Aggression-Power	Power/Achievement
Hedonism	Aesthetic		Sex, Play		Hedonistic		Relaxation-Fun-Friendship	Sensation Seeking
Altruistic	Social	Social	Nurturance	Social	Altruistic	Interpersonal Concern	Affection-Support	Altruism
Affiliation	Social	Social	Affiliation	Social			Relaxation-Fun-Friendship	Sensation Seeking
Tradition	Religious	Religious			Religious			Personal Growth
Security			Succorance, Infavoidance	Conventional			Reduce Tension-Conflict-Threat	Stress Avoidance
Commerce	Economic	Economic	Acquisition	Conventional				Power/Achievement
Aesthetics	Aesthetic	Aesthetic	Sentience	Artistic	Artistic			Sensation Seeking
Science	Theoretical	Theoretical	Understanding	Investigative	Scientific			

Source: Gregory, 1992. Reprinted with permission.

Recognition Motives

The need to be recognized and gain the attention of others is distinct from the power motive. Although Spranger (1928), Allport, Vernon, and Lindzey (1960), and Novacek and Lazarus (1990) combine power with recognition, Murray (1938) distinguishes between power and recognition by proposing achievement and dominance needs (power) and exhibition needs (recognition). Gregory (1992) proposes that recognition may apply to all of Holland's types because the theme tends to resemble a trait more than a type.

Power Motives

Spranger's political attitude highlights achievement, aggression, status, and dominance. Allport, Vernon, and Lindzey (1960) describe the political man as one who primarily focuses on achieving power. Murray's needs for achievement and dominance fit closely with the power motive. The power motive is clearly aligned with Holland's enterprising type. This type seeks leadership positions, values freedom and ambition, and has a life goal of being in charge. Holland describes enterprising types as power seeking, dominant, enthusiastic, and energetic.

Hedonism Motives

None of Spranger's attitudes are closely aligned with hedonistic motives. Murray's needs for sex and play contain elements that are similar to hedonism; erotic pleasure is the basis of the need for sex, and having fun is the basis of the need for play. Holland has no type analogous to the hedonistic motive. Novacek and Lazarus identify a sensation-seeking dimension that emphasizes sexual pleasure, fun, free time, and excitement.

Altruistic Motives

Altruistic motives resemble affiliation motives; Spranger's social attitude and Holland's social type capture part of this construct. However, the distinction between affiliation and altruism is nicely characterized in Murray's need for nurturance. Nurturance focuses on helping, protecting, caring for, and curing those in need, while affiliation concerns desires for friendship and being around others. Novacek and Lazarus (1990) identified a dimension called altruism, which they describe as the desire to help and support others as well as being willing to make sacrifices for them.

Affiliation Motives

Spranger's social attitude highlights desires for interaction and positive interpersonal relations. Murray's need for affiliation is one of the best-known motives in his taxonomy; it emphasizes a desire for friendship. Holland's social type wants to be helpful, identifies with do-gooders/bleeding hearts, and seeks out opportunities for social interaction.

Tradition Motives

The tradition motives resemble Spranger's religious attitudes, which are concerned with moral issues and conservative values. Novacek and Lazarus identified a personal growth dimension that contains the moral, ethical, and spiritual themes associated with the tradition motives, particularly in the aspiration to be fair and just, and the need to develop a philosophy of life. None of Holland's types endorse the tradition motives, with the possible exception of social types, who are idealistic, want to help others, value equality, and identify with spiritual leaders.

Security Motives

As seen in Table 10, the security motives are not well-mapped by constructs identified by the major motivational theorists. Gregory (1992) points out that these motives are also more like traits than types. Because the construct concerns needs for certainty, control, and order, it resembles Murray's definition of the needs for succorance and infavoidance. The succorance need entails the desire to be protected and cared for, whereas the infavoidance need implies a cautious, controlled attitude. There is some overlap between the security motives and Holland's description of conventional types as conforming, conservative, and methodical.

Commerce Motives

Interest in business and money making are the keys to commercial motives, and this dimension can be traced back to Spranger's economic attitude, which emphasized the desire to control resources and to acquire material possessions. Allport, Vernon, and Lindzey's economic man is interested in business and the accumulation of wealth. Holland's conventional type is interested in business, identifies with successful business people, and wants to work in finance and commerce. These types are described as conservative, conforming, unimaginative, and methodical.

Aesthetic Motives

Spranger's conception of the aesthete was a person who enjoys the pleasures of the body and the arts. Murray's need for sentience, which he described as seeking out sensuous feelings and impressions, is similar to Spranger's aesthetic attitude. Holland's (1987, p. 5) artistic type values the world of beauty, identifies with artists of various disciplines, and aspires to work in artistic pursuits. Holland describes artistic types as creative, sensitive, imaginative, and nonconforming.

Science Motives

Spranger's theoretical attitude emphasizes a preference for naming, classifying, and logical analysis. Similarly, Allport, Vernon, and Lindzey proposed that the theoretical man seeks to discover truth through empirical, critical, and logical means. Holland's investigative type values logic, analysis, and the pursuit of knowledge. This type enjoys science and identifies with scientists. Holland describes the investigative type as intellectual, scholarly, analytical, and curious.

INITIAL DEVELOPMENT

The MVPI contains 200 items presented in the form of statements to which a respondent indicates "agree," "uncertain," or "disagree." Each scale contains 20 items that were derived rationally from hypotheses about the likes, dislikes, and aversions of the "ideal" exemplar of each motive. Each scale is composed of five themes: (a) Lifestyles, which concern the manner in which a person would like to live; (b) Beliefs, which involve "shoulds," ideals, and ultimate life goals; (c) Occupational Preferences, which include the work an individual would like to do, what constitutes a good job, and preferred work materials; (d) Aversions, which reflect attitudes and behaviors that are either disliked or distressing; and (e) Preferred Associates, which include the kind of persons desired as coworkers and friends.

There are no correct or incorrect responses for the MVPI items; therefore, there is no need for validity or faking keys. There is no item overlap among the 10 scales. The items were screened for content that might seem to be offensive or an invasion of privacy. There are no items concerning sexual preferences, religious beliefs, criminal or illegal behavior, racial/ethnic attitudes, or attitudes about disabled individuals. There are no items that could be used to determine physical or mental disabilities; the MVPI is not a medical examination.

SUMMARY OF THE CURRENT MVPI STRUCTURE

The MVPI is a relatively new inventory. Its structure includes 10 scales that were developed around five themes: lifestyles, beliefs, occupational preferences, aversions, and preferred associates. This structure has remained constant since the inventory was introduced in the early 1990s.

FUTURE DEVELOPMENT PLANNED FOR THE MVPI

Perhaps the biggest challenge that lies ahead for the MVPI is taking advantage of the rich assessment data that it produces in the form of more sophisticated reports. The MVPI is still in its infancy relative to the history of personality-based assessment inventories. Interpretive information continues to evolve, and as this information forms interpretive patterns, it will be incorporated into reports.

One area that will clearly develop over the next few years is the role of the MVPI in assessing the work environments that leaders create. We believe that the values of leaders are largely responsible for the work environments that leaders create. Those with values consistent with the leader will find the environment satisfying. In contrast, those with inconsistent values may be dissatisfied and seek alternative employment opportunities. This is such an important concept that we are adding interpretive information to the MVPI scales that focus on the environment that a leader will create (see Chapter 7). We anticipate that this concept will be increasingly important in understanding MVPI results, particularly in light of the demand for leadership talent in the growing world economy.

GENERAL INTERPRETATION GUIDELINES FOR THE MVPI

- The MVPI can provide useful feedback in a broad variety of situations. For example, MVPI feedback can help candidates or hiring managers determine how happy an individual will be in a particular job. MVPI results can also give managers information on how to motivate specific employees. Group MVPI results can be used to help teams better understand areas of conflict and help organizations quantify their unique culture.

- The MVPI can be used in a wide variety of employee selection and development situations.

- The relative degree of person-job fit can be determined by comparing a person's higher scores on the MVPI with the prevailing values of the organization.

- Scores at the 65th percentile and above are considered to be High. These are the true drivers that people actively seek out in their lives. Managers should pay close attention to these scores when motivating employees.

- Scores between the 36th and 64th percentiles are considered to be Average. These are the things that interest the individual, but at a lesser degree than his/her drivers.

- Scores at the 35th percentile and below are considered to be Low. These are the things to which an individual is indifferent. Low scores, however, do not necessarily imply de-motivation, but they do indicate things that an individual is not interested in or motivated by.

- If a profile has no scores in the High range, then the scores in the Average range are considered to be true drivers.

- The leader's MVPI profile will determine the working environment they will create for their employees.

- The MVPI profile for top leadership will be a key indicator of organizational culture.

- The interpretive statements for each scale are empirically based.

MVPI FACTS

- The initial version of the MVPI was developed in the early 1990s. Like the Hogan Personality Inventory (HPI) and the Hogan Development Survey (HDS), the MVPI has undergone several revisions. The current version of the MVPI was published in 1996.

- The MVPI assesses the things that individuals enjoy and that indicate what kinds of jobs, work, and environments they will find most satisfying.

- The MVPI is an excellent tool to determine how well a person will fit with a job and with a team, department, or organization.

- The MVPI has 200 items that comprise 10 primary scales. The data are presented in terms of percentiles.

- More than 500,000 people have taken the MVPI.

- The MVPI is a Level B assessment.

MVPI GLOBAL PORTABILITY

The current version of the MVPI has only been available for a little over a decade. Even with its short history, it has proven its worth in the international marketplace as a valuable tool in understanding the motives and driving values of individuals. Perhaps an even more important use for the inventory from an international perspective is in understanding the type of environment a leader will create within a given culture. As with the HPI, we have engaged in a large-scale translation effort over the past decade. At the time of this printing, the MVPI is available online in the following languages:

- Bahasa (BM)
- Brazilian Portuguese (BP)
- Castilian Spanish (CA)
- Czech (CS)
- Danish (DA)
- French Parisian (FR)
- German (GR)
- Icelandic (IS)
- Japanese (JA)
- Kenyan (KE)
- Korean (KO)

- Norwegian (NO)
- Polish (PL)
- Simplified Chinese (ZH)
- Slovak (SK)
- South African (AE)
- Spanish (ES)
- Swedish (SV)
- Traditional Chinese (ZC)
- Turkish (TR)
- UK English (UK)
- US English (US)

Although we are at the early stages of developing an international research archive for the MVPI, we are rapidly expanding our norm data and validation research. The results we have obtained to date regarding norms and validity for the MVPI continue to support its global portability.

CHAPTER 7

MOTIVES, VALUES, PREFERENCES INVENTORY SCALES

Recognition	*Appreciation is a wonderful thing: it makes what is excellent in others belong to us as well.*	– Voltaire
Power	*You can go a long way with a smile. You can go a lot farther with a smile and a gun.*	– Al Capone
Hedonism	*Fun is a good thing, but only when it spoils nothing better.*	– George Santayana
Altruistic	*It is one of the most beautiful compensations of life that no man can sincerely try to help another without helping himself.*	– Ralph Waldo Emerson
Affiliation	*I like pigs. Dogs look up to us. Cats look down on us. Pigs treat us as equals.*	– Winston Churchill
Tradition	*Tradition is the illusion of permanence.*	– Woody Allen
Security	*Any society that would give up a little liberty to gain a little security will deserve neither and lose both.*	– Benjamin Franklin
Commerce	*If your only goal is to become rich, you will never achieve it.*	– John D. Rockefeller
Aesthetics	*It's very beautiful, but it's not fashion—it's something else. It's costume.*	– Pierre Cardin
Science	*The problems that exist in the world today cannot be solved by the level of thinking that created them.*	– Albert Einstein

SCALE 1 – RECOGNITION

The Recognition scale measures values associated with fame, visibility, and publicity; an interest in being acknowledged and rewarded; and a lifestyle organized around opportunities for self-display. Important areas of concern include a desire to be recognized, noticed, and famous.

- Low Scorers – Prefer working in environments where they can share credit; they tend to create environments that focus on bottom-line results and sharing credit.

- High Scorers – Value public acknowledgement for hard work and individual/team success; they will create an environment that publicly rewards job performance and values high-profile projects.

Performance Implications of High Scores (65%–100%)

Individuals with High scores are perceived as colorful, outgoing, and socially confident. They care deeply about being the center of attention and having their accomplishments acknowledged in public. These individuals tend to be interesting, imaginative, self-confident, and dramatic, but also independent and unpredictable. They appear to handle pressure and criticism well, prefer to work in teams, communicate well with others, and contribute many ideas. They are dramatic, can have trouble admitting their mistakes, and may be reluctant to share credit. They will seek work assignments that provide opportunities to be noticed, such as sales, entertainment, teaching, and customer service and will want to lead a group that has an opportunity for visibility.

Performance Implications of Average Scores (36%–64%)

Individuals with Average scores are perceived as social, confident, and appropriate. They prefer work environments where there are opportunities to be with others, and where they will be recognized for their achievements, but they are also willing to share credit with others. Although public recognition is not the primary motivator in their lives, they are not likely to remain silent when they are due some credit for important accomplishments.

Performance Implications of Low Scores (0%–35%)

Individuals with Low scores are perceived as quiet, restrained, and modest. They tend to be reserved and uncommunicative, and avoid calling attention to themselves. They value sharing credit, are indifferent to personal recognition, and do not mind working by themselves in behind-the-scenes roles.

Recognition and Leadership

Leaders with High scores for Recognition seek fame, acknowledgment, and appreciation from others. They expect to be admired, and can be annoyed when they are not. On the one hand, this puts pressure on their staff to be appropriately admiring; on the other hand, leaders with High scores for Recognition tend to be indifferent to such needs among their subordinates, which can create unnecessary tensions. This is a culture with the leader as the star.

Recognition and Culture

A high Recognition culture is one in which accomplishment, productivity, and apparent success are recognized in a prompt and public fashion. In addition, the organization self-consciously strives to ensure that clients and competitors recognize and understand the significance of its performance. The stars will be the heroes of the organization; the outcasts will be the critics of others' performance.

SCALE 2 – POWER

The Power scale measures values associated with competition, achievement, and being perceived as influential; an interest in challenge; and a lifestyle organized around worldly success. Important areas of concern include a desire for challenge, competition, achievement, and success.

- Low Scorers – Do not value managing others and directing workflow processes and procedures; they prefer confrontation-free environments and individual contributor roles.

- High Scorers – Value leadership and authority and prefer to tell others what to do versus taking orders; they value influence and are perceived as indispensable.

Performance Implications of High Scores (65%–100%)

Individuals with High scores are perceived as leaderlike, assertive, and strategic about their careers. They value achievement and accomplishment, and they evaluate themselves in terms of what they are able to get done. These individuals prefer environments where there are opportunities to get ahead, achieve, and succeed. Ideal occupation areas include management, sales, marketing, consulting, and entrepreneurship. These individuals are ambitious, energetic, visionary, leaderlike, controlling, and willing to disagree with their superiors. Others describe them as having leadership skills, challenging limits, and being socially competent. They care deeply about being successful and having opportunities for upward mobility and will tend to leave when such opportunities are not available.

Performance Implications of Average Scores (36%–64%)

Individuals with Average scores are perceived as confident, willing to lead, and having an agenda for their careers. They accept challenging projects, take the initiative, and value assignments with responsibility and opportunities to be in charge. These individuals want to be successful and will take pride in their achievements, but they also realize there is more to life than their job.

Performance Implications of Low Scores (0%–35%)

Individuals with Low scores are perceived as unassertive, reluctant to lead, and modest. They tend to be quiet and careful about following procedures, and they will not disagree with their superiors. These individuals are uninterested in competition, achievement, and personal advancement; consequently, they are usually not very strategic about their careers. They value getting along, following orders, and not being responsible for the performance of others.

Power and Leadership

Leaders with High scores for Power are achievement-oriented, want to make a difference, and want to create a legacy. They value accomplishment and have little tolerance for sloth. On the one hand, they will create a pragmatic, results-oriented culture where things get done; on the other hand, they may create a culture in which there is too much top-down control.

Power and Culture

A culture characterized by high Power is aggressive, competitive, and results-oriented. It keeps track of its performance vis-à-vis the competition; it sets ambitious goals for itself; it minimizes wasted motion, meetings, and pointless discussions; and it evaluates itself on what it is able to accomplish. The heroes of the organization will be those who have contributed the most in a substantive, measurable way. The outcasts will be the lazy and/or ineffectual.

SCALE 3 – HEDONISM

The Hedonism scale measures values associated with good company and good times; an interest in pleasure, excitement, and variety; and a lifestyle organized around entertaining friends, good food, and having fun. Important areas of concern include a desire for fun, excitement, and a lifestyle organized around good food, good drinks, and entertainment.

- Low Scorers – Value businesslike and professional environments; they will create serious and structured work environments.

- High Scorers – Value colorful and entertaining environments; they will create fun and open-minded environments.

Performance Implications of High Scores (65%–100%)

Individuals with High scores are perceived as lively, flirtatious, and pleasure seeking. They tend to be dramatic, impulsive, and the life of the party. They prefer work environments with opportunities to have fun or entertain others. Ideal occupation areas include sales, hospitality, travel, and entertainment. These individuals are expressive, changeable, easily bored, unconcerned with details, and they may not learn from their mistakes. Consequently, they may need to be reminded to follow through and put business before pleasure.

Performance Implications of Average Scores (36%–64%)

Individuals with Average scores are perceived as relaxed, informal, and fun-loving. They usually put business before pleasure and keep commitments, but may also be impulsive and sometimes overindulgent. These individuals can usually strike a proper balance between work and play and between having fun and being task-focused. They prefer a flexible work environment that allows leaders to set their own priorities, and which allows people to balance serious work with lighthearted interludes.

Performance Implications of Low Scores (0%–35%)

Individuals with Low scores are perceived as self-disciplined, socially appropriate, and formal. They tend to be reserved, concerned with details, and careful about what they say and do. These individuals prefer to work in a restrained and task-focused environment, and will tend to have difficulties with people who do not share their devotion to duty. Others will view them as buttoned-down, no nonsense, and serious. They often seem reluctant to relax and have a good time—especially when there is work to be done.

Consequently, they may need to be reminded occasionally to take time out to "smell the roses."

Hedonism and Leadership

Leaders with High scores for Hedonism are motivated by variety and fun, and they enjoy entertaining others. They will tend to create a culture marked by office parties, celebration of staff accomplishments, and an overall sense of fun. However, not everyone has a sense of humor, and some staff will think these leaders lack seriousness.

Hedonism and Culture

A high Hedonism culture is characterized by an ethos of "work hard/play hard"; people strive to perform at a high level, and then periodically take time to relax, celebrate, and have a good time together. There is a clear awareness that having fun is as much a part of the culture as effortful striving, and there may even be a "party budget." The heroes of the organization will be those who are the most fun to be around. The outcasts will be "party poopers."

SCALE 4 – ALTRUISTIC

The Altruistic scale measures values associated with improving society and actively helping others, an interest in helping the less fortunate, and a lifestyle organized around making the world a better place to live. Important areas of concern include the desire to serve others, improve society, and help the less fortunate.

- Low Scorers – Place less value on helping others; they place more value on their own work and how organizational decisions will impact their ability to get things done.
- High Scorers – Value helping others and creating an environment that places emphasis on customer service.

Performance Implications of High Scores (65%–100%)

Individuals with High scores are perceived as honest, sympathetic, and concerned about others. They tend to be sensitive, considerate, unassertive, and kind. They prefer work in which they can help others, including careers in teaching, medicine, hospitality, social work, counseling, and human resources. These individuals are idealistic, good-natured, and care about social justice, the plight of the have-nots, and the welfare of the environment. They listen well and are sensitive to staff and client needs, but may not be very forceful. They enjoy helping others, promote staff morale, foster open communication, and help others (including subordinates) enhance their careers.

Performance Implications of Average Scores (36%–64%)

Individuals with Average scores are perceived as responsible, socially aware, and considerate. They keep their staff informed, respond to advice, and consider staff morale. These individuals can usually maintain a balance between a focus on the bottom line and a concern for staff welfare. Although they enjoy helping others, they probably will not devote their lives to public service or spend time doing volunteer work for charitable organizations, and are more likely to contribute money instead of personal time to help others.

Performance Implications of Low Scores (0%–35%)

Individuals with Low scores are perceived as tough, uncommunicative, and somewhat materialistic. They tend to be assertive, forceful, direct, outspoken, and willing to confront people-related problems. These individuals are able to focus on their work, can filter out unnecessary demands, and will not be distracted by the crises and emotional storms of others. They prefer task-oriented work environments, are more concerned with productivity than staff morale or development, and tend not to be interested in helping the less fortunate citizens of society.

Altruistic and Leadership

Leaders with High scores for Altruistic enjoy helping and encouraging others. They will tend to create a culture marked by fair treatment, civil behavior, respect for individuals, and an emphasis on personal growth and development. Not surprisingly, not everyone cares about civility and fairness, and these people will think the leaders do not care about results.

Altruistic and Culture

A high Altruistic culture is one that cares about the welfare and well-being of the staff. People are encouraged to develop their talents and fulfill their potential, and they are provided the resources and assistance to do so. Everyday interaction is characterized by respect, consideration, and mutual support. Such an organization is also involved in the larger social community. The heroes of the organization will be those who are the most dedicated and selfless. Selfish people will be the outcasts of these organizations.

SCALE 5 – AFFILIATION

The Affiliation scale measures values associated with frequent and varied social contact, an interest in working with others, and a lifestyle organized around social interaction. Important areas of concern include a need for frequent and varied social contact and a lifestyle organized around meetings and get-togethers.

- Low Scorers – Tend to be task-oriented, distant, enjoy working alone, and may not want to be part of a team.

- High Scorers – Value working with others, being highly visible in the organization, social interaction, and creating a sense of commitment to tasks or groups.

Performance Implications of High Scores (65%–100%)

Individuals with High scores are perceived as energetic, outgoing, and talkative. They tend to be charming, socially insightful, adaptable, and spontaneous. These individuals enjoy working in team environments and dislike working alone. They enjoy meeting new people, networking, and developing strategic alliances. They seem approachable, trusting, adaptable, and open to criticism. They are often described as good corporate citizens who are willing to follow company policy, but others may see them as being somewhat dependent on the approval of upper management.

Performance Implications of Average Scores (36%–64%)

Individuals with Average scores are perceived as approachable, expressive, and friendly. Although socializing with friends or colleagues is not a primary motivator, they will prefer a work environment that requires some teamwork and group process and will dislike working alone for extended periods. These individuals are comfortable around strangers, are open communicators, and will provide both information and feedback to their staff.

Performance Implications of Low Scores (0%–35%)

Individuals with Low scores are perceived as withdrawn, uncommunicative, and uncomfortable around strangers. They prefer to work alone, and they value their private time. These individuals are independent, quiet, self-restrained, and not deeply concerned with pleasing others. They are most comfortable with work environments in which people mind their own business and solve their own problems. They do not desire constant or rapidly changing social contact, are not concerned with social approval, and may not want to work in a team environment.

Affiliation and Leadership

Leaders with High scores for Affiliation love social interaction of almost any kind. As a result, they will tend to create a culture marked by frequent, even constant, communication among and between units, lots of meetings, and frequent and spontaneous special purpose work teams. People who are more introverted and/or task-oriented will think the culture values activity over productivity.

Affiliation and Culture

A high Affiliation culture is one with a near compulsion for social interaction. The official and unofficial practices and procedures will be designed to maximize social contact. This includes calling many scheduled and unscheduled meetings, frequent communication within and between units, and organizing the office space so as to encourage interaction. The heroes of the organization will be those who are most popular; the outcasts will be the loners.

SCALE 6 – TRADITION

The Tradition scale measures values associated with history and convention, an interest in high standards and appropriate social behavior, and a lifestyle organized around well-established principles of conduct. Important areas of concern include traditional morality, family values, and a lifestyle guided by well-established norms of social behavior.

- Low Scorers – Tend to value liberal, flexible, and unconventional environments; they tend to be flexible concerning the similarity between their own and the organization's values and prefer self-direction.

- High Scorers – Are motivated by environments that share their same values. Typically, these values are conservative in nature; they will be de-motivated in an environment that does not share their beliefs and values.

Performance Implications of High Scores (65%–100%)

Individuals with High scores are perceived as mature, commonsensical, and responsive to advice. They defend established procedures, are careful about experimenting, maintain formal relations with coworkers, and have conservative lifestyles. These individuals value rules, standards, and prefer stable and predictable work environments. They care about maintaining tradition, custom, and socially acceptable behavior. They tend to be trusting, considerate, evenhanded, and good-natured, but also somewhat cautious, set in their ways, and resistant to change.

Performance Implications of Average Scores (36%–64%)

Individuals with Average scores are perceived as trusting, responsible, and coachable. They are somewhat formal, fairly conservative in their views, and prefer to follow established procedures. Although they may enjoy doing things in new ways, they also appreciate the role of tradition and history as guides to behavior.

Performance Implications of Low Scores (0%–35%)

Individuals with Low scores are perceived as unconventional, independent, and unresponsive to advice. They challenge established procedures, change directions quickly, and appreciate diverse viewpoints. These individuals value change, modernity, and a progressive lifestyle. They tend to be liberal and nontraditional in their beliefs and prefer modern, dynamic, and flexible work environments. They tend to be described as progressive, unpredictable, flexible, impulsive, and willing to take risks.

Tradition and Leadership

Leaders with High scores for Tradition value respect for authority and tradition, duty, and hard work and will create a culture marked by formality, rules, and uniform procedures. Leaders with Low scores value innovation, diversity, and respect for uniqueness and will create a culture marked by informality, experimentation, and openness to alternative perspectives.

Tradition and Culture

A high Tradition culture will be typified by dress codes, grooming standards, a clear hierarchy and reporting structure, and rules about decorating desks and office space. There will be symbols attesting to patriotism and respect for authority (e.g., flags, pictures of government officials or venerated figures of the past) and perhaps designated times when incumbents join in public displays of respect for authority (e.g., prayers or flag raising ceremonies). There may also be small museums or libraries commemorating the organization's history. The heroes of the organization will be the people at the top of the hierarchy; the outcasts will be the nonconformers.

SCALE 7 – SECURITY

The Security scale measures values associated with certainty, predictability, and risk-free environments, an interest in structure and order, and a lifestyle organized around minimizing risk, uncertainty, and criticism. Important areas of concern include a need for structure, order, and a lifestyle organized around planning for the future and minimizing financial risk, employment uncertainty, and criticism.

- Low Scorers – Enjoy environments where they are given freedom to take chances, test the limits, and make quick changes.
- High Scorers – Are motivated by cautious, risk-free environments that provide predictability and consistency; they create environments that focus on high-quality, low-risk decisions rather than new or untested markets.

Performance Implications of High Scores (65%–100%)

Individuals with High scores are perceived as cautious, conforming, and quiet. They care deeply about safety, financial security, and avoiding mistakes. These individuals prefer a stable and predictable work environment that promises good job security, and they dislike performance appraisal and ambiguity. Others describe them as polite, attentive to details, punctual, and easy to supervise, but somewhat shy and uncomfortable around strangers. They tend to be inhibited, unassertive, and risk avoidant; consequently, they tend to earn less than they might because they are unwilling to take risks with their careers.

Performance Implications of Average Scores (36%–64%)

Individuals with Average scores are perceived as careful, responsible, and slow to act. They tend to be uncomfortable with risky and ambiguous situations, and would rather err on the side of safety than take chances with their careers or finances. These individuals tend not to seek feedback, take initiative, or be innovators. They are most likely to perform well in situations where the chances of success are certain or where the future of the organization is secure.

Performance Implications of Low Scores (0%–35%)

Individuals with Low scores are perceived as outgoing, assertive, and adventurous. They enjoy taking risks and testing limits, tolerate ambiguity and uncertainty, and like feedback on their performance. These individuals are leaderlike and tend to be described as independent, open to criticism, and willing to take risks. They are unconcerned about job security and prefer environments where risk taking, innovation, and taking the initiative are rewarded.

Security and Leadership

Leaders with High scores for Security dislike risk taking and appreciate structure and predictability. They will create a risk-averse culture marked by caution, fallback options, and fail-safe strategies. Leaders with Low scores for Security are unafraid of risk, will take chances to advance the business, and will bounce back quickly from failure.

Security and Culture

A high Security culture will be characterized by a concern about errors, mistakes, leaks, and alien intrusions and will put careful processes in place to guard against undesired eventualities, both real and imagined. These will include security procedures, access codes, oversight plans to guarantee compliance with authorized methods, and an overarching emphasis on minimizing risk. The heroes of the organization will be those who make the fewest mistakes and excel in calling others out; the outcasts will be people who are tolerant of others' mistakes and are flexible about the rules.

SCALE 8 – COMMERCE

The Commerce scale measures values associated with business activities, money, and financial gain, an interest in realizing profits and finding business opportunities, and a lifestyle organized around investments and financial planning. Important areas of concern include an interest in earning money, realizing profits, finding business opportunities, and a lifestyle organized around investments and financial planning.

- Low Scorers – Are unconcerned with the bottom line and/or material success, and will not spend their spare time working on finance-related issues.

- High Scorers – Value finding ways to make money, both for themselves and the organization; they are interested in budget and compensation issues and value activities such as financial forecasting and cost benefit analysis.

Performance Implications of High Scores (65%–100%)

Individuals with High scores are perceived as ambitious, active, and energetic. They tend to be hardworking, task-oriented, planful, organized, practical, socially adroit, and mature. These individuals tend to pay close attention to budgets and compensation issues, and are comfortable working within specified guidelines. They are serious about their work, attentive to detail, businesslike, direct, and focused on the bottom line. These individuals care deeply about monetary matters, material success, and income as a form of self-evaluation. They are most happy in work environments with opportunities to make money and to get ahead.

Performance Implications of Average Scores (36%–64%)

Individuals with Average scores are perceived as serious, focused, and hardworking. They tend to maintain a balance between profitability, fun, people issues, and the bottom line. These individuals are usually calm, fair, and attentive to morale and financial issues. They are neither indifferent to financial considerations nor preoccupied with them. Consequently, money will not be a major motivator in their personal or work lives, and other priorities will interest them more than compensation.

Performance Implications of Low Scores (0%–35%)

Individuals with Low scores are perceived as friendly, unselfish, and generous. They tend to be more interested in ideas and having fun than in money, fame, or success. These individuals are sympathetic, relaxed, and loyal to their employees, and they value relationships over profitability. Consequently, they may be well-liked, but may not push people for results. They are indifferent to commercial values, are unconcerned about material success, and will not spend their spare time reading about (or working on) finance-related issues.

Commerce and Leadership

Leaders with High scores for Commerce are motivated by the bottom line. They will create a culture characterized by financial discipline, a single-minded search for profits, and energetic efforts to reduce costs. Others may think these leaders tend to emphasize profits over people and finances over feelings.

Commerce and Culture

A high Commerce culture will emphasize profitability and cost containment. The heroes of the culture will be "rainmakers," or persons who raise money, develop business, or devise new and effective methods for reducing costs. There will be a constant, relentless focus on the "bottom line," sometimes over the short run and possibly at the expense of the long term. The heroes of the organization will be those who generate revenues and cut costs; the outcasts will be wastrels and spendthrifts.

SCALE 9 – AESTHETICS

The Aesthetics scale measures values associated with creative and artistic self-expression; an interest in art, literature, and music; and a lifestyle guided by imagination, culture, and attractive surroundings. Important areas of concern include interest in art, literature, music, and a lifestyle guided by issues of style, culture, good taste, and a desire to entertain.

- Low Scorers – Value practical problem solving and running things by the book, and are less concerned with the appearance of work products or their environment.

- High Scorers – Value innovation and problem solving; they are the most motivated in environments that allow experimentation, exploration, and creativity; they value quality as much as quantity.

Performance Implications of High Scores (65%–100%)

Individuals with High scores are perceived as spontaneous, fun-loving, and creative. They appreciate opportunities to use their imagination and are happiest in work environments that allow experimentation, exploration, and creative problem solving. These individuals enjoy innovation and will care about the appearance of work products. At times, their imagination and enthusiasm for the new, the original, and the interesting may make it difficult for them to concentrate on the old, the dull, and the repetitive. Others may see them as unpredictable, disorganized, preferring to solve problems on their own, easily bored, and testing the limits.

Performance Implications of Average Scores (36%–64%)

Individuals with Average scores are perceived as colorful, enthusiastic, and expressive. They enjoy innovation, can change direction and focus easily, and are able to combine creativity with practicality. Although these individuals have some artistic interests and values, they are not dominant factors in their life. Consequently, they are more likely to be concerned with the content rather than the appearance of work products.

Performance Implications of Low Scores (0%–35%)

Individuals with Low scores are perceived as steady and practical, with conventional taste in lifestyle issues. They are indifferent to aesthetic values or creative self-expression and have practical interests and a businesslike style. These individuals tend to be stable, predictable, levelheaded, and dependable. They keep their emotions under control, persist with boring tasks, and use a practical approach to problem solving. They tend to be unconcerned with issues of personal autonomy or the appearance of work products and tend to not be interested in innovation and may even resist it.

Aesthetics and Leadership

Leaders with High scores for Aesthetics worry about the quality, look, and feel of work products. They will create a culture that emphasizes a sense of high concept and style with a lot of attention to issues of appearance and layout. Others may think they waste money on nonessentials, but for such leaders, stylish appearance trumps cost every time.

Aesthetics and Culture

A high Aesthetics culture will be characterized by a self-conscious attention to style, appearance, quality, and "good taste." The furniture, wall coverings, rugs, and restrooms will be high quality, often the result of advice from external consultants. Stationery, logos, and reception areas (all aspects of the public face of the organization) will be carefully designed to send a message to clients and staff regarding quality and standards of style. The heroes of the organization will be those with the best taste; the philistines will be the outcasts.

SCALE 10 – SCIENCE

The Science scale measures values associated with learning; an interest in new ideas, technology, and analytical problem solving; and a lifestyle organized around exploring and understanding how things work. Important areas of concern include an interest in new ideas and technology and a rational and data-based approach to problem solving.

- Low Scorers – Are uninterested in science or technical advances, and they are more comfortable working with people than technology; they will tend to be more intuitive in their decision making and problem-solving efforts; and they will only rely upon data as a support or influence mechanism.

- High Scorers – Value problem-solving environments where they can stay current with new technical and business information and involve new technology in work procedures; they will create an environment that values analytical problem solving, curiosity, and objective decision-making processes.

Performance Implications of High Scores (65%–100%)

Individuals with High scores are perceived as curious, analytical, and comfortable with technology. They enjoy analyzing problems, understanding how things work, and getting below the surface noise to get to the truth. These individuals tend to be bright and well-organized, but may lack leadership skills. They prefer environments where they can use data to identify trends, solve problems, or create meanings, and they tend to stay informed about new technical and business information. They may also be perceived as easily bored, impatient, argumentative, easily annoyed, and preferring analysis to action.

Performance Implications of Average Scores (36%–64%)

Individuals with Average scores are perceived as good organizational citizens who are not easily bored and can focus on team goals. They can make intuitive decisions, persist with repetitive tasks, follow company rules, and are comfortable with technology. These individuals tend to strike a balance between analysis and action and try to stay up-to-date on new technical and business information. They should be helpful in solving problems, but are as likely to engage others' assistance in finding solutions as they are to research ideas on their own.

Performance Implications of Low Scores (0%–35%)

Individuals with Low scores are perceived as uncomfortable with technology, having practical interests, and focused on personal goals. They tend to be uninterested in science and technology, and they prefer an intuitive and spontaneous approach to problem solving. These individuals want action, not analysis, and are more comfortable working with people than with technology. They tend to be sympathetic, open to feedback, and responsive to criticism. Others describe them as responsible, flexible, and willing to make mistakes.

Science and Leadership

Leaders with High scores for Science are logical, disciplined, empirical, and prefer to make data-based decisions. They will create a culture that emphasizes rationality and accountability, but which may be slow to react and make decisions. Leaders with Low scores value intuition, instinct, and experience. They will create a culture that emphasizes doing things "well enough" and making decisions that are good enough rather than well-grounded in data.

Science and Culture

A high Science culture will be characterized by an emphasis on the rigor and defensibility of plans, goals, decisions, and public statements. People's positions and opinions must be justified with logic and data. Anyone's views can be (and usually are) challenged, and they must be defended satisfactorily. Few courses of action will be chosen arbitrarily or idiosyncratically; policies and procedures will typically be based on evidence and rationality. The heroes of the organization will be the smart people; the outcasts will be the "airheads" and slow learners.

PART 2

METHODS OF INTERPRETATION

CHAPTER 8

CONFIGURAL INTERPRETATION

My philosophy of life is that if we make up our mind what we are going to make of our lives, then work hard toward that goal, we never lose—somehow we win out.

– Ronald Reagan

The preceding chapters provide basic information regarding how to interpret each of the Hogan inventories: the Hogan Personality Inventory (HPI), the Hogan Development Survey (HDS), and the Motives, Values, Preferences Inventory (MVPI). We presented the information on a scale-by-scale basis, focusing on the performance implications of a particular range of scale scores. This information is a necessary and useful first step in understanding the inventories, but it only scratches the surface of the interpretive power that can be gained from them.

The next step in this learning process is called configural interpretation. Configural interpretation involves looking beyond a single scale of an inventory to gain deeper insight into performance by combining the results of more than one scale. The ability to make configural interpretations depends on the experience of the person reviewing the inventory results. There are 28 scales associated with the three inventories. Mathematically, that works out to 756 possible two-scale combinations and countless other 3, 4, 5, or more scale combinations. It would not be possible (nor fruitful) to write out interpretations for all these combinations. However, experience reveals that certain combinations are more common than others and recognizing them can dramatically improve the interpretive power to be gained from the inventories.

The purpose of this chapter is to give users some insight into configural interpretation. We will use the HPI as the foundation for building toward increasingly complex interpretations. After we have explored interpretations for the HPI, we will use a job family approach to examine HPI results in conjunction with HDS results and, finally, MVPI results. We conclude this chapter with a brief consideration of "syndrome" configurations.

HPI INTERPRETATION

The easiest and perhaps most comprehensive way to illustrate configural interpretations for the HPI is to provide a look-up table for the seven scales, taken two at a time. This approach will result in 84 dyads, illustrated in two "look-up" tables. Table 11 illustrates the structure of the "look-up" tables. The actual "look-up" tables appear in Table 12 and Table 13.

Table 11: Structure of "Look-up" Tables

	High Scores (>65%)
Table 12 = Low Scores (<35%)	
	Low Scores (<35%)
	High Scores (>65%)
Table 13 = High Scores (>65%)	
	Low Scores (<35%)

This approach will not address middle-range scores; however, it provides a starting point when considering the performance implications of two scales in combination. It is important to emphasize that the interpretive information provided in the following tables is a simple "thumbnail" perspective to be used solely as a starting point.

Table 12: HPI Low Score Configurations

Low			Impact of the Combination
	High	Ambition	Driven to compete, achieve, and win while constantly worrying about possibly failing and then being criticized.
	Low	Ambition	Fears failure and avoids it by choosing low-pressure roles with few demands.
	High	Sociability	Needs social interaction, but constantly worries about being rejected or criticized, which results in diminished social skills.
	Low	Sociability	Prone to worry and self-doubt, fears being criticized, and will avoid stressful social gatherings and public appearances.
	High	Inter. Sens.	Will try to build conflict-free relations, will be upset when conflicts arise, and will blame self when they occur.
	Low	Inter. Sens.	Will be blunt and confrontational during interactions, but afterwards will worry about and feel guilty over damaging a relationship.
Adjustment	High	Prudence	Will follow rules, pay attention to details, and work very hard, while staying alert for signs of criticism and disapproval.
	Low	Prudence	May have issues with anger management and personal discipline and may engage in bursts of "organizing activity."
	High	Inquisitive	Bouts of creative activity will be interrupted by bouts of self-doubt and self-examination.
	Low	Inquisitive	Will resist change or new ideas because they will disrupt routine, and the unknown will cause anxiety.
	High	Learn. App.	Will be driven to stay up-to-date to avoid feeling anxious about not being "in the know" about new developments.
	Low	Learn. App.	May not stay up-to-date due to the stress and worry that may result from learning things that might create future change.

124

Table 12 (continued): HPI Low Score Configurations

Low			Impact of the Combination
Ambition	High	Sociability	Will be an energetic and lively person with few well-defined career goals and little focus on achievement.
	Low	Sociability	A clear follower who will allow others to lead and will happily go along as a team player.
	High	Inter. Sens.	A pleasant and agreeable person who will seem rather meek, noncompetitive, and unwilling to challenge others.
	Low	Inter. Sens.	Will tend to be argumentative or disagreeable, but with little desire to "win" such interactions or even make a point.
	High	Prudence	Will rely on rules and procedures to accomplish assigned tasks, but will rarely take any initiative or deviate from assigned tasks.
	Low	Prudence	Will take shortcuts and find the easy way to do a job with the least effort and to a minimum standard of performance.
	High	Inquisitive	Curiosity about new ideas and techniques, but without necessarily doing anything or committing to any course of action.
	Low	Inquisitive	Will follow standard routines while working, but will avoid changes or innovations that might create new demands or additional work.
	High	Learn. App.	Interested in learning new methods and techniques, but will rarely take the initiative to use them.
	Low	Learn. App.	Prefers to learn on the job and is uninterested in training, applying new knowledge, or using new technology.
Sociability	High	Inter. Sens.	Will be reluctant to start new relationships, but will be quite skilled at maintaining existing relationships.
	Low	Inter. Sens.	A quiet, even shy person who nonetheless is rather tough and willing to confront others when necessary.
	High	Prudence	Will be task-oriented, planful, organized, and hardworking, but with little or no public fanfare or self-promotion.
	Low	Prudence	Will be careless about rules and procedures, impulsive and defiant, but these behaviors may be hard to notice.
	High	Inquisitive	Will be quiet and reserved, but curious about what is going on; should be a good listener.
	Low	Inquisitive	Little interest in interacting with others and no interest in change or innovation.
	High	Learn. App.	Focused on individual learning opportunities and knowledge acquisition, but without the stress of group interactions.
	Low	Learn. App.	Prefers to learn in an experiential, hands-on fashion without being exposed to social scrutiny.

Table 12 (continued): HPI Low Score Configurations

Low			Impact of the Combination
	High	Prudence	Will be blunt and direct and tend to confront people who do not work hard, stay focused, or pay attention to detail.
Inter. Sens.	Low	Prudence	Will be impulsive, self-absorbed, confrontational, and a poor team player, but can work with little supervision.
	High	Inquisitive	Will be curious, open-minded, and intellectually engaged, with a propensity to play the devil's advocate and challenge others' views.
	Low	Inquisitive	Should be a tough-minded pragmatist with little tolerance for wooly-minded abstractions or risky innovations.
	High	Learn. App.	Should seem bright, well-informed, eager to learn, and willing to challenge the ideas of others.
	Low	Learn. App.	Uses his/her experience as the basis for an argumentative, challenging interpersonal style while discounting the value of formal learning.
Prudence	High	Inquisitive	Curious, thoughtful, and creative, open to new ideas and innovations, and willing to implement and try new things.
	Low	Inquisitive	Tends to be impulsive, distractible, disorganized, and rarely reflects on the meaning or consequences of such behavior.
	High	Learn. App.	Will seem bright, well-informed, interested in training, and willing to try new methods, techniques, and technology.
	Low	Learn. App.	Will prefer to learn by experience, but will not pay much attention to the lessons of experience or the consequences of failure.
Inquisitive	High	Learn. App.	Will be a quick study who values staying up-to-date, but with little interest in innovations that lack clear practical implications.
	Low	Learn. App.	Will lack curiosity and be unwilling to try anything new without first-hand experience regarding its positive, tangible impact.

126

Table 13: HPI High Score Configurations

			Impact of the Combination
High			
	High	Ambition	Calm, poised, self-confident, hardworking, upwardly mobile, somewhat aggressive, and eager to be in charge.
	Low	Ambition	Easygoing and self-satisfied; comfortable following rather than leading; perceived as lacking energy, passion, and drive.
	High	Sociability	Outgoing, talkative, self-confident, and entitled; expecting to be liked and successful.
	Low	Sociability	Quiet, self-confident, strong, silent type who will handle stress easily and without any noticeable drama.
	High	Inter. Sens.	Confident, friendly, relationship-oriented interpersonal style that creates a perception of modesty and inner strength.
	Low	Inter. Sens.	Will seem confident, self-assured, and perhaps arrogant with a direct, challenging, and blunt interpersonal style.
Adjustment	High	Prudence	Hardworking, persistent, organized, dependable, mature, and very strong under stress and pressure.
	Low	Prudence	Calm and steady under pressure, but disorganized and impulsive, sometimes creating havoc for others who have to fill in.
	High	Inquisitive	Curious, open-minded, and able to generate new ideas with great confidence, often elevating them above the ideas of others.
	Low	Inquisitive	Confident, self-assured, and unflappable, but with little interest in change, innovation, or enhanced understanding of current processes.
	High	Learn. App.	Bright, self-confident, well-informed, self-assured, and possibly arrogant, but able to support opinions with logic and data.
	Low	Learn. App.	Self-confident, stable, and self-assured, but perhaps smug and complacent with little interest in acquiring new knowledge.

127

Table 13 (continued): HPI High Score Configurations

High			Impact of the Combination
Ambition	High	Sociability	Forceful, energetic, and hardworking; will communicate vigorously and reach out to others as a career development strategy.
	Low	Sociability	Quiet and reserved, but intense and driven to succeed; will lead by example because action speaks louder than words.
	High	Inter. Sens.	Strong desires for achievement and success will be facilitated by real talent for building and maintaining relationships.
	Low	Inter. Sens.	Hardworking, competitive, and achievement-oriented, combined with a blunt and challenging interpersonal style.
	High	Prudence	Unusually hardworking and achievement-oriented, within a framework of conscientiousness and attention to detail.
	Low	Prudence	Competitive and achievement-oriented, while regarding rules, processes, and procedures as barriers to be overcome.
	High	Inquisitive	Hardworking, achievement-oriented, and leaderlike and a source for providing new ideas and vision.
	Low	Inquisitive	Hardworking and eager to succeed, but by doing something well and avoiding changes that may disrupt what is working.
	High	Learn. App.	Hardworking, competitive, and leaderlike, but smart and up-to-date and will not suffer fools gladly.
	Low	Learn. App.	Hardworking and achievement-oriented, but impatient with training, strongly prefers to learn on the job.
Sociability	High	Inter. Sens.	Gregarious, outgoing, and talkative, but will be seen as warm, friendly, approachable, and charming.
	Low	Inter. Sens.	Good at starting relationships, but will have trouble maintaining them due to his/her blunt interpersonal style.
	High	Prudence	Strong task orientation that will involve endless discussions of minute details in the name of accurate communication.
	Low	Prudence	Flexible, spontaneous, outgoing interactive style that may allow conversations to venture into gray or marginally-appropriate areas.
	High	Inquisitive	Interested in meeting new people and exploring new ideas, but might be regarded as lacking focus or easily distracted by the next new thing.
	Low	Inquisitive	Outgoing and approachable; primarily interested in the mundane or routine with little interest in the big picture.
	High	Learn. App.	Smart and up-to-date with a breezy and approachable interpersonal style who is quick to move on new and different topics.
	Low	Learn. App.	Gregarious, outgoing, and talkative, but has little interest in current events or new developments in business or technology.

128

Table 13 (continued): HPI High Score Configurations

High			Impact of the Combination
Inter. Sens.	High	Prudence	Serious and conscientious; has high standards of performance, but tolerant rather than self-righteous or picky.
	Low	Prudence	Pleasant, tolerant, and agreeable, but with relatively low standards about timely and quality performance.
	High	Inquisitive	Cordial and pleasant, has a lively imagination, and willing to explore ideas regardless of how impractical they may be.
	Low	Inquisitive	Warm and engaging, has a rather prosaic imagination and little interest in the big picture.
	High	Learn. App.	Bright and well-informed, but does not flaunt his/her knowledge or criticize those who are less educated.
	Low	Learn. App.	Pleasant and sociable colleague with little interest in formal learning, current events, or new developments in technology.
Prudence	High	Inquisitive	Strong interest in discussing ideas and innovation with a tendency to be mired in the details during implementation.
	Low	Inquisitive	Strict adherence to rules, processes, and procedures with little interest in innovation, particularly when things seem to be working;
	High	Learn. App.	Smart, well-informed, hardworking, careful person with good judgment, but reluctant to challenge established procedures.
	Low	Learn. App.	Careful, conscientious, hardworking person with little interest in training and development; comfortable with what he/she already knows.
Inquisitive	High	Learn. App.	Bright, up-to-date, productive, and always on the lookout for new methods, technology, or paths to the future.
	Low	Learn. App.	Interested in new ideas and developments, but prefers to hear about them versus read about them; open-minded, but intellectually lazy.

The preceding dyads represent the most fundamental level of configural interpretation. They illustrate the interpretive power that can be gained by looking beyond a single scale to the way personality characteristics interact. If we go a step further, we can observe behavioral patterns that can only be understood after considering three or more HPI scales in combination. The following are three examples (sometimes called syndromes) that produce relatively consistent behavioral patterns.

- Creativity – The creativity syndrome is defined by scores above the 65th percentile on Inquisitive and Ambition, and scores below the 35th percentile on Prudence. High Inquisitive reflects the cognitive style associated with creativity; low Prudence reflects the necessary flexibility and willingness to challenge convention; high Ambition reflects the energy necessary to bring one's tasks to completion.

- Arrogance – Persons who score above the 90th percentile on Inquisitive, Adjustment, Ambition, and Sociability and above the 65th percentile on Prudence will seem very competent and will make an excellent impression on others. Beyond their competencies, however, they may be arrogant. They may see themselves as more competent than others do, promote their own career goals at the expense of the organization for which they work, ignore negative feedback, and be insensitive to the needs and expectations of others, especially subordinates. Not surprisingly, if you give them this feedback, they may ignore it.

- Delinquency – The Prudence scale is the best single indicator of delinquent tendencies on the HPI. Although all delinquents will have low Prudence scores, not everyone with a low Prudence score will be delinquent. By considering scores on Adjustment and Sociability, a much more accurate judgment can be made. Specifically, the combination of low scores for Adjustment and Prudence and a high score for Sociability suggests a person who is alienated and unhappy (low Adjustment), hostile to rules and authority (low Prudence), but impulsive and attention seeking (high Sociability). The syndrome itself is relatively infrequent in normal (e.g., nonprison) populations; when it occurs, it signals a person whose identity includes being tough, defiant, and scornful of the normal rules and conventions of society.

These are three examples of behavior patterns that are best understood after considering multiple HPI scales. We could easily spend the rest of this guide documenting behavior patterns that can be explained through configural interpretation. In fact, we discover new patterns regularly, and avid users of our inventories discuss specific profiles and their behavioral implications on a daily basis.

Another approach to understanding combinations of HPI scores is to consider the demands of a job or occupation. This is perhaps the most common use of the HPI, and it provides a framework for organizing configural interpretations. The premise for this approach is determining the probability of success. The probability of an individual being successful in a job increases dramatically when his/her profile matches the demands associated with that job. For example, the HPI profile for an Air Traffic Controller (a job demanding a calm demeanor, low distractibility, high conscientiousness, and comfort with routine) would be quite different from a Used Car Salesperson (a job demanding passion, interpersonal skills, resilience, and flexibility). We can capitalize on these differences by examining a range of demands associated with various job families to create a useful configural scoring guide.

Job families are groups of similar occupations classified based on work performed, skills, education, training, and credentials needed. We have identified seven job families for this guide, derived from the nine "job classifications" used by the Equal Employment Opportunity Commission (EEOC) for employers in the United States. They include Managers and Executives, Professionals, Technicians and Specialists, Operations and Trades, Sales and Customer Support, Administrative and Clerical, and Service and Support. We combined the EEOC job classifications for Craft Worker, Operative, and Laborer into one group (Operations and Trades) because of the overlap in competencies required for success in these classifications.

We used this classification scheme as a guide because: (a) a large percentage of employers within the United States are familiar with the EEOC job classifications; (b) the job classifications are clear and easy to use for reporting purposes; and (c) it provides a way to organize configural interpretations that is comprehensive without resorting to the mind-numbing exercise of considering "X" things taken "X" at a time. We begin by considering the configural results for the Managers and Executives job family using just the HPI (see Table 14). We will then add the HDS and MVPI results to develop a complete configural template for this job family. We conclude this chapter with a configural template for each of the remaining six job families.

Table 14 illustrates the HPI configural results for the Managers and Executives job family. The matrix highlights the key scales (not all seven scales are key) associated with performance in the job family, an indication of the ideal range (Low = <35%; Average = 36% to 64%; High = >65%) in which a score should fall, a brief description of what is covered by the job family, and a description of the typical performance of a person who has this type of profile. Keep in mind that success in a job can come in many forms. The following profile simply highlights the scales that are most important to success. The job families are broad, and for specific jobs, more precise ranges and additional scales may prove useful in predicting success.

Table 14: Job Family 1 (Managers and Executives)

HPI Profile				
Scales	**Score Range**			**Description**
	Low	**Avg.**	**High**	
Adjustment		X	X	The Managers and Executives job family consists of employees assigned to positions of administrative or managerial authority over the human, physical, and/or financial resources of the organization (e.g., supervisors, team leaders, managers, directors, and vice presidents). If the target job fits this description, then look for the following pattern of scores: average to high scores for Adjustment, Ambition, and Interpersonal Sensitivity, and average scores for Prudence. This is the profile of a person who is calm and stable (Adjustment), competitive and achievement-oriented (Ambition), and friendly and agreeable (Interpersonal Sensitivity). This person will also be conscientious and rule-following (Prudence), but not overly rigid or inflexible about rules and procedures.
Ambition		X	X	
Sociability				
Inter. Sens.		X	X	
Prudence		X		
Inquisitive				
Learn. App.				

HDS INTERPRETATION

We begin with the HDS by examining three configurations that follow directly from the factor structure of the inventory, and then consider some simple relationships between the HDS and the HPI.

As noted in Chapter 4, the HDS has a three-factor structure. There is a "Moving Away" factor (Excitable, Skeptical, Cautious, Reserved, and Leisurely), a "Moving Against" factor (Bold, Mischievous, Colorful, and Imaginative), and a "Moving Toward" factor (Diligent and Dutiful). Although it is rare to see all of the scales associated with a factor elevated to the high-risk level, it is common to see elevations on all the scales within a factor. When this occurs, it is similar to the syndromes described in reference to combinations of scales on the HPI. Such syndromes result in a unique combination of behaviors. The following are descriptions of each of the three syndromes defined by elevations on all of the scales within each factors.

- Moving Away – A person exhibiting this syndrome will be prone to florid emotional displays that swing between passionate enthusiasm and intense distaste regarding people or projects (Excitable). The person would be keenly alert for signs of betrayal and/or disapproval, and if these signs are detected would "go postal"—challenge, accuse, confront, and retaliate (Skeptical). Beneath the prickly exterior, this person is insecure and afraid of being criticized (Cautious), deeply resentful of superiors (Leisurely), but quiet, withdrawn, and preferring to work alone (Reserved). Therefore, the insecurity and resentment might be hard to detect.

- Moving Against – A person exhibiting this syndrome will be bright, charismatic, and self-confident to the point of being arrogant (Bold), excitement seeking and limit testing (Mischievous), self-dramatizing, exuberant, and impulsive (Colorful), and creative and innovative to the point of seeming eccentric (Imaginative). Interestingly, it is common to see this syndrome in a leader's profile because the positive behaviors associated with these scales cause individuals to be noticed and create a leaderlike aura that others may find attractive. The potential downside is that one or more of these scales may be in the high-risk range, and derailing tendencies will emerge.

- Moving Toward – This syndrome is defined by a high degree of conscientiousness and need for guidance. Managers initially appreciate people like this because they will go to great lengths to make sure every detail of an assignment is completed and nothing falls through the cracks (Diligent). They will also look to their manager for direction and will avoid taking any action other than what their manager has clearly and unambiguously directed (Dutiful). Over time, these people will lose respect in the organization because they will be seen as followers, incapable of taking independent action. They may also get in trouble with their manager because of the time needed to direct them regarding the minutest details. In other words, the credit they gain with their followership may wear on a busy manager who needs staff to take more initiative as business demands increase.

The three factors can also be defined from the point of view of strategies that an individual uses to influence people. These three "influence" factors are:

- Intimidation – "You force me to express in no uncertain terms how much I have become disappointed with you." (Excitable) "I am being mistreated and taken advantage of, and so I am fully justified in responding in kind." (Skeptical) "I have no option but to point out all the potential problems that could occur, because otherwise you will make changes that could have disastrous consequences." (Cautious) "You say that I am not listening to you. You must realize that if you could say anything that is of interest to me, I would listen." (Reserved) "The only reason I have ignored you is because you always interrupt me at a time when you should be doing your own work." (Leisurely)

- Seduction – "Some of us just have the talent for this sort of thing, and so if you follow my lead, things will go well." (Bold) "There are all sorts of complexities to this problem, especially from the point of view of relationships among decision-makers. I can have those folks eating out of my hand." (Mischievous) "Many people enjoy being with me, and so why not just join me and we can get things moving again?" (Colorful) "The reason we are having trouble is because no one can see new the possibilities as well as I can. If you can trust me and take this new path, we can leave all these problems behind." (Imaginative)

- Control – "You will give me everything I need because I get things done, they are done right, and they are done ahead of schedule." (Diligent) "I have been loyal to you, letting you make the decisions and following you without question. Now that I need your support, I am sure you won't let me down." (Dutiful)

If you have ever known someone whose scores on the HDS are all low, you can understand that an entire profile of low HDS scores usually reveals a very bland individual who has little influence on others.

These HDS combinations of scales provide significant interpretive power. The interpretive power can be further magnified by considering the HDS in conjunction with the HPI. We refer to the HDS as a measure of the "dark side" of personality, in contrast to the HPI, which measures the "bright side." This simple nomenclature is actually quite useful for understanding the configural interpretations required when considering HPI-HDS results jointly.

We do not see a person's "dark side" on a regular basis. Generally, we see a person's "bright side," which may be augmented by some of the more positive behaviors associated with the HDS scales. For example, people with high Prudence scores often have fairly high scores on Diligent, indicating conscientiousness and detail orientation. Similar relationships can be observed between other HPI and HDS scales. While these relationships are not inevitable, they occur often enough to provide a useful organizing structure when considering simple HPI-HDS configurations. Table 15 illustrates these relationships with a brief configural interpretation for each.

Table 15: Relationships between the HPI and HDS Scales

HDS Scales				HPI Scales			HDS Scales	
Description	Scales	High Score	Low Score	Scales	High Score	High Score	Scales	Description
Emotional individual who can be volatile or explosive	Excitable	↓	↑	Adjustment	↓	↑	Bold	Self-confident individual who seems arrogant
Follower who will avoid making decisions	Cautious	↓	↑	Ambition	↓	↑	Bold	A driven person who refuses to admit to or learn from mistakes
Socially withdrawn individual with a very tough style	Reserved	↓	↑	Sociability	↓	↑	Colorful	Gregarious person who loves personal attention
						↑	Leisurely	An individual that uses "yes" to avoid agenda conflict
Argumentative person who does not trust others	Skeptical	↓	↑	Inter. Sens.	↓			
						↑	Dutiful	Relationship-oriented person who says "yes" to everything
Rule-averse person who will test the system	Mischievous	↓	↑	Prudence	↓	↑	Diligent	A rigid person who cares about every painstaking detail
Routine-oriented person who only does what he/she is told	Dutiful	↓	↑	Inquisitive	↓	↑	Imaginative	An open, creative person who lacks focus or discipline

When these combinations occur, the inevitable question is, at what point does a useful combination of attributes on two inventories turn into a derailing combination? We can provide a useful example by considering a configural interpretation of the Managers and Executives job family (see Table 16). Recall that an average Prudence score predicts a manager who is conscientious and rule-following, but not excessively rigid or inflexible about rules and procedures. An elevated score on the Diligent scale would be consistent with this interpretation. If the score on the Diligent scale is in the high-risk level, we would observe that this manager would be overly focused on details and unable to see the big picture. If the manager also had high scores on Prudence, we would observe not only an excessive focus on details, but also rigid adherence to rules and requiring everyone to do things by the book—the manager's book. The result will be a micromanager who drives subordinates crazy with his/her rigidity and need for control.

Now that we have seen the enhanced interpretive power that can be gained by considering HPI-HDS scores in combination, let us return to the Managers and Executives job family and add the HDS to the equation. Again, only key scales will be considered, with the proviso that significant elevations on any HDS scale can be problematic and potentially derail an individual with an otherwise strong profile.

We will highlight the scales from two perspectives. First, we will discuss the performance enhancements that can be gained when scores fall in the designated range. Second, we will consider the performance issues that may occur if scores fall outside the designated range. This is consistent with the general rule regarding HDS scales that too much of a good thing will allow negative, derailing behaviors to surface.

Table 16: Job Family 1 (Managers and Executives – continued from Table 14)

HPI Profile

Scales	Score Range			Description
	Low	Avg.	High	
Adjustment		X	X	The Managers and Executives job family consists of employees assigned to positions of administrative or managerial authority over the human, physical, and/or financial resources of the organization (e.g., supervisors, team leaders, managers, directors, and vice presidents). If the target job fits this description, then look for the following pattern of scores: average to high scores for Adjustment, Ambition, and Interpersonal Sensitivity, and average scores for Prudence. This is the profile of a person who is calm and stable (Adjustment), competitive and achievement-oriented (Ambition), and friendly and agreeable (Interpersonal Sensitivity). This person will also be conscientious and rule-following (Prudence), but not overly rigid or inflexible about rules and procedures.
Ambition		X	X	
Sociability				
Inter. Sens.		X	X	
Prudence		X		
Inquisitive				
Learn. App.				

Table 16 (continued): Job Family 1 (Managers and Executives – continued from Table 14)

HDS Profile

Scales	Score Range				Performance Enhancers	Derailment Risks
	No	Low	Mod.	High		
Excitable					This is the profile of a person with a healthy degree of skepticism (Skeptical) regarding what others tell him/her, who seems confident and in charge (Bold), charismatic and willing to test limits without crossing the line (Mischievous), engaging and attractive (Colorful), creative and somewhat unconventional (Imaginative), and who will attend to details and follow up when needed (Diligent).	This person needs to avoid unnecessary mistrust (Skeptical), ignoring mistakes and criticism (Bold), creating trust issues because of limit-testing behavior (Mischievous), grabbing the spotlight and competing with subordinates (Colorful), offering ideas without evaluating them (Imaginative), and missing the big picture while micromanaging details (Diligent).
Skeptical		X				
Cautious						
Reserved						
Leisurely						
Bold		X	X			
Mischievous		X	X			
Colorful		X	X			
Imaginative		X	X			
Diligent		X				
Dutiful						

MVPI INTERPRETATION

Adding the MVPI into the interpretive mix is a bit more challenging than combining the HPI with the HDS, primarily because how a person's values match his/her job requires some organizational context. This is so because, although a person's values may be consistent with a particular job or career, they may be inconsistent with the culture of an organization. Inconsistencies (or misalignments) between a person's values and the organizational culture can often cause a person to leave for another organization. This does not mean the person disliked the job he/she was performing; it means that he/she would prefer to do that job in another organization where the culture is more compatible with his/her values.

We can use the Managers and Executives job family to illustrate this issue. Typically, people who value leadership roles have at least average scores on the Power scale. They want to be in charge and take responsibility for getting things done. They dislike environments where they have little control over their fates or the fate of the business for which they are responsible. Now, consider an organization searching for a new manager. Assume the managers in this organization all have average scores on Power, but in addition, they have high scores on Tradition and low scores on Hedonism. The culture of this organization would feature patriotic, spiritual, and family values as a backdrop. Fun and entertainment would be discouraged. Candidates with a moderate Power score should fit right in. However, candidates with high scores on Hedonism and low scores on Tradition would find the organization to be far too serious and would greatly prefer organizations where fun was tolerated and even encouraged.

Situations like this occur more often than people realize. They typically result in turnover, and the reason usually has more to do with "fit" than with competence. We present this example in order to illustrate the importance of the match between the values of an individual and an organization. The match does not have to be one-to-one. However, as the values of the individual and the organization diverge, the probability of turnover increases.

The MVPI is useful for configural interpretation even when organizational data are unavailable. In such cases, the interpretation will focus on "fit" with a job or career. The values of scientists working alone in laboratories will be different from managers of used car salespersons. This is the perspective we will use when considering the MVPI component of the configural interpretations related to the job families.

We now add the MVPI to the HPI and HDS profile for the Managers and Executives job family (see Table 17). We will focus on the key scales only, highlight score ranges, and describe performance enhancers and cultural conflicts. The cultural conflicts will reflect components of an organizational environment that may create dissatisfaction for the person in this job family.

Table 17: Job Family 1 (Managers and Executives – Continued from Table 14 and Table 16)

HPI Profile

Scales	Score Range			Description
	Low	Avg.	High	
Adjustment		X	X	The Managers and Executives job family consists of employees assigned to positions of administrative or managerial authority over the human, physical, and/or financial resources of the organization (e.g., supervisors, team leaders, managers, directors, and vice presidents). If the target job fits this description, then look for the following pattern of scores: average to high scores for Adjustment, Ambition, and Interpersonal Sensitivity, and average scores for Prudence. This is the profile of a person who is calm and stable (Adjustment), competitive and achievement-oriented (Ambition), and friendly and agreeable (Interpersonal Sensitivity). This person will also be conscientious and rule-following (Prudence), but not overly rigid or inflexible about rules and procedures.
Ambition		X	X	
Sociability				
Inter. Sens.		X	X	
Prudence		X		
Inquisitive				
Learn. App.				

Table 17 (continued): Job Family 1 (Managers and Executives – Continued from Table 14 and Table 16)

HDS Profile

Scales	Score Range				Performance Enhancers	Derailment Risks
	No	Low	Mod.	High		
Excitable					This is the profile of a person with a healthy degree of skepticism (Skeptical) regarding what others tell him/her, who seems confident and in charge (Bold), charismatic and willing to test limits without crossing the line (Mischievous), engaging and attractive (Colorful), creative and somewhat unconventional (Imaginative), and who will attend to details and follow up when needed (Diligent).	This person needs to avoid unnecessary mistrust (Skeptical), ignoring mistakes and criticism (Bold), creating trust issues because of limit-testing behavior (Mischievous), grabbing the spotlight and competing with subordinates (Colorful), offering ideas without evaluating them (Imaginative), and missing the big picture while micromanaging details (Diligent).
Skeptical		X				
Cautious						
Reserved						
Leisurely						
Bold		X	X			
Mischievous		X	X			
Colorful		X	X			
Imaginative		X	X			
Diligent		X				
Dutiful						

Table 17 (continued): Job Family 1 (Managers and Executives – Continued from Table 14 and Table 16)

MVPI Profile					
Scales	**Score Range**			**Performance Enhancers**	**Cultural Conflicts**
	Low	**Avg.**	**High**		
Recognition				This is the profile of a person who wants to be in control and take responsibility for results (Power), who will pay close attention to the bottom line and the financial success of a venture (Commerce), and will use data to make decisions, but will not become overly enamored with data or succumb to analysis paralysis (Science).	This person will be unhappy in cultures where there is little control over one's fate (Power), where the financial success of the venture is disregarded (Commerce), where data are overanalyzed in a way that slows decision making, or where decisions are made intuitively with little supporting rationale (Science).
Power		X	X		
Hedonism					
Altruistic					
Affiliation					
Tradition					
Security					
Commerce		X	X		
Aesthetics					
Science		X			

REMAINING SIX JOB FAMILIES

Tables 18–23 present the configural interpretations for the six remaining job families. These tables have been constructed in the same way as the Managers and Executives job family. Each table illustrates a profile for a job family that would be considered ideal (in the absence of organizational context).

144

Table 18: Job Family 2 (Professionals)

HPI Profile				
Scales	**Score Range**			**Description**
	Low	**Avg.**	**High**	
Adjustment		X	X	The Professionals job family consists of experts with a broad educational background who rely primarily on knowledge and intelligence to do their work. Examples include scientists, physicians, attorneys, accountants, teachers, and human resource professionals. If the target job fits this description, then look for the following pattern of HPI scores: average to high scores for Adjustment, Ambition, Interpersonal Sensitivity, Prudence, and Inquisitive. This is the profile of a person who is calm and even-tempered (Adjustment), achievement-oriented (Ambition), congenial and tactful (Interpersonal Sensitivity), conscientious and rule-abiding (Prudence), and bright and creative (Inquisitive).
Ambition		X	X	
Sociability				
Inter. Sens.		X	X	
Prudence		X	X	
Inquisitive		X	X	
Learn. App.				

Table 18 (continued): Job Family 2 (Professionals)

HDS Profile						
Scales	**Score Range**				**Performance Enhancers**	**Derailment Risks**
	No	**Low**	**Mod.**	**High**		
Excitable					This is the profile of a person who will challenge others' ideas and data (Skeptical), have an agenda and work toward achieving it (Leisurely), appear self-confident, even fearless (Bold), and offer ideas that seem unusual, creative, and somewhat unconventional (Imaginative).	This person will need to avoid challenging others' motives (Skeptical), acting unilaterally, or failing to involve others who do not agree with his/her agenda (Leisurely), he/she will need to be sure not to ignore feedback or failure (Bold), or offer too many ideas without getting anything done (Imaginative).
Skeptical		X	X			
Cautious						
Reserved						
Leisurely		X				
Bold		X				
Mischievous						
Colorful						
Imaginative		X	X			
Diligent						
Dutiful						

145

Table 18 (continued): Job Family 2 (Professionals)

MVPI Profile

Scales	Score Range			Performance Enhancers	Cultural Conflicts
	Low	Avg.	High		
Recognition				This is the profile of a person who likes some control over his/her work (Power), enjoys helping others (Altruistic), does not mind working alone (Affiliation), is potentially creative (Aesthetics), and tends to be a knowledge worker—or, at least, knowledge plays a central role in the work product (Science).	This person will not flourish in cultures where there is little control over one's fate (Power), helping others is the core of the job (Altruistic), all work is team-based and interdependent (Affiliation), creativity is unimportant (Aesthetics), and data is irrelevant to decision making (Science).
Power		X			
Hedonism					
Altruistic		X			
Affiliation	X				
Tradition					
Security					
Commerce					
Aesthetics		X			
Science		X	X		

Table 19: Job Family 3 (Technicians and Specialists)

HPI Profile				
Scales	**Score Range**			**Description**
	Low	**Avg.**	**High**	
Adjustment		X	X	The Technicians and Specialists job family consists of occupations that require applying highly specialized knowledge in the skilled manipulation (e.g, operation, repair, cleaning, and/or preparation) of specialized technology, tools, and/or machinery to perform very specific functions within the organization. Examples include computer technology specialists, industrial drafters, specialized equipment operators, and service technicians. If the target job fits this description, then look for the following pattern of HPI scores: average to high scores for Adjustment, Ambition, Prudence, and Learning Approach. This is the profile of a person who is calm and stable (Adjustment), achievement-oriented and competitive (Ambition), patient and conscientious (Prudence), and interested in acquiring new knowledge (Learning Approach).
Ambition		X	X	
Sociability				
Inter. Sens.				
Prudence		X	X	
Inquisitive				
Learn. App.		X	X	

148

Table 19 (continued): Job Family 3 (Technicians and Specialists)

HDS Profile						
Scales	**Score Range**				**Performance Enhancers**	**Derailment Risks**
	No	**Low**	**Mod.**	**High**		
Excitable	X	X			This is the profile of a person who keeps his/her emotions under control (Excitable), will not break rules to achieve results (Mischievous), will be attentive to processes and follow through on details (Diligent), and will comply with and support senior management (Dutiful).	This person will need to avoid seeming to lack any passion (Excitable), following rules or procedures that do not make sense (Mischievous), focusing on details while ignoring the big picture or micromanaging others (Diligent), or becoming overly reliant upon authority figures and failing to take appropriate initiative (Dutiful).
Skeptical						
Cautious						
Reserved						
Leisurely						
Bold						
Mischievous	X	X				
Colorful						
Imaginative						
Diligent		X	X			
Dutiful		X	X			

Table 19 (continued): Job Family 3 (Technicians and Specialists)

MVPI Profile					
Scales	**Score Range**			**Performance Enhancers**	**Cultural Conflicts**
	Low	**Avg.**	**High**		
Recognition				This is the profile of a person who enjoys working with others and being part of a team (Affiliation) and prefers work environments that value sound operating procedures and performance standards (Tradition), in which people care about how things work and find ways to make them work better (Science).	This person will not flourish in cultures that value individual contribution over team accomplishments (Affiliation), that have little regard for doing things the right way (Tradition), and where decisions are made without adequate evaluation of data (Science).
Power					
Hedonism					
Altruistic					
Affiliation		X	X		
Tradition		X			
Security					
Commerce					
Aesthetics					
Science		X	X		

149

Table 20: Job Family 4 (Operations and Trades)

HPI Profile				
Scales	**Score Range**			**Description**
	Low	**Avg.**	**High**	
Adjustment		X	X	The Operations and Trades job family consists of skilled, semiskilled, and unskilled occupations who gain job knowledge and skills primarily through experience and on-the-job training. Examples include craft workers, heavy machine operators, landscapers, and factory workers. If the target job fits this description, then look for the following pattern of HPI scores: average to high scores for Adjustment and Prudence and average scores for Ambition and Learning Approach. This is the profile of a person who is calm and stable (Adjustment), team-oriented, but willing to take initiative (Ambition), conscientious and rule-abiding (Prudence), and willing to learn the key requirements of the job necessary to be successful (Learning Approach).
Ambition		X		
Sociability				
Inter. Sens.				
Prudence		X	X	
Inquisitive				
Learn. App.		X		

Table 20 (continued): Job Family 4 (Operations and Trades)

HDS Profile

Scales	Score Range				Performance Enhancers	Derailment Risks
	No	Low	Mod.	High		
Excitable	X				This is the profile of a person who stays calm and keeps his/her emotions under control (Excitable), avoids risky decisions or working outside sanctioned limits (Cautious), attends to processes and follows through on details (Diligent), and respects and supports management (Dutiful).	This person will need to avoid seeming to lack enthusiasm (Excitable), refusing to act or make decisions due to a fear of failure (Cautious), focusing on details and ignoring the big picture or micromanaging details and other people (Diligent), or seeming overly reliant upon authority figures and refusing to take initiative (Dutiful).
Skeptical						
Cautious		X	X			
Reserved						
Leisurely						
Bold						
Mischievous						
Colorful						
Imaginative						
Diligent		X	X			
Dutiful		X	X			

151

Table 20 (continued): Job Family 4 (Operations and Trades)

MVPI Profile					
Scales	**Score Range**			**Performance Enhancers**	**Cultural Conflicts**
	Low	Avg.	High		
Recognition				This is the profile of a person who enjoys working with others and being part of a team (Affiliation), who prefers work environments that emphasize old-fashioned virtues of hard work and respect for authority (Tradition), wants a stable work environment and long-term employment (Security), and solves problems in a pragmatic way (Science).	This person will be unhappy in cultures that value individual contribution over the accomplishments of the team (Affiliation), that encourage diversity and radical experimentation (Tradition), where jumping from job to job is the norm (Security), and where decisions are made based on impulse and not data (Science).
Power					
Hedonism					
Altruistic					
Affiliation		X	X		
Tradition		X			
Security		X			
Commerce					
Aesthetics					
Science		X			

Table 21: Job Family 5 (Sales and Customer Support)

HPI Profile

Scales	Score Range			Description
	Low	Avg.	High	
Adjustment		X		The Sales and Customer Support job family consists of employees who build the credibility and sales of an organization through interacting and establishing long-lasting relationships with clients. Examples include sales executives, telemarketers, customer service representatives, and account managers. If the target job fits this description, then look for the following pattern of HPI scores: average to high Ambition and Prudence and average Adjustment and Interpersonal Sensitivity. This is the profile of a person who is competitive and achieving (Ambition) and patient and conscientious (Prudence). This person will also be calm and self-confident (Adjustment), but open to feedback. In addition, this person will be friendly and engaging (Interpersonal Sensitivity), but able to handle conflict appropriately.
Ambition		X	X	
Sociability				
Inter. Sens.		X		
Prudence		X	X	
Inquisitive				
Learn. App.				

153

Table 21 (continued): Job Family 5 (Sales and Customer Support)

HDS Profile						
Scales	**Score Range**				**Performance Enhancers**	**Derailment Risks**
	No	**Low**	**Mod.**	**High**		
Excitable	X	X			This is a profile of a person who tends to be low on the "Moving Away" scales (Excitable, Skeptical, Cautious, Reserved, and Leisurely) because of a need to build and maintain relationships. In addition, this person will be self-confident without being arrogant (Bold). If the job has a heavy sales component versus service component, low to moderate elevations on the other "Moving Against" scales (Mischievous, Colorful, and Imaginative) may be helpful.	This person will need to avoid seeming to lack passion, which sometimes accompanies very low scores on the "Moving Away" scales. It is also important to avoid seeming arrogant, and for positions closer to traditional sales, the charisma associated with the other "Moving Against" scales should not turn into deceitful (Mischievous), attention seeking (Colorful), or eccentric (Imaginative) behaviors.
Skeptical	X	X				
Cautious	X	X				
Reserved	X	X				
Leisurely	X	X				
Bold		X	X			
Mischievous		X	X			
Colorful		X	X			
Imaginative		X	X			
Diligent						
Dutiful						

154

Table 21 (continued): Job Family 5 (Sales and Customer Support)

MVPI Profile					
Scales	**Score Range**			**Performance Enhancers**	**Cultural Conflicts**
	Low	Avg.	High		
Recognition		X		This is the profile of a person who wants to be recognized and recognizes the accomplishments of others (Recognition), wants to be in control and take responsibility for results (Power), will pay close attention to the financial success of a venture (Commerce), and will use data to make important decisions (Science).	This person will not be happy in cultures that do not celebrate personal achievement (Recognition), where there is little control over one's fate (Power), that are unconcerned about financial success (Commerce), or where decisions are made impulsively or compulsively (Science).
Power		X	X		
Hedonism					
Altruistic					
Affiliation					
Tradition					
Security					
Commerce		X	X		
Aesthetics					
Science		X			

Table 22: Job Family 6 (Administrative and Clerical)

HPI Profile

Scales	Score Range			Description
	Low	Avg.	High	
Adjustment		X	X	The Administrative and Clerical job family consists of employees who plan, direct, or coordinate the support services of an organization. Examples include secretaries, professional assistants, receptionists, and mail clerks. If the target job fits this description, then look for the following pattern of HPI scores: average to high Adjustment, Ambition, and Prudence and average Interpersonal Sensitivity. This profile is of a person who is calm and stable (Adjustment), competitive and achievement-oriented (Ambition), and patient and conscientious (Prudence). This person will also be friendly and agreeable (Interpersonal Sensitivity), but able to handle conflict appropriately.
Ambition		X	X	
Sociability				
Inter. Sens.		X		
Prudence		X	X	
Inquisitive				
Learn. App.				

156

Table 22 (continued): Job Family 6 (Administrative and Clerical)

HDS Profile

Scales	Score Range				Performance Enhancers	Derailment Risks
	No	Low	Mod.	High		
Excitable	X	X			This is a profile of a person who tends to have low scores on the "Moving Away" scales (Excitable, Skeptical, Cautious, Reserved, and Leisurely), needs to build and maintain relationships, will also have low to moderate scores on the "Moving Toward" scales (Diligent and Dutiful), ensuring that he/she pays attention to detail and respects, complies with, and supports management (Dutiful).	Low scores on the "Moving Away" scales present virtually no derailment risk for people in these positions. Moreover, elevations on these scales (and the negative behaviors that accompany them) are problematic in this job family because of the way they negatively impact relationships. In contrast, high detail orientation (Diligent) and followership (Dutiful) are useful and even encouraged.
Skeptical	X	X				
Cautious	X	X				
Reserved	X	X				
Leisurely	X	X				
Bold						
Mischievous						
Colorful						
Imaginative						
Diligent		X	X			
Dutiful		X	X			

157

Table 22 (continued): Job Family 6 (Administrative and Clerical)

MVPI Profile					
Scales	**Score Range**			**Performance Enhancers**	**Cultural Conflicts**
	Low	**Avg.**	**High**		
Recognition				This is the profile of a person who enjoys helping others (Altruistic) and working with others and being part of a team (Affiliation), prefers work environments that value hard work and respect for tradition and authority (Tradition), and prefers stable work environments that offer long-term employment (Security).	This person will be unhappy in cultures that do not value their people (Altruistic), that value individual contribution over the accomplishments of the team (Affiliation), that disregard getting things done the right way (Tradition), and where jumping from job to job is the norm (Security).
Power					
Hedonism					
Altruistic		X			
Affiliation		X	X		
Tradition		X	X		
Security		X			
Commerce					
Aesthetics					
Science					

Table 23: Job Family 7 (Service and Support)

HPI Profile				
Scales	**Score Range**			**Description**
	Low	**Avg.**	**High**	
Adjustment		X	X	The Service and Support job family consists of employees who provide protective services, such as police officers, firefighters, and guards, or services for others (e.g., jobs in food service, recreation, and entertainment). If the target job fits this description, then look for the following pattern of HPI scores: average to high Adjustment, Ambition, and Prudence and average Interpersonal Sensitivity. This profile is of a person who is calm and stable (Adjustment), competitive and achievement-oriented (Ambition), and patient and conscientious (Prudence). This person will also be friendly and agreeable (Interpersonal Sensitivity), but able to handle conflict appropriately.
Ambition		X	X	
Sociability				
Inter. Sens.		X		
Prudence		X	X	
Inquisitive				
Learn. App.				

159

Table 23 (continued): Job Family 7 (Service and Support)

HDS Profile						
Scales	**Score Range**				**Performance Enhancers**	**Derailment Risks**
	No	**Low**	**Mod.**	**High**		
Excitable					This is the profile of a person who is reasonably self-confident when faced with challenging situations (Bold), is self-controlled and able to follow established procedures (Mischievous), will attend to details and avoid careless mistakes (Diligent), and will happily follow the instructions of superiors (Dutiful).	This person will need to avoid becoming overly self-confident, but act confidently within the bounds of their training (Bold), avoid bending rules or making exceptions (Mischievous), not become preoccupied with trivial details (Diligent), and be willing to take action in ambiguous and changing circumstances without external guidance and direction (Dutiful).
Skeptical						
Cautious						
Reserved						
Leisurely						
Bold		X				
Mischievous	X					
Colorful						
Imaginative						
Diligent		X	X			
Dutiful		X	X			

160

Table 23 (continued): Job Family 7 (Service and Support)

MVPI Profile					
Scales	**Score Range**			**Performance Enhancers**	**Cultural Conflicts**
	Low	**Avg.**	**High**		
Recognition				This is the profile of a person who enjoys helping others and providing assistance that makes a difference in their lives (Altruistic), likes to work with others and be part of a team (Affiliation), and prefers working in an environment that respects traditional values, hard work, and lawful authority (Tradition).	This person will not be happy in an organization that does not respect its people (Altruistic), values individual contribution over the accomplishments of the team (Affiliation), and disregards getting things done the right way (Tradition).
Power					
Hedonism					
Altruistic		X	X		
Affiliation		X	X		
Tradition		X	X		
Security					
Commerce					
Aesthetics					
Science					

161

SYNDROME CONFIGURATIONS

A consideration of configural interpretation would not be complete without a brief description of "syndrome" configurations. Syndromes are essentially combinations of scales that, when observed, often indicate a particular behavioral repertoire that will persist throughout a person's overall pattern of behavior. The following are some examples that we commonly encounter.

Leading – High (*HPI Ambition, MVPI Power*); Moderate to High (*HPI Inquisitive, HDS Bold*)
A driven person (Ambition) who will enjoy being in charge and drive results (Power). He/she will be open to new ideas and potentially offer new insights (Inquisitive) and will be reasonably self-confident in front of people (Bold).

Competing – High (*HPI Ambition, HDS Bold, MVPI Power*)
A competitive person (Ambition) who will be fearless and self-confident even in the face of failure (Bold) and care deeply about being successful or winning (Power).

Managing – High (*HPI Ambition*); Moderate to High (*HPI Prudence, HDS Diligent, MVPI Commerce*)
A status-seeking person (Ambition) who is conscientious about executing a business plan (Prudence), mindful of the details (Diligent), and attentive to the bottom line (Commerce).

Creating – High (*HPI Ambition and Inquisitive, HDS Imaginative, MVPI Aesthetics*); Low (*HPI Prudence*)
An aspiring and energetic person (Ambition) who will be open to new ideas (Inquisitive), think outside the "nine dots" (Imaginative), pay close attention to issues of taste and style (Aesthetics), and challenge tradition and conventional wisdom (Prudence).

Intimidating – High (*HPI Ambition, HDS Reserved*); Low (*HPI Interpersonal Sensitivity and Sociability, MVPI Affiliation*)
An aggressive person (Ambition) who is tough and insensitive (Reserved), interpersonally blunt and abrasive (Interpersonal Sensitivity), uncommunicative (Sociability), and prefers to work alone (Affiliation).

Ingratiating – High (*HPI Sociability and Interpersonal Sensitivity, HDS Dutiful, MVPI Affiliation*)
A gregarious and friendly person (Sociability) who avoids conflict (Interpersonal Sensitivity), willingly follows the lead of others (Dutiful),

tries to be a good corporate citizen, and seeks the approval of management (Affiliation).

Resisting – High (*HPI Prudence, HDS Leisurely, Cautious, and Diligent, MVPI Security*); Low (*HPI Inquisitive*)

A rigid, inflexible person (Prudence) who is stubborn and prone to procrastinating (Leisurely), avoids making decisions (Cautious), fussy about details (Diligent), is worried about any change that might threaten his/her job (Security), and hostile to innovation or new ideas (Inquisitive).

Risk Taking – High (*HPI Adjustment and Sociability, HDS Mischievous*); Low (*HPI Prudence, MVPI Security*)

A calm person who seems unaffected by the stress of risk (Adjustment), comfortable with the high profile associated with risk taking (Sociability), enjoys testing limits (Mischievous), views rules as obstacles to be overcome (Prudence), and seeks out environments where risk taking is rewarded (Security).

Empty Suit – High (*HPI Ambition, Sociability, and Interpersonal Sensitivity, HDS Cautious*); Low (*MVPI Power*)

A person who is interested in career advancement (Ambition), relies heavily upon the ability to meet people and network (Sociability), build relationships (Interpersonal Sensitivity), avoids risky decisions (Cautious), and the possibility of being held accountable for results (Power).

SUMMARY

Configural interpretation takes practice, and there is no substitute for it. The more you review HPI, HDS, and MVPI profiles, the more you will come to understand the intricacies of configural interpretation and value the results. The good news is that there is always something to learn as you ponder a person's scores across the three inventories. The bad news is that it is not possible to provide a definitive guide to configural interpretation. This chapter was only designed to start you thinking about configural interpretation. We provided some common beginning points, including dyad interpretations on the HPI, job family interpretations, and syndromes that take into account multiple scales and that rely upon all three inventories. We view the job family interpretations as a very useful place to start any interpretive process. They provide ideal profiles that can be compared with a profile under consideration. The differences between an ideal profile and one that is being reviewed will be the source of an interpretation that is interesting, meaningful, and most of all, accurate.

CHAPTER 9

CONFLICT INTERPRETATION

That man is a creature who needs order yet yearns for change is the creative contradiction at the heart of the laws which structure his conformity and define his deviancy.

– Freda Adler

As you have learned, Hogan publishes three different inventories, each measuring different attributes of a person. The Hogan Personality Inventory (HPI) measures normal personality, or the way a person reacts to normal, day-to-day situations. The Hogan Development Survey (HDS) measures those characteristics that occur under stressful conditions, conditions of uncertainty, or in novel situations (i.e., when the person is not sure how to respond). These characteristics will impede a person's ability to get along with others and get ahead in his/her career. Finally, the Motives, Values, Preferences Inventory (MVPI) measures a person's workplace preferences and motivations, those things he/she values with respect to culture and climate, and his/her personal motivations. The MVPI is used to understand (a) the kind of culture or climate a person will find motivating, (b) the type of job or career a person will find motivating, and (c) the type of culture or environment a person will create as a leader.

So far the guide has focused on interpretation of individual inventory results and common configurations within and across inventories. We now turn to less common configurations. These configurations have often been described as conflicts between inventories or scales. Actually, they are more complex combinations that require thoughtful interpretation. For example, what happens when common configurations do not occur? What if a person exhibits high Adjustment and Ambition, but not high Bold; or high Ambition and Adjustment occur along with very low Excitable? It is inevitable that you will encounter conflicting results when using our inventories. This will be true whether you use a single inventory, where conflicts may emerge between scales; multiple inventories, where conflicts may emerge across inventories; or a combination of both of these situations. There is a reason we offer three Hogan inventories, and we encourage people to use them as a suite. They measure different attributes of a person, and they are free to correlate, and at times, appear to conflict with one another.

In the past, these conflicts have been treated as anomalies that result from careless responding on the part of the person completing the inventories. More and more, we see that much can be learned from these conflicts, and in fact, they often manifest themselves in observable behavior. Instead of trying to explain away these "conflicts," we find that these conflicts are real, they exist in the person completing the inventories, and they are often a significant source of concern or conflict in that person's life. A great deal of developmental benefit can be derived from these discrepancies when a person comes to understand them and how they are manifested behaviorally. Furthermore, performance improvements can be realized when a person addresses negative behaviors associated with these conflicts.

The purpose of this chapter is to explore the interpretation of conflicting results from the inventories. We will examine some conflicts that we have encountered within each inventory and then look at conflicts that may arise across inventories. Again, this is not meant to be an exhaustive review. Rather, it is an introduction to interpreting conflicting results that we have observed.

HOGAN PERSONALITY INVENTORY CONFLICTS

Thousands of behaviors can be observed in reference to various combinations of the seven scales and 41 subscales (or HICs) on the Hogan Personality Inventory. Conflicts typically arise in three ways. First, similar behavioral descriptions and/or competencies can be associated with multiple scales. When a person is described by others as tenacious, this "competency" may be the result of high Ambition (works really hard and strives to get ahead) or high Prudence (attends to every detail). The competency is appropriately labeled, but the competency is comprised of components of two or more personality characteristics.

Second, two personality scales can conflict, which might give rise to situational application of key behaviors. For example, high Ambition (normally associated with aggressive, competitive behaviors) may not appear in certain situations when high Interpersonal Sensitivity is also present. For example, a manager may set very high expectations for a project (Ambition), but have difficulty confronting others when they do not meet those expectations (Interpersonal Sensitivity). It can be difficult to determine which of these two characteristics will emerge in any given situation. However, it is likely that the manager will feel conflicted in these situations. The conflict is very real and may negatively impact job performance.

Third, conflicts may arise within a particular personality scale because of specific subscale results. For instance, within the Prudence scale, a person scoring high on Moralistic, Mastery, and Virtuous may be a strict rule follower, yet very inattentive to details because of low scores on Not Spontaneous, Impulse Control, and/or Avoids Trouble. Table 24 illustrates some common conflicts encountered with HPI results.

There are two points to be made from the above. First, personality inventories (the HPI included) take thousands of human behaviors and organize them into discrete, manageable units of analysis (i.e., scales and subscales). The inventory, in essence, reduces human variability in a world in which behavior is free to vary. For example, a person who scores high on Ambition can be independent and willing to set high expectations, but also fiercely competitive and unwilling to listen to others' viewpoints. Second, few personal interactions involve only one personality characteristic. Interactions are multifaceted, and personality

characteristics combine to form new and interesting behaviors. The scales used
to describe these characteristics will, at times, appear to complement and, at
other times, compete with each other.

Table 24. Hogan Personality Inventory Conflicts

Conflict	Interpretation
Behaviors that appear inconsistent with primary scale results	
Low Adjustment	Low Adjustment can supplant otherwise strong results because of emotion.
High Ambition	High Ambition can help compensate for other scale weaknesses (e.g., low Prudence), but can be very exhausting and lead to poor time management.
High Sociability	High Sociability can mask potential weaknesses in other scales for short periods of time, such as in interviews.
High Prudence	High Prudence can mask other personality characteristics because of the task focus and willingness to follow rules.
Behaviors that may be in conflict because of scale scores	
High Ambition and Low/High Adjustment	With high Ambition, the person will set high expectations; however, when combined with low Adjustment, the typical style will be to focus on negative, exception-driven leadership; when combined with high Adjustment, the typical style will be to focus on goal- or accomplishment-oriented leadership.
Opposites on Ambition and Sociability	High Ambition with low Sociability results in high expectations and goals that are not proactively communicated to others; high Sociability and low Ambition results in frequent conversations that have minimal goal focus.
High Ambition and High Interpersonal Sensitivity	High Ambition people set high expectations for themselves and others, are driven, competitive, and want to lead and win; high Interpersonal Sensitivity people are empathic, agreeable, and want to get along with others; it is difficult to want to be both the leader and friend to subordinates.
Opposites on Sociability and Interpersonal Sensitivity	High Sociability and low Interpersonal Sensitivity results in wanting to be around people who do not want to be around you; low Sociability and high Interpersonal Sensitivity results in not wanting to be around people who want to be around you, which can result in a perception of being aloof.
High Prudence and High Inquisitive	Results in a person that is open to new ideas, somewhat creative, and able to see connections between seemingly unrelated pieces of information, but may be too inflexible and detail-oriented to get anything off the ground and implemented.

Table 24 (continued): Hogan Personality Inventory Conflicts

Conflict	Interpretation
Behaviors that may be in conflict because of subscale scores	
Opposites on Good Attachment and Moralistic	Both of these subscales are associated with following rules—Good Attachment is about respecting and following authority figures, while Moralistic concerns following your own rules in a consistent manner. High Good Attachment and low Moralistic results in a desire to respect authority in the face of disrespecting the rules those authority figures may create; low Good Attachment and high Moralistic results in a lack of respect for authority and their rules, but a willingness to adhere to the rules you care about and find acceptable.
Self-confidence and Not Autonomous	Self-confidence concerns socially displayed confidence while Not Autonomous is associated with concern for others' approval and acceptance. High Self-confidence and high Not Autonomous results in outward self-confidence tempered by approval needs from authority figures (and possible demand characteristics); low Self-confidence and low Not Autonomous results in an independent, but self-doubting individual.
Opposites on Prudence (top 3 and bottom 3 subscales)	In general, look for a trend here (i.e., if Prudence is average or low, is it mainly due to lower scores on the top 3 or bottom 3 subscales). High top 3 and low bottom 3 results in a good organizational citizen that is disorganized and fails to plan; low top 3 and high bottom 3 results in a person who does not particularly care for or follow other people's rules, but is quite detail-oriented and planful in areas of interest and self-import.
Opposites on Experience Seeking and Thrill Seeking	People often think of these subscales as highly dependent and do not always see the differences between them. Experience Seeking concerns the willingness to try new things. Thrill Seeking is associated with trying new (and possibly dangerous) activities. High Experience Seeking and low Thrill Seeking represents an interest in variety, but a lack of interest in potentially dangerous thrills; low Experience Seeking and high Thrill Seeking represents an interest in the thrill derived from high adrenalin activities, but little interest in variety for the sake of variety.

HOGAN DEVELOPMENT SURVEY CONFLICTS

Conflicts that arise on the HDS are different from those on the HPI. Here we look at elevations on scales that result in competing derailers. The biggest conflicts arise when conflicting elevations occur on performance risks that cross the super factors (Moving Away, Moving Against, and Moving Toward). Because these super factors are associated with social distance, elevations that cross factors inherently create conflict in terms of social distance. For example, if a person possesses a strong Moving Against profile, but also scores high on Dutiful, conflict would arise from need for the person to remain closely aligned with superiors, while he/she would behave so as to drive superiors away. Table 25 illustrates some common conflicts encountered with HDS results.

Table 25: Hogan Development Survey Conflicts

Conflict	Interpretation
Excitable and Leisurely	High scores on both scales indicate that under stressful conditions and conditions of uncertainty, these people will show stress reactions and emotions without restraint (high Excitable). However, they will keep opinions concerning people and their performance to themselves and rarely expose their true negative feelings about others (high Leisurely). So, others will see these people as showing signs of stress, but likely will not know the reason for the stress.
Cautious and Mischievous	High Cautious scores are typically associated with slowing down processes and procedures because of a fear of failure, while high Mischievous scores are associated with extreme impulsivity. On the one hand, these people likely will show a great deal of restraint (which can frustrate others who are willing to move forward more quickly), and this restraint is most readily apparent in unknown or novel situations. On the other hand, when they are comfortable or show strong convictions about a project or direction, these people will jump into the project with almost reckless abandon. They also will tend to be rather stubborn concerning what they will do and how they will perform in these situations. The end result is that others will feel frustrated and annoyed at the inconsistent behavior and the hurry up/wait dichotomy.

Table 25 (continued): Hogan Development Survey Conflicts

Conflict	Interpretation
Cautious and Dutiful	People with high scores on both Cautious and Dutiful tend to have a great deal of internal conflict because they have a strong desire to slow down processes and procedures (especially those that are foreign to them) for a fear of failure (Cautious), while having a strong sense of duty and loyalty to authority figures and superiors (Dutiful), resulting in an aversion to rocking the boat or going against orders. When directed into roles or projects that are uncertain or uncomfortable, the person will have a great deal of internal conflict, and the resulting stress likely will inhibit successful job performance.
Reserved and Bold	High scorers on Reserved display two different types of stress reactions. Some of these people show extreme aloofness or introversion and withdraw from others, with a tendency to focus on personal accomplishment. A second portion of high scorers on Reserved are extremely interpersonally insensitive (i.e., they either close themselves off from social contact or they force themselves into social situations in a painfully objective manner). Combine either of these characteristics with extreme arrogance and overinflation of self-worth (high Bold), and you have a person who is unwilling to admit faults and limitations, which can be detrimental in stressful situations and situations of uncertainty. This is one of those combinations where the conflict is between two super factors (e.g., the person will clearly Move Away from some, typically subordinates, while also Moving Against others, typically superiors).
Reserved and Colorful	There is both internal and external conflict for those who have high scores on Reserved and Colorful. These people will tend to withdraw from others or otherwise act in a painfully objective manner (Reserved). They may also demonstrate strong attention-seeking behaviors (Colorful). In some situations, where the two characteristics stay separate, others will be baffled and uncertain as to which characteristic will be manifested. In other situations, where the two characteristics coincide, the person will use their moody and poor social responses (Reserved) as the main factor in obtaining the attention they desire (Colorful).

Table 25 (continued): Hogan Development Survey Conflicts

Conflict	Interpretation
Leisurely and Diligent	High scores on Leisurely can be marked by a general and intense stubbornness with respect to being asked to follow rules and processes or to perform activities that the person finds undesirable (Leisurely). With the addition of high Diligent, these individuals know there is a right way to do things and strongly believe that their way is not only the best way, but the only way. These people (a) do not follow the rules or procedures of others, (b) strongly promote their own agendas and ways to accomplish tasks, and (c) do not proactively let others know how they will be doing things. The end result is a reputation for inflexibility and an inability to be counted on to perform in a team-oriented manner.
Leisurely and Dutiful	These two scales have as a common denominator (at the high end), an unwillingness to confront others, resulting in two different outcomes. People who score high on Leisurely will agree to terms they find distasteful (because acquiescence will typically reduce conflict and therefore stress), but will not follow through. This will lead others to believe they cannot count on the person. People who score high on Dutiful will not publicly go against their boss or popular positions with which they disagree. In essence, these people will lose their organizational voice, as their viewpoints and opinions are not shared in public. Both situations leave others feeling as if the person does not support them and is not a team player.
Mischievous and Diligent	On the surface, these two scales seem to be polar opposites. One is associated with extreme flexibility and impulsivity (Mischievous), while the other is associated with micromanagement (Diligent). However, they both have at their core an unwillingness to follow others' rules and procedures. When a person scores high on both of these scales, the person is very opinionated and has strong beliefs concerning how things should be accomplished. These beliefs are so strong that the person will both shun (or work against) others' ideas they find to be distasteful or contraindicated (Mischievous), while just as strongly indicating and trying to force others to perform in ways that they believe are the best (sometimes only) way to accomplish tasks.

MOTIVES, VALUES, PREFERENCES INVENTORY CONFLICTS

The MVPI is a measure of internal drive resulting from motives and values. It is not a measure of personality. The MVPI scales are virtually orthogonal or unrelated to one another (i.e., high or low scores on one scale do not impact the scores on other scales). Conflicts that arise on the MVPI tend to create confusion for a person, in that what the person wants out of life may be difficult to obtain simply through work (e.g., a high Commerce score for a person working as a school teacher). In this section, we look at differences on scales that essentially result in competing values.

Some of the more difficult conflicts occur when the elevations cross what have been called super factors on the MVPI (**Status** – Recognition, Power, Hedonism; **Social** – Altruistic, Affiliation, Tradition; **Financial** – Security, Commerce; **Decision Making Style** – Aesthetics and Science). Individuals with elevated scores crossing factors can be pulled in different directions (e.g., Status and Social). Because the scales within a super factor combine to form a powerful motivating force, conflicts across the factors can cause an individual to seek satisfaction in competing settings such as home life versus work life. In contrast, when alignment exists, conflict is minimized and the opportunity for greater focus in one direction is possible. For example, a person with a high score in both Commerce and Altruistic is motivated both by making money and by helping others. Some of these people can find satisfaction for both characteristics in their job (e.g., working in a profitable organization with a strong commitment to community service). A person finding satisfaction in a single setting will likely be more satisfied than a person who is trying to satisfy these characteristics in multiple settings (e.g., a high-paying job that requires many hours of work and also a heavy social calendar loaded with volunteer efforts outside of work). The difference between these two situations is alignment, with the latter potentially pulling the individual in two directions. Table 26 illustrates some common conflicts encountered with MVPI results.

Table 26: Motives, Values, Preferences Inventory Conflicts

Conflict	Interpretation
Recognition and Affiliation	High Recognition individuals want to be noticed and receive acknowledgement for their accomplishments. This may not be forthcoming if the individual is low on Affiliation, and therefore, not motivated by meeting new people, social networking, or sharing his/her accomplishments with people.
Altruistic and Power	High Altruistic often results in putting one's self-interests aside in favor of the greater good, which can be counterproductive to the drive and goal orientation associated with high Power.
Affiliation and Altruistic	High Affiliation individuals prefer social, team-oriented work environments that may not be consistent with low Altruistic, which can result in a preference for task-oriented environments and performing in ways to maximize personal benefit.
Commerce and Security	High Commerce individuals gauge their success through money, which often requires risk, while high Security often results in a preference for low-risk environments.
Aesthetics and Science	Although both of these scales are associated with the motivation to dig through symptoms to determine underlying problems, they do so in different ways. High Aesthetics individuals are motivated by quality control while high Science individuals are motivated by data and statistics. Opposite preferences for these two values can create conflict in the desire for subjectivity associated with Aesthetics (i.e., quality is motivated and defined by the look and feel of an end product) and the desire for objectivity associated with Science (i.e., quality is motivated by statistical and mathematical parsimony, regardless of the complexity of the system).
Affiliation and Power	High team orientation and the motivation to be well-liked and connected to others can result from high Affiliation. This can conflict with the desire for personal accomplishment and being motivated by telling others what to do (versus being told what to do) often arising from high Power.
Tradition and Hedonism	High Tradition often results in a desire for a mature, conservative lifestyle (or at least a consistent lifestyle organized around deep-seated rules and procedures). This may be inconsistent with the motivation to pleasure seek, sometimes in a haphazard manner, associated with high Hedonism.

Conflicts Between Inventories

Conflicts between inventories often yield very valuable insights. As we stated at the beginning of this chapter, these "conflicts" reflect a behavioral pattern that is different from what we would expect given the correlations among the scales across the three inventories.

Some conflicts create more tension than others. As an example, a person with a low score on Adjustment and a high score on Excitable might have learned a number of techniques to control the Excitable tendencies, while continuing to display passion, urgency, and sometimes overemotion on a daily basis. In contrast, much lower behavioral tension occurs for a person with low Sociability and high Affiliation who might enjoy working quietly in the background as a member of a highly visible team.

The following section offers descriptions of some of the more common alternative interpretations we have observed across the inventories. We have tried to highlight those that occur frequently and present challenges from an interpretation standpoint. We start by explaining the relationship we would typically expect, and then move into alternate ways in which the scales can and do interact and what that means from a behavioral standpoint.

HDS Conflicts and the Role of the HPI

Most of the descriptions that follow have less to do with true conflicts and more to do with alternative interpretations for high scores on HDS scales. In many of these cases, the HPI plays a role in the way behaviors are manifested (and potentially interpreted by others) in the workplace.

Excitable

In general, people who score high on Excitable will typically score low on Adjustment. Low Adjustment individuals tend to be tense and self-critical and will negatively evaluate their own performance. When under stress, these characteristics lead to typical high Excitable behaviors such as yelling at people. The low Adjustment aspect of this combination will result in worrying about yelling at people after the fact.

From time to time, a person with high Excitable will score high on Adjustment. In these situations, it is good to look at the Ambition and sometimes the Prudence scales on the HPI. A person very high on Ambition and Adjustment will tend to set very high expectations for themselves and others. Often these expectations will be set at levels that are higher than employees can typically handle. The end result is that the excitement in the workplace tends to be shown by the employees because they have such a high sense of urgency imposed upon them to get work completed. In other words, the boss yells (high Excitable), but thinks the staff deserve it (high Adjustment) for not meeting his/her unrealistic expectations (high Ambition). The employees are stressed by the boss's behavior and may themselves exhibit "excited" behaviors.

The stress levels of employees also will be heightened if you take the above interpretation and add in high Prudence. High Prudence will be accompanied by expectations that others will work according to a very specific and very well-defined set of rules, procedures, and project specifications. When people do not perform this way, the high Prudence person will tend to let them know. By putting people under these exacting and almost impossible standards, and criticizing them when they do not meet the expectations (this is the assessment taker's high Excitable coming out), the stress level of employees will also increase as they realize they will not be able to please the person.

Cautious

Typically, high Cautious is associated with a high score on Prudence (following rules and current processes, not being impulsive, being concerned with what others think) and/or a low score on Ambition (not having the personal drive or energy to change things or do them differently than is already being done now). In this scenario, the person's lack of drive and energy associated with changing rules and procedures leads, under stress and pressure, to the person slowing down decisions, not making decisions, being slow to recognize when change would be good, and in general being seen by others as a "red tape" performer.

From time to time, a person with high Cautious can have a high Ambition score. In this situation, look to the Adjustment score that likely is low. This person will set very high expectations (high Ambition). However, they will do so around negative things (low Adjustment). In other words, they motivate others through negative goals (e.g., "If we do not fix a, b, and c, we will all get fired"), rather than positive, proactive goals (e.g., "If we work very hard, look at where we can take this company"). The Cautious characteristics come out here as a real fear of failure and anxiety over what bad things could happen. Three things are important to note concerning people with this profile. First, many leaders will have this high Ambition, low Adjustment, high Cautious combination. Second, fear-based motivation can and does work. Finally, although fear-based motivation can work, it comes at a high cost in terms of the well-being of the leader and the team. It is exhausting working under these conditions.

Reserved

Although Reserved is only one scale on the HDS, under stress and pressure, the person will react in one of two very different ways. It is important to identify the type of reserved reaction that likely will be forthcoming, and we look to the Sociability and Interpersonal Sensitivity scales for answers. As we refer to these two scales, it is important to understand that all high Reserved people have a difficult time reading social cues and do not understand how their actions affect others.

A person with low scores on Sociability and high scores on Reserved will be seen as distant and aloof. He/She will tend to work behind closed doors, literally shutting off the rest of the world and concentrating on his/her own work versus the team's work. As a leader, a person with this profile will often be visibly absent when most needed by employees.

If the high Reserved person scores low on Interpersonal Sensitivity, the end result is a very abrupt, sometimes painfully objective style. The things they say to others may be correct and may be data based, but there will certainly be better ways to say them. Others will describe the person as interpersonally insensitive, very direct, and sometimes harsh and mean. Others will do their best to avoid the person, especially when a stressful situation is involved (i.e., the people interacting with the high Reserved person will "Move Away" from that person).

Colorful

Typically, high Colorful scores are associated with higher scores on Sociability, and to a lesser extent, with high Ambition. Under normal conditions, the person is socially outgoing, willing to tell people what they think, and motivated by getting their point across (high Ambition, or more specifically, high scores on the No Social Anxiety subscale). When under stress and pressure, these characteristics are extended past the positive and lead the person to become hyper-social, to interrupt others, to forget their listening skills, and in general become rather attention seeking.

A subset of people with high Colorful scores will not have high scores on Sociability. This group of people often has lower scores on the Prudence scale. People with lower Prudence scores can be both impulsive and also willing to do things that are novel and unconventional. As such, these people may not be the most socially outgoing, but their mannerisms, dress, or eccentric behaviors will quietly lead others to notice them. Their Colorful mannerisms are more behavioral than social.

Diligent

In most situations, high scores on Diligent are associated with high scores on Prudence. High scorers on Prudence pay attention to details and like to follow rules and procedures. Under stress, these characteristics will manifest themselves as micromanagement, equal importance given to all tasks regardless of impact, and a general overadherence to rules and procedures without thought for practicality.

For many people, however, high Diligent is not always associated with high Prudence. Typically in these situations, Ambition and Interpersonal Sensitivity can help explain behaviors. Under normal conditions, these people will set high expectations for themselves and others and will know exactly how they like things (high Ambition). Furthermore, when these expectations are not met, the person will let others know about it, sometimes in a painfully objective manner (low Interpersonal Sensitivity). Under stress, the Diligent takes over and looks like a dogmatic adherence to expectations and a general high level of being nitpicky with respect to these expectations.

Bold

High Bold scores are often associated with high Adjustment. High Adjustment is associated with being very calm and even-tempered and being very self-accepting. When derailment enters the picture in the form of a high Bold score, a high level of arrogance can be exhibited that includes an unwillingness to admit minor faults and limitations. For the most part, people with this combination of scores will tend to be calm in how they present their boldness. They will not show a sense of urgency, will remain calm under all conditions, and will have a real unwillingness to admit to even minor faults and limitations.

As an alternative, many people will have a high Ambition score associated with high Bold. For these people, the arrogance and overconfidence is much more verbal and outgoing. These folks will tend to be boastful, over promise on projects and deadlines, actively argue with others when confronted with negative information, and brag about past accomplishments and future opportunities. In their eyes, they are superior to others and are not afraid to let others know this "fact" (e.g., "Is it really bragging if I can do everything I say I can, or is it just a statement of fact?").

MVPI Conflicts and the Role of the HPI

The MVPI is *not* a measure of personality and should not be treated that way. We like to think of these two assessments in the following manner: the MVPI tells us what a person wants out of life, and the HPI tells us those behaviors and characteristics the person uses to achieve the things that motivate them. Also, it is possible for a person to lack the personality characteristics necessary to attain the things that motivate them. When providing feedback based on these two assessments, it is important to make this distinction. Therefore, conflicts are really within the person (i.e., they have a motive that is not being met because they have not developed the personality characteristics to make it happen). The following represent the most common conflicts that cause dissatisfaction and can be de-motivating.

Power and Ambition

In general, people who are motivated by being in charge and telling others what to do versus being told what to do (high Power) will tend to be driven, energetic, and competitive (high Ambition). When these scales do not match up, typically the person's Ambition is high and his/her Power is low. In this scenario, look at the Interpersonal Sensitivity scale, which is often high. High Interpersonal Sensitivity (associated with wanting to be well-received and liked by others) impacts the person's competitiveness and drive (Ambition), especially in negative situations. Power is motivation to be in charge no matter the situation. People with high Interpersonal Sensitivity only want to be in charge when things are going well. As such, their Power score may show up as low even though they are ambitious and driven.

Altruistic and Interpersonal Sensitivity

Typically, people who are motivated by helping others and are focused on customer service (high Altruistic) will be empathic to others' needs and generally agreeable (high Interpersonal Sensitivity). When scores oppose one another, two different patterns may emerge. First, you may have a person who wants to help others (high Altruistic), but does so by giving "tough love" feedback that concentrates on the negative (low Interpersonal Sensitivity). Second, you may have a person who is very nice, agreeable, and easy to get along with (high Interpersonal Sensitivity), but who does so not to help others, but to focus on personal needs and goals (low Altruistic).

Affiliation and Sociability

In most individuals, those who are motivated by social networking and finding similarities with others (high Affiliation) will be outgoing, extraverted, and socially aggressive. However, sometimes a person may be very motivated to interact with others (high Affiliation), but will be more of a reactive communicator and wait for others to start and drive communication (low Sociability). This is a situation where a person has not developed the personality characteristics to proactively address his/her motivations. Also, some people can be very socially outgoing (high Sociability) for the purpose of communicating with others, while having little desire for group affiliation (low Affiliation).

Security and Prudence

High scores on Security (i.e., motivated by risk-free environments) are often accompanied by high scores on Prudence (i.e., planful and organized). Low scores on Security (i.e., motivated by risky environments) will be associated with low scores on Prudence (i.e., willing to take chances and do things on impulse).

It is conceivable for a person to be motivated by working in secure environments (high Security), but be somewhat impulsive in decision making and/or not want to follow others' rules and procedures (low Prudence). More commonly, we find people who are motivated by trying new things and doing things differently (low Security), but will be very planful and organized (high Prudence) in the way they implement these endeavors.

HDS and MVPI Conflicts

Much like the conversation with the HPI and MVPI, the most important thing to remember when looking at data between the HDS and MVPI is that they are two different types of measures. The HDS is a measure of personality derailments, while the MVPI is a measure of internal motives that are not always readily apparent to others. It is quite possible that some people have developed personality characteristics that inhibit their ability to successfully attain their motivations. When providing feedback on these two assessments, it is important to make this distinction. Again, conflicts occur within the person (i.e., they have a motive that is not being met because they have a personality characteristic that inhibits attainment of that motive). The following are examples of these types of conflicts.

Power and Bold

People with high Power scores will be focused on finding environments where they can be in charge. They will often be self-confident people, sometimes to the point where they will become arrogant and overly feedback-resistant under stress (high Bold). These people will typically be moved into leadership positions by their superiors, though their subordinates may have different beliefs regarding their leadership skills. This is a case of too much of a good characteristic turning into a development need.

Altruistic and Reserved

Potential conflicts can occur when both of these scores are high. For example, if a person is motivated by helping others (high Altruistic), but does so by either (a) having limited interaction with the person or (b) sharing painfully objective feedback (high Reserved), a conflict will likely occur. In this scenario, the person receiving help may not appreciate the help regardless of the motivation involved.

Affiliation and Colorful

This is another situation where too much of a good thing can lead to bad outcomes. We typically find that high scores on Affiliation are associated with high scores on Colorful. When thinking about the derailment aspects of the HDS, you can see that this may not be beneficial. People with high Affiliation are motivated to meet new people and interact with them. High Colorful people are often so consumed with hearing themselves speak that those with whom affiliation is hoped will find the interaction distasteful and may not want to share the affiliation.

Security and Mischievous

People who score high on Security (i.e., motivated by risk-free environments) will typically score low on Mischievous (i.e., be planful and responsible). In some situations, a person may be motivated by working in secure environments (high Security), but become very impulsive and haphazard under conditions of stress (high Mischievous). Even worse consequences can occur when individuals are willing to take risks (low Security), extremely impulsive, and rash when making decisions (Mischievous). This can lead to very poor decision making.

Conflicts When Leading Others

The final area to be covered with respect to the interpretation of conflicts has to do with those encountered when assessing for leadership. Effectively leading others requires a complex set of behaviors that are related to numerous scales across all three inventories. Furthermore, it is fair to say that there is no such thing as a perfect leadership profile. It is true, however, that some profiles are much better suited to leading people than others. It is also true that even the best leadership profiles may contain some conflicts, and the conflicts may prove to be accretive or a hindrance to performance.

The approach that we have taken for this section is to examine seven crucial roles a leader must fill in order to be effective. We examine these roles in terms of the behaviors performed, the inventory scales associated with each role, and potential conflicts and performance implications that may arise among the scales. For each role, we first discuss those motives and values associated with being willing to perform the tasks (MVPI). We follow this by describing those characteristics that will facilitate task and job performance (HPI) and finish with those characteristics that will inhibit job performance (HDS). Conflicts can occur in any of these scenarios where the characteristics do not coincide with one another.

Establishing a Vision

- **Description** – Leaders must be able to evaluate the market or competitive environment and establish a target or end state for the team that will result in beating the competition. This includes the ability to make connections between seemingly unrelated pieces of information in order to come up with more complex and complete strategies and solutions.

- **Key scales that facilitate performance** – Three scales are associated with Establishing a Vision. The Aesthetics scale is important to vision, as it is associated with being motivated by decision quality and the desire to dig through symptoms to get to underlying problems. From a personality perspective, high scores on Inquisitive are associated with being visionary and making connections between seemingly unrelated pieces of information. Finally, when under stress and pressure, leaders with an Imaginative score that is too high may make poor decisions, in that their solutions may be rash or odd. They also may fail to take the time to sell their ideas to others, which can undermine their credibility.

Setting Expectations

- **Description** – Leaders must be able to establish goals and objectives for various team members that align with the vision, and if accomplished, will result in moving the team closer to achieving the vision.

- **Key scales that facilitate performance** – Three scales are associated with setting expectations. First, the leader must be motivated to lead. This is associated with high scores on the Power scale. From a personality perspective, high scores on Ambition are associated with setting lofty expectations for oneself and others and, in general, being competitive and willing to take charge. When under stress and pressure, those who score too high on Bold may diminish their performance by exaggerating their own self-worth and making commitments that cannot be fulfilled. In essence, a little Bold goes a long way, and too much Bold can create a variety of profile conflicts. Interestingly, too little Bold can also create conflicts, in that the leader may appear to lack self-confidence in setting expectations.

Communicating

- **Description** – Once leaders set expectations around a vision, they must be able to verbalize the vision and expectations to team members in a clear and concise manner that facilitates understanding and inspires action.

- **Key scales that facilitate performance** – From a motivational perspective, the leader must be motivated to network and to create an environment of open, positive, team-oriented communications. This type of environment is created by people who score higher on Affiliation. From a personality perspective, a moderately high level of Sociability will facilitate job performance because of its association with more extraverted behaviors, such as getting out from behind the desk and in front of others (where the vision and expectations can be routinely articulated). Sometimes too much Sociability can become distracting, or worse, lead to poor listening.

  With respect to derailment, there are two scales associated with inhibiting job performance. First, high scorers on Colorful can be disruptive and exhausting. Second, high scores on Reserved can have the opposite effect. Those with high scores will tend to either close themselves off from others or be overly insensitive, causing others to shy away from sharing information. Either way, high scores on these HDS scales can inhibit job performance.

Learning and Decision Making

- **Description** – Leaders must be able to sort through mounds of data and identify what is important and what to do about it (which may range from nothing all the way up to changing the vision).

- **Key scales that facilitate performance** – Learning and decision making for an effective leader are associated with three different motives and values including Science, Security, and Commerce. People scoring higher on Science will tend to be motivated to conduct data analyses, search for relevant research, and identify technological advancements to generate solutions to specific problems. In general, they will value data-based solutions to most problems. Security is associated with the type of environment in which decisions will be made. Low scorers will be willing to take risks in their decisions, while high scorers will be more interested in maintaining the status quo. The extent to which either of these scores is beneficial or inhibitive to the organization is based on the organization's environment and culture. Finally, those scoring higher on Commerce will tend to focus their decision-making strategies on making money both for themselves and for the organization. Furthermore, financial arguments will typically be used to sell ideas to others.

From a personality perspective, how the person learns will be based on the Learning Approach scale. High scorers will tend to focus on new events, current theories, and cutting-edge ideas in the field. Others may see these leaders as quite forward thinking. Low scorers will tend to focus on how to apply new thoughts and ideas. They likely will concern themselves with quickly implementing and trying out new ideas or processes to see what works.

Two derailment characteristics can inhibit learning and decision making. First, high Cautious individuals will tend to slow down decision making processes, mainly due to a fear of failure. New concepts and ideas may sit idle while additional analyses are conducted. Also, high Skeptical leaders will tend to be more apt to point out the potential negative (versus positive) outcomes associated with new ideas. These characteristics, when taken together, can lead to low morale and unwillingness to share ideas for fear of negative feedback.

Managing Priorities

- **Description** – Leaders must be able to multitask and handle many different foci at once. Some of these activities will require a high degree of attention to detail, others will simply require monitoring, and some must be dismissed to avoid unnecessary distractions. Good leaders know how to manage these priorities.

- **Key scales that facilitate performance** – The main motivational scale associated with managing priorities is Security. Higher scorers will tend to create a structured environment where risks and uncertainty are minimized, expectations are spelled out, and performance standards are explicit. They will be motivated to be safe rather than sorry, which means that details are an important aspect of the workplace environment. Lower scorers, on the other hand, will tend to create flexible environments where quick changes in direction are expected and easily handled. Details may not be viewed as extremely important.

Prudence, from a personality perspective, is associated with how performance is maintained in the workplace. Higher scorers will be structured, disciplined, and pay attention to rules, processes, and procedures. They will work hard to take the vision presented to the organization and put structure and details around it. Lower scorers will tend to be more flexible and nimble and be willing to make fast changes in direction if necessary. They may sometimes miss details and be overly impulsive, which can lead to false starts.

Two basically opposing derailment characteristics can impact how the leader manages priorities. When feeling stress and pressure, high scorers on

Diligent will tend to micromanage others and nit pick at them when they do not perform up to expectations. In the opposite direction, leaders who score high on Mischievous will not always make these performance expectations known or follow them consistently, which can cause real confusion and stress in others who are not sure what to do or which rules and procedures to follow.

Managing People

- **Description** – Leaders must be able to manage people, which can range from confronting performance problems to maintaining open lines of communication to working effectively across boundaries.

- **Key scales that facilitate performance** – The Power and Recognition scales are related to the environment a leader will create with respect to managing expectations. Higher scores on Power will be associated with valuing the leadership role and being motivated by ensuring others will meet performance expectations. Higher scores on Recognition will value the recognition that leadership roles provide. They will prefer an environment where they get public recognition for a job well done. Also, they will create an environment where recognition is used as a source of motivation to others.

  Part of effective leadership has to do with addressing job performance. Leaders who score high on Interpersonal Sensitivity, when asked to assume positions of authority, will be well-liked by subordinates and peers, but will have difficulty confronting others when they do not meet performance expectations. On the other hand, low scorers will tend to be very willing to confront poor performance, but may do so in a very abrupt and possibly insensitive manner. Here we have another case where leaders who score in the middle range tend to be the most effective, while those scoring at either extreme on the scale tend to encounter conflicts.

  When under stress and pressure, two performance risks can be particularly problematic when managing people. First, leaders scoring high on Leisurely may avoid confronting poor performers, allowing them to remain in the dark regarding performance problems. Second, managing others has to do with standing up and letting others know when there is disagreement. High scorers on Dutiful will tend to withhold opinions and go along, at least publicly, with the group. Both high Leisurely and Dutiful will cause conflict for a leader because of the tendency to step away from people management challenges (albeit in different ways).

Creating the Work Environment

- **Description** – Leaders must be able to create a work environment that motivates team members over time and allows them to contribute in a meaningful way to achieving the vision.

- **Key scales that facilitate performance** – From a motivational perspective, the Altruistic score is associated with how the leader will treat his/her employees and create an environment where employees believe they are cared for and their careers are important. People who score high on Altruistic will be very concerned with creating an environment focused on customer service and employee assistance and development. They will focus on staff morale, communicate with staff regularly, request and listen to feedback, and encourage a quality-focused environment.

  In day-to-day work environments, high scorers on Adjustment will set the tone by creating a relatively stress-free environment that focuses on the positive and how to achieve goals. Staff will look to high scorers to define how to react to organizational issues and initiatives, and these people will respond in a calm and even-tempered manner. From time to time, their lack of emotion may lead others to believe that they lack urgency, or at least, urgency around specific projects.

  Under stressful environments, two HDS scales negatively impact performance. First, high scorers on Excitable will tend to forget that others may not be able to handle the work loads to which they have become accustomed. Others may come to feel that the leader is piling on too much work and creating an environment that is unsympathetic to mistakes.

  The second scale that may affect performance is Reserved. High-scoring leaders will tend to react to others' performance in an interpersonally insensitive manner particularly with respect to mistakes. This may cause others to not want to try new things because it may never be good enough.

All seven of these roles are essential to the success of a leader. It should be clear by the sheer number of scales cited that a perfect profile is very unlikely, perhaps impossible. What should also be clear is that there are a number of ways profile conflicts can occur for a leader. Accurately interpreting conflicts can be of enormous benefit in the leader's development. It is not uncommon for a leader to respond to an effective interpretation with comments indicating how they have struggled with a particular conflict and to describe the value they gained from the interpretive insights.

SUMMARY

This chapter explored some of the interpretation conflicts that you are likely to encounter as you use the three inventories. In many ways, effective interpretation of conflicting scale results is the key role for someone interpreting inventory results. Computers (and the reports they generate) can only go so far in providing interpretive content. There will always be nuisances and conflicting information that can be found when interpreting these inventories. Sometimes this information has little impact in understanding the results. Other times the impact can be quite profound. By recognizing and effectively interpreting conflicting results, you will be able to add significant value in understanding the results of our inventories.

CHAPTER 10

HOGAN PERFORMANCE MODEL

Leadership is not magnetic personality—that can just as well be a glib tongue. It is not "making friends and influencing people"—that is flattery. Leadership is lifting a person's vision to high sights, the raising of a person's performance to a higher standard, the building of a personality beyond its normal limitations.

– Peter F. Drucker

The material we have covered so far focuses on interpreting the inventories based on a person's score on one or more scales. This approach is effective when there are no other data involved or additional data simply provide contextual information for an interpretation. However, situations often arise in which inventory results are only one piece of a larger performance puzzle that requires integration. We developed the Hogan Performance Model for such situations. The model is essentially a heuristic that provides guidance when considering multiple data sources in relation to performance.

The model has three components. Attributes describe "why we do what we do." Competency Domains describe "what and how we do it." Job Performance represents the requirements necessary to be successful in a job. If you have assessment information on Attributes and Competency Domains, you can relate that information to job requirements. The following section illustrates the Hogan Performance Model (see Figure 1) with a brief description of each component.

Figure 1: Hogan Performance Model

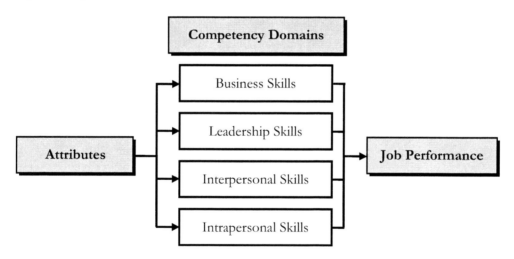

ATTRIBUTES

Attributes are concerned with "why people do what they do" and are best predicted by inventories that are capable of looking beyond a sample of behaviors to provide a description of broad, general trends in behavior that are rooted in reputation. If you will recall our discussion from Chapter 1, we made a distinction between **reputation** and **identity**. Reputation concerns what you do, while identity concerns why you do it. Our inventories are windows into a person's reputation, reflecting past behavior that has consistently been proven to be the best single predictor of future behavior. Directly measuring identity is difficult, if not impossible. However, by measuring reputation we provide an effective link between attributes (why you do what you do) and competency domains (what and how you do it).

Attributes can include personality characteristics, cognitive abilities, and motivational characteristics (see Figure 2). The Hogan Personality Inventory (HPI) and Hogan Development Survey (HDS) provide excellent measures of personality characteristics. A measure of critical thinking such as the Hogan Business Reasoning Inventory (HBRI) would be a good measure of cognitive abilities. Motivational characteristics speak to our wants, desires, and interests and are often founded in our values. The Motives, Values, Preferences Inventory (MVPI) will provide a good understanding of motivational characteristics. Understanding personality characteristics, cognitive abilities, and motivational characteristics is the foundation for understanding performance effectiveness. These attributes dictate "why you do what you do" and are usually quite enduring across a person's career.

Other data or assessment tools that purport to measure "signs" (as opposed to "samples") of behavior would group under the Attribute component of our model, as they largely try to explain "why you do what you do." This notion is quite important because there are more than 2,500 test vendors in the United States alone. They offer countless numbers of inventories, all purporting to measure some aspect of the Attributes component of our model. Furthermore, it is often the case that multiple inventories are used to measure similar things from a slightly different perspective and add little more than noise to the understanding of "why you do what you do."

There are two important things to consider when using data targeting the Attributes component. First, have the data sufficiently covered personality characteristics, cognitive abilities, and motivational characteristics? Second, to what extent do the data sources overlap or conflict in understanding "why you do what you do"? To the extent you can sort out the answers to these questions, you will, as they say, "be able to separate the wheat from the chaff" with respect to these data sources. For example, there is little point to including two measures of personality in a measurement process if both measures were developed to assess the Five-Factor Model (FFM) of personality. The measures would likely be highly correlated with one another and would produce little in the way of additional explanatory value, while increasing the cost and time of the assessment process. To reiterate, the key to measuring Attributes is to measure personality characteristics, cognitive abilities, and motivational characteristics as efficiently as possible.

Figure 2: Measuring Attributes

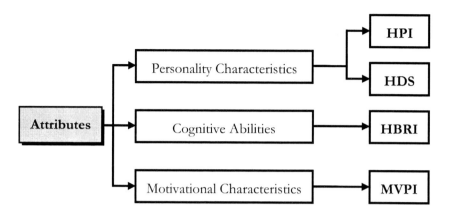

COMPETENCY DOMAINS

Competency Domains are clusters of competencies that tend to go together. They are best measured using on-the-job behavioral examples, actual "samples" of behavior, or ratings of job behavior. For personnel selection, the most common methods for gathering this information are the job application, the résumé, and the job interview. Structured job interviews seem to yield the best results. However, certain types of bio-data have also proven to be quite useful. Once on the job, the most common way for competency data to be collected is through a multi-rater assessment. These assessments can take many forms, but their underlying features are relatively similar. Someone is asked to complete a rating or ratings on the person being assessed. These ratings address the performance of job behaviors in terms of proficiency or frequency.

Four domains capture most of the competencies that commonly occur in business (Hogan and Warrenfeltz, 2003). Business Skills include competencies that can be done on one's own and usually involve information processing. Leadership Skills include competencies used in managing others. Interpersonal Skills encompass competencies used in getting along with others. Finally, Intrapersonal Skills refer to self-regulatory competencies considered to be at the core of how one approaches any work assignment. The Competency Domains have an important developmental relationship to one another. Intrapersonal Skills develop early in life, followed by Interpersonal, Leadership, and Business Skills. The earlier in life a skill is developed, the more difficult it is to change. For example, it is much easier to develop problem-solving skills (Business Skills Domain) than work attitude (Intrapersonal Skills Domain). This distinction should be considered when choosing development targets. The following diagram (see Figure 3) illustrates the four Competency Domains with actual competencies aligned to them. As we will see in later chapters, the

Competency Domains are quite robust and can be used to structure virtually any competency model.

Figure 3: Competency Domains

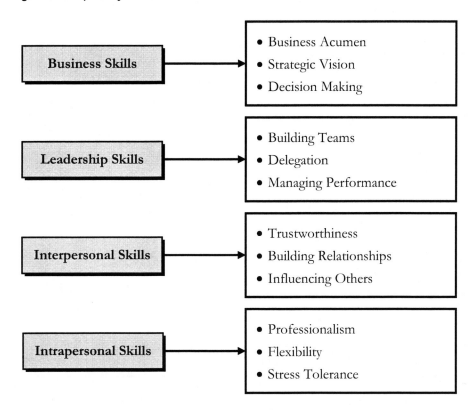

We have examined the relationships between the four domains and the scales on our inventories. These relationships depend on the competencies that have been used to populate the domains, but we have seen results that are relatively stable regardless of the competencies evaluated (as long as they are effectively classified into the domains). The results also make some intuitive sense when one considers important aspects of the scales in relation to the domains. The following diagram (see Figure 4) illustrates these relationships. We have also provided a brief description of each domain from the standpoint of an effective leadership profile.

Figure 4: Hogan Inventory Scales Organized by the Domains

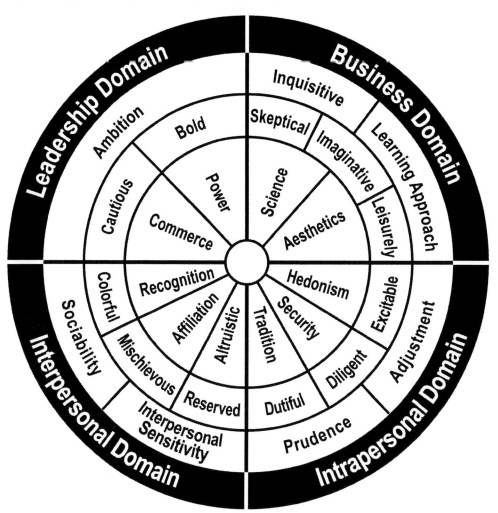

- **Business Domain** – Openness to new ideas, creativity, and a willingness to learn (moderate to high Inquisitive, Learning Approach, and Imaginative) with a healthy degree of skepticism (moderate Skeptical) and an interest in one's own agenda (moderate Leisurely) are important to success in this domain as a leader. In addition, it is important to value data and creativity (moderate to high Science and Aesthetics).

- **Leadership Domain** – Strength in this domain for a leader is marked by competitiveness (high Ambition), aggressive self-confidence (moderate Bold), willingness to take measured risks (low Cautious), desire to be in charge (high Power), and an interest in the financial success of the venture (high Commerce).

- **Interpersonal Domain** – It is important for a leader to possess an approachable style with a willingness to take tough stands on important issues (moderate Sociability, Interpersonal Sensitivity, and Reserved). A degree of charisma (moderate Colorful, Mischievous, and Recognition) with a willingness to help others (moderate Altruistic) and take a team approach (moderate to high Affiliation) will be important in motivating team members.

- **Intrapersonal Domain** – A balanced emotional demeanor (moderate Adjustment and low Excitable) with an organized "can do" approach (moderate Prudence, Diligent) will be important to success. In addition, those having some respect for authority and possessing integrity (moderate Dutiful and Tradition) with a willingness to add fun to the workplace (moderate Hedonism) and take prudent career risks (low Security) will often advance quickly.

JOB PERFORMANCE

The final component of the model is Job Performance. Interestingly, it is perhaps the least understood component. This statement may sound counterintuitive, but consider the following:

1. Evaluating job performance has probably occupied as much journal space as the topic of leadership, and there is still not an agreed-upon model for job performance. Entire books are available on the topic of performance measurement, with no consensus on even a definition.

2. No two companies (not even ones with similar jobs) evaluate job performance in the same way.

3. The most common method for evaluating job performance is through supervisory ratings, which are consistently unreliable, riddled with personal bias, and often bear little relationship to future performance.

4. Supervisory ratings are almost always associated with administrative outcomes (raises, promotions, terminations, etc.), which further limit them as true measures of performance.

5. When hard measures are used, such as sales figures, number of units produced, service provided, etc., they are usually confounded with any number of other organizational factors that limit their utility. Corporate auditors even question the value of such hard measures as legitimate indicators of return on investment.

With all the drawbacks, job performance is still the only truly important criterion variable for the Hogan Performance Model. We define effective job performance as whatever the organization decides to be effective job performance. This makes job performance a situation-specific variable in a model that will otherwise generalize to virtually any organization.

We mentioned at the outset that this model was an organizing heuristic for considering multiple data sources. The bad news is that the inability to define effective job performance in a way that generalizes across organizations is a key limiting factor when using this model. Model components follow from the point at which job performance is defined. For example, we might define the performance metric for a used car salesperson as the number of cars sold. Once job performance is defined, we can determine the appropriate competencies and key attributes. The good news is that once job performance is defined, the Hogan Performance Model provides a simple organizing structure for building an effective employee selection or development system.

GENERAL APPROACH FOR COMPETENCY ASSESSMENT

The Hogan Performance Model provides the backdrop for offering a general approach for assessing competencies. This is perhaps one of the most often requested areas of guidance for using Hogan inventories. Many companies spend considerable time and money developing competencies that they believe capture successful performance on the job. They are not particularly interested in a direct comparison of our inventories to job success. Rather, they are interested in the way our inventories assess their competencies. The thinking here is quite straightforward within our performance model. The company has linked job performance to competencies. If we can group their competencies into our domain model and link the domains to our inventories (via scale relationships), we essentially have a sound predictive model that could easily be demonstrated through basic validation research. The following diagram (see Figure 5) illustrates these relationships with a brief description of the links that are built through data collection techniques.

Figure 5: Using the Hogan Performance Model to Predict Performance

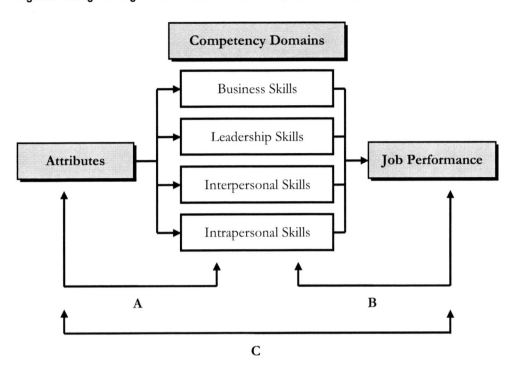

- **Relationship A** – Illustrates the relationship between Attributes and competencies (Competency Domains). Empirical research completed by Hogan Assessment Systems (HAS) has been used to demonstrate these relationships. Our research is now sufficiently robust, so validity generalization procedures can be used to demonstrate these links.

- **Relationship B** – Illustrates the link between competencies (Competency Domains) and Job Performance. Content validity is often used by organizations to justify this link, but there are many examples of actual empirical work completed to demonstrate this link.

- **Relationship C** – Illustrates the classic criterion validation link between Attributes and Job Performance. HAS has conducted hundreds of these studies and has archived them as part of our effort to extend the use of validity generalization data to virtually any job in the economy.

The importance of these relationships is clear. They allow HAS to use validity generalization methods to determine the relationships between our inventories, competencies (structured according to the four domains), and ultimately, job performance. We have spent more than 30 years accumulating an extensive research archive on these relationships. Much of this research is the direct result of company-specific validation work in which we collected and analyzed data on our inventories, competencies, and job performance. One of the most important outcomes of this work is the meta-analytic validity data we have amassed that empirically support the relationships between our inventories and competencies associated with effective performance across a variety of jobs. This allows us to use all methods of validity generalization to evaluate predictor-criterion relations for jobs.

Table 27 illustrates these relationships for 32 competencies organized according to the four domains to which they most closely align. These competencies represent those we have encountered frequently in our research. We have included in the table a capsule definition of the competency, the HPI scales that would facilitate performance, and the HDS scales that might hinder performance. An average correlation coefficient precedes each HPI scale where sufficient meta-analytic data were available to compute one. We have omitted MVPI data from these tables because of the impact of the cultural issues associated with specific organizations.

The "Preferred Score Range" for the HPI is indicated by an "X" in Table 27. The Preferred Score Range provides guidance to those interpreting our inventories in terms of competency performance. A score falling in the designated range is likely to facilitate effective performance of the competency. In contrast, a score falling outside the range will reduce the likelihood of effective competency performance. As the number of scores that fall inside the designated ranges increases, the likelihood of effective competency performance increases, and consequently, performance in a job that requires the competency improves.

The "Avoid Score Range" for the HDS is indicated by an "O" in Table 27. The Avoid Score Range provides guidance to those interpreting our inventories in terms of barriers to competency performance. A score falling in the designated range is likely to hinder effective performance of the competency. In contrast, a score falling outside the range will likely not reduce effective competency performance and, in certain circumstances, increase the likelihood of effective competency performance. As the number of scores that fall inside the designated ranges increases, the likelihood of ineffective competency performance increases, and consequently, performance in a job that requires the competency declines.

Table 27: Competencies from the Hogan Archive with their Associated HPI and HDS Scales

Business Domain												
		HPI Scales That Facilitate Performance*					**HDS Scales Likely To Hinder Performance****					
				Preferred Score Range				**Avoid Score Range**				
Competency	**Definition**	**r**	**Scale**	**Low**	**Avg.**	**High**	**Scale**	**No**	**Low**	**Mod.**	**High**	
Business Acumen	Possessing basic knowledge of business processes and procedures	.46	Adjustment		X	X	Excitable			O	O	
		.51	Ambition			X	Bold	O			O	
		.25	Inquisitive		X	X	Cautious			O	O	
		N/A	Learn. App.			X	Imaginative	O			O	
							Dutiful			O	O	
Strategic Vision	Recognizing long-term business opportunities and implications	.29	Inquisitive		X	X	Imaginative	O			O	
							Dutiful			O	O	
Tactical Reasoning	Evaluating the risks and opportunities in day-to-day business transactions	.17	Adjustment		X	X	Excitable			O	O	
		.20	Prudence		X	X	Bold	O			O	
		.17	Learn. App.		X	X	Diligent	O			O	
							Mischievous			O	O	

* An (X) indicates that scores falling within this range will facilitate performance on the competency.

** An (O) indicates that scores falling within this range will likely hinder performance on the competency.

Table 27 (continued): Competencies from the Hogan Archive with their Associated HPI and HDS Scales

Business Domain

Competency	Definition	HPI Scales That Facilitate Performance*		Preferred Score Range			HDS Scales Likely To Hinder Performance**	Avoid Score Range			
		r	Scale	Low	Avg.	High	Scale	No	Low	Mod.	High
Problem Solving	Identifying a workable solution from a range of alternatives	.13	Adjustment		X	X	Excitable				O
		.12	Prudence		X		Bold	O			O
		N/A	Learn. App.		X	X	Diligent			O	O
							Mischievous	O			O
Decision Making	Evaluating potential courses of action from a range of alternatives	.20	Ambition		X	X	Bold	O			O
		.20	Inquisitive		X		Cautious			O	O
		.15	Learn. App.		X		Imaginative	O			O
							Dutiful			O	O
Continuous Learning	Taking advantage of opportunities to learn and stay current	.16	Ambition		X	X	Bold	O			O
		.11	Inquisitive		X	X	Cautious			O	O
		N/A	Learn. App.		X	X	Imaginative	O			O
							Dutiful	O			O

* An (X) indicates that scores falling within this range will facilitate performance on the competency.

** An (O) indicates that scores falling within this range will likely hinder performance on the competency.

Table 27 (continued): Competencies from the Hogan Archive with their Associated HPI and HDS Scales

Business Domain

Competency	Definition	HPI Scales That Facilitate Performance*					HDS Scales Likely To Hinder Performance**				
		r	Scale	Preferred Score Range			Scale	Avoid Score Range			
				Low	Avg.	High		No	Low	Mod.	High
Training Performance	Excelling in opportunities to learn and develop new skills and abilities	.28	Ambition		X	X	Bold			O	O
		.22	Inquisitive		X	X	Cautious			O	O
		.25	Learn. App.			X	Imaginative	O			O
							Dutiful	O			O
Job Knowledge	Possessing the basic knowledge necessary to perform a job or function	.15	Adjustment		X		Excitable				O
		.14	Ambition		X		Bold			O	O
		N/A	Inquisitive		X		Cautious	O			O
		N/A	Learn. App.		X	X	Imaginative			O	O
							Dutiful	O			O

* An (X) indicates that scores falling within this range will facilitate performance on the competency.

** An (O) indicates that scores falling within this range will likely hinder performance on the competency.

Table 27 (continued): Competencies from the Hogan Archive with their Associated HPI and HDS Scales

Leadership Domain

Competency	Definition	r	HPI Scale	Low	Avg.	High	HDS Scale	No	Low	Mod.	High
							HDS Scales Likely To Hinder Performance**				
		HPI Scales That Facilitate Performance*		Preferred Score Range					Avoid Score Range		
Achievement	Striving to accomplish high goals or standards	.20	Ambition			X	Cautious				O
							Bold	O			O
Building Teams	Acquiring the talent necessary to beat the competition	.31	Adjustment		X	X	Excitable			O	O
		.24	Ambition		X	X	Bold	O			O
		.24	Inter. Sens.		X		Cautious			O	O
							Skeptical	O			O
							Leisurely	O			O
Delegation	Getting work done through others	.35	Adjustment		X	X	Excitable	O			O
		N/A	Ambition		X	X	Bold	O			O
		N/A	Prudence	X	X		Cautious			O	O
							Mischievous	O			O
							Diligent			O	O

* An (X) indicates that scores falling within this range will facilitate performance on the competency.

** An (O) indicates that scores falling within this range will likely hinder performance on the competency.

Table 27 (continued): Competencies from the Hogan Archive with their Associated HPI and HDS Scales

Leadership Domain

Competency	Definition	r	Scale (HPI)	Low	Avg.	High	Scale (HDS)	No	Low	Mod.	High
					Preferred Score Range					**Avoid Score Range**	
Employee Development	Improving the ability of team members to beat the competition	.29	Ambition		X	X	Cautious			O	O
		N/A	Sociability		X		Bold	O			O
		N/A	Learn. App.		X	X	Reserved			O	O
							Colorful			O	O
Initiative	Taking action without being told to do so						Cautious			O	O
		.32	Ambition		X	X	Bold	O			O
		N/A	Prudence	X	X		Mischievous	O			O
							Dutiful			O	O
Leadership	Building teams that beat the competition						Excitable			O	O
		.15	Adjustment		X	X	Bold	O			O
		.29	Ambition		X	X	Cautious			O	O
		N/A	Sociability		X		Reserved			O	O
							Colorful	O			O

HPI Scales That Facilitate Performance
HDS Scales Likely To Hinder Performance

* An (X) indicates that scores falling within this range will facilitate performance on the competency.

** An (O) indicates that scores falling within this range will likely hinder performance on the competency.

Table 27 (continued): Competencies from the Hogan Archive with their Associated HPI and HDS Scales

Leadership Domain

Competency	Definition	HPI Scales That Facilitate Performance*						HDS Scales Likely To Hinder Performance**				
					Preferred Score Range					Avoid Score Range		
		r	Scale	Low	Avg.	High		Scale	No	Low	Mod.	High
Managing Performance	Providing feedback regarding the accomplishment of objectives	.27	Adjustment		X	X		Excitable				O
		N/A	Ambition		X	X		Bold	O			O
		N/A	Inter. Sens.		X			Cautious			O	O
								Skeptical	O			O
								Leisurely			O	O
Resource Management	Allocating time, people, and equipment to beat the competition	.32	Ambition		X	X		Cautious	O		O	O
		.33	Sociability		X			Bold	O			O
		.25	Inquisitive		X	X		Reserved			O	O
								Colorful			O	O
								Dutiful			O	O
								Imaginative	O			O

* An (X) indicates that scores falling within this range will facilitate performance on the competency.

** An (O) indicates that scores falling within this range will likely hinder performance on the competency.

Table 27 (continued): Competencies from the Hogan Archive with their Associated HPI and HDS Scales

Interpersonal Domain

Competency	Definition		HPI Scales That Facilitate Performance*	Preferred Score Range			HDS Scales Likely To Hinder Performance**	Avoid Score Range			
		r	Scale	Low	Avg.	High	Scale	No	Low	Mod.	High
Trustworthiness	Securing the confidence of others through consistent words and actions	.13	Inter. Sens.		X		Skeptical			O	O
		.24	Prudence		X	X	Leisurely			O	O
		.17	Adjustment		X		Mischievous			O	O
							Diligent	O			O
							Excitable			O	O
							Bold			O	O
Respect for Others	Working to understand and empathize with the position of others	.23	Inter. Sens.		X	X	Skeptical			O	O
		.36	Adjustment		X		Leisurely			O	O
		.23	Prudence		X	X	Excitable			O	O
		N/A	Sociability		X		Bold			O	O
							Mischievous			O	O
							Diligent	O			O
							Reserved			O	O
							Colorful			O	O

* An (X) indicates that scores falling within this range will facilitate performance on the competency.

** An (O) indicates that scores falling within this range will likely hinder performance on the competency.

205

Table 27 (continued): Competencies from the Hogan Archive with their Associated HPI and HDS Scales

Interpersonal Domain

Competency	Definition	HPI Scales That Facilitate Performance*					HDS Scales Likely To Hinder Performance**				
		r	Scale	Preferred Score Range			Scale	Avoid Score Range			
				Low	Avg.	High		No	Low	Mod.	High
Interpersonal Communication	Interacting effectively with others to convey thoughts and ideas	.10	Inter. Sens.		X		Skeptical			O	O
		.11	Adjustment		X	X	Leisurely			O	O
		.13	Ambition		X	X	Excitable			O	O
		N/A	Sociability		X		Bold				O
							Cautious			O	O
							Reserved			O	O
							Colorful			O	O
Building Relationships	Establishing and maintaining positive rapport with others	.10	Inter. Sens.			X	Skeptical			O	O
		.17	Adjustment		X	X	Leisurely			O	O
		.15	Ambition		X	X	Excitable			O	O
		N/A	Sociability		X		Bold	O			O
							Cautious			O	O
							Reserved			O	O
							Colorful			O	O

* An (X) indicates that scores falling within this range will facilitate performance on the competency.

** An (O) indicates that scores falling within this range will likely hinder performance on the competency.

Table 27 (continued): Competencies from the Hogan Archive with their Associated HPI and HDS Scales

Interpersonal Domain

Competency	Definition		HPI Scales That Facilitate Performance*	Preferred Score Range			HDS Scales Likely To Hinder Performance**	Avoid Score Range			
		r	Scale	Low	Avg.	High	Scale	No	Low	Mod.	High
Influencing Others	Utilizing the power of persuasion to gain the support of others	.25	Inter. Sens.		X		Skeptical	O			O
		.21	Sociability		X		Leisurely	O			O
		.38	Ambition		X	X	Reserved	O			O
		.25	Adjustment		X		Colorful			O	O
							Cautious			O	O
							Bold	O			O
							Excitable			O	O
Service Orientation	Responding to others in a timely manner to satisfy their needs	.14	Inter. Sens.			X	Skeptical			O	O
		.17	Adjustment		X		Leisurely			O	O
		.15	Prudence		X		Excitable			O	O
		N/A	Sociability		X		Bold			O	O
							Mischievous			O	O
							Diligent	O			O
							Reserved			O	O
							Colorful			O	O

* An (X) indicates that scores falling within this range will facilitate performance on the competency.

** An (O) indicates that scores falling within this range will likely hinder performance on the competency.

Table 27 (continued): Competencies from the Hogan Archive with their Associated HPI and HDS Scales

Interpersonal Domain

Competency	Definition		HPI Scales That Facilitate Performance*	Preferred Score Range			HDS Scales Likely To Hinder Performance**	Avoid Score Range			
		r	Scale	Low	Avg.	High	Scale	No	Low	Mod.	High
Teamwork	Working cooperatively with others to accomplish goals or objectives						Skeptical				O
		.13	Inter. Sens.		X	X	Leisurely				O
		.19	Adjustment		X		Excitable			O	O
		.20	Prudence		X	X	Bold			O	O
		N/A	Sociability		X		Mischievous			O	O
							Diligent	O			O
							Reserved			O	O
							Colorful			O	O
Sales Ability	Using persuasion skills to get a customer to make a purchase						Skeptical			O	O
		.14	Inter. Sens.		X		Leisurely			O	O
		.16	Adjustment		X		Excitable			O	O
		.24	Ambition		X	X	Bold	O			
							Cautious			O	O

* An (X) indicates that scores falling within this range will facilitate performance on the competency.

** An (O) indicates that scores falling within this range will likely hinder performance on the competency.

Table 27 (continued): Competencies from the Hogan Archive with their Associated HPI and HDS Scales

Intrapersonal Domain

Competency	Definition		HPI Scales That Facilitate Performance*	Preferred Score Range			HDS Scales Likely To Hinder Performance**	Avoid Score Range			
		r	Scale	Low	Avg.	High	Scale	No	Low	Mod.	High
Dependability	Reliably following through on commitments made to others	.17	Adjustment	X	X		Excitable			O	O
		.17	Prudence		X	X	Bold			O	O
		N/A	Sociability		X		Mischievous			O	O
							Diligent	O			O
							Reserved			O	O
							Colorful			O	O
Flexibility	Willingness to take alternative actions given appropriate justification	.17	Adjustment		X	X	Excitable			O	O
		.21	Ambition		X	X	Bold	O			O
							Cautious			O	O
Detail Orientation	Attending to all steps and follow-ups necessary to accomplish a task	.14	Prudence		X	X	Mischievous			O	O
							Diligent	O			O

* An (X) indicates that scores falling within this range will facilitate performance on the competency.

** An (O) indicates that scores falling within this range will likely hinder performance on the competency.

Table 27 (continued): Competencies from the Hogan Archive with their Associated HPI and HDS Scales

Intrapersonal Domain

Competency	Definition	r	HPI Scale	Preferred Score Range Low	Preferred Score Range Avg.	Preferred Score Range High	HDS Scale	Avoid Score Range No	Avoid Score Range Low	Avoid Score Range Mod.	Avoid Score Range High
Safety Orientation	Staying attuned to potential accidents and taking action to avoid them	.21	Adjustment		X	X	Excitable			O	O
		.27	Ambition		X		Bold			O	O
		.21	Prudence			X	Cautious	O			O
		N/A	Inquisitive	X			Mischievous			O	O
							Diligent	O			O
							Dutiful	O			O
							Imaginative			O	O
Planfullness	Looking forward in addressing tasks to anticipate steps and contingencies	.14	Ambition		X	X	Bold			O	O
		.14	Prudence		X	X	Cautious	O			O
							Mischievous			O	O
							Diligent	O			O

* An (X) indicates that scores falling within this range will facilitate performance on the competency.

** An (O) indicates that scores falling within this range will likely hinder performance on the competency.

Table 27 (continued): Competencies from the Hogan Archive with their Associated HPI and HDS Scales

Intrapersonal Domain

Competency	Definition	HPI Scales That Facilitate Performance*					HDS Scales Likely To Hinder Performance**				
		r	Scale	Preferred Score Range			Scale	Avoid Score Range			
				Low	Avg.	High		No	Low	Mod.	High
Stress Tolerance	Maintaining stable performance under the pressures of work or life	.30	Adjustment			X	Excitable			O	O
		.16	Inter. Sens.		X	X	Bold	O			O
		.19	Prudence		X		Skeptical			O	O
							Leisurely	O			O
							Mischievous	O			O
							Diligent	O			O
Work Attitude	Approaching work with a positive "can do" mindset	.36	Adjustment			X	Excitable			O	O
		.22	Prudence	X	X		Bold	O			O
		N/A	Inter. Sens.			X	Mischievous	O			O
							Diligent			O	O
							Skeptical			O	O
							Dutiful	O			O

* An (X) indicates that scores falling within this range will facilitate performance on the competency.

** An (O) indicates that scores falling within this range will likely hinder performance on the competency.

Table 27 (continued): Competencies from the Hogan Archive with their Associated HPI and HDS Scales

Intrapersonal Domain

Competency	Definition	HPI Scales That Facilitate Performance*		Preferred Score Range			HDS Scales Likely To Hinder Performance**	Avoid Score Range			
		r	Scale	Low	Avg.	High	Scale	No	Low	Mod.	High
Professionalism	Conducting oneself with high standards and integrity						Excitable			O	O
		.17	Adjustment		X	X	Bold	O			O
		.19	Ambition		X	X	Cautious	O			O
		.18	Inter. Sens.		X		Skeptical	O			O
		.16	Prudence		X	X	Leisurely			O	O
							Mischievous			O	O

* An (X) indicates that scores falling within this range will facilitate performance on the competency.

** An (O) indicates that scores falling within this range will likely hinder performance on the competency.

SUMMARY

In this chapter, we presented the Hogan Performance Model, which was designed to provide those using our inventories with a heuristic to organize a wide range of data related to job performance. The model includes a domain structure that organizes competencies and allows for direct links to be determined between competencies and our inventories through validity generalization methods. We concluded this chapter with a detailed look at 32 competencies we have commonly encountered in our research, and for which we have considerable validity data linking them directly to our inventories. This approach is important because it will lay the foundation for considering the relationship between our inventories and commercially available competency models. It also provides those using our inventories with the initial guidance needed to link our inventories to the competencies identified by their organizations or the organizations to which they are providing consulting services.

CHAPTER 11

COMPETENCY INTERPRETATION

The first requisite for success is the ability to apply your physical and mental energies to one problem incessantly without growing weary.

– Thomas A. Edison

GENERAL APPROACH FOR COMPETENCY INTERPRETATION

One of the most often requested areas of guidance for using Hogan inventories is interpreting Hogan inventories in light of a specific competency model. In the last chapter, we outlined the Hogan Performance Model and illustrated its application in understanding competencies that we have commonly encountered in our research. We will extend this approach to other commercially available competency models in this chapter. The purpose here will be to demonstrate the ability of our inventories to provide insight regarding competencies that are not directly associated with Hogan research. This generalization is important because of the vast array of competencies in use throughout the business world. If we can adequately create interpretive bridges to competencies beyond those we have directly dealt with in our research, then similar bridges can be developed for virtually any competency structure.

The following is a six-step process for developing a bridge between our inventories and other competency models:

1. **Develop a clear description of the job in question.** This should include an overview of the industry and organization, a description of key job components and challenges, and a listing of any cultural factors that might be important to success.

2. **Develop a competency structure based on the description of the job.** This may be predetermined if a company has developed a competency model for the job. If a commercially available competency structure is being used, the company offering the structure will likely have a methodology for developing a competency model. It is also possible to develop a competency model based on input from internal subject matter experts or through assistance from a consultant with expertise in developing competency models. However, competencies that have been researched and empirically supported are always preferred over homegrown models that do not have a research foundation.

3. **Organize the competencies according to the four domains associated with the Hogan Performance Model outlined in Chapter 10.** This is essentially a sorting task whereby competencies are sorted into a domain based on the highest degree of overlap with a domain. For example, competencies that are mostly information processing oriented are sorted into the Business Skills Domain, while those clearly associated with leading people are sorted into the Leadership Skills Domain.

4. **Select the absolute critical competencies that you want to relate to Hogan inventories.** This is an important step because you have to balance the desire to cover everything with the reality of selecting competencies that cover critical aspects of the job and can be reasonably measured using Hogan inventories. Keep in mind that you are not dropping competencies from the job. You are simply selecting those that can be effectively measured with our inventories, while reserving assessment of the remaining competencies with different techniques, such as an interview.

5. **Align scales from the Hogan inventories with the competencies.** This can be done by using the information in Chapter 10 to select a scale or scales that are likely to correlate with a particular competency. Keep in mind that simpler relationships usually work best. For example, a competency like Stress Tolerance can be very complex and may have any number of behaviors associated with it. However, in relating it to Hogan scales, it is better to keep things simple and rely upon the Adjustment scale of the Hogan Personality Inventory (HPI) as a good indicator of Stress Tolerance.

6. **Set the score range that you are going to look for on the Hogan scale(s) that would indicate a high probability of successful performance.** For example, if planning and organizing were a competency and Prudence were the Hogan scale selected for measuring the competency, you would need to establish the range you were looking for that would maximize the probability of success without screening out all the applicants. In other words, if you said a high probability of success was only possible with scores in the 80% to 90% range on Prudence, you would screen out a large number of potentially qualified applicants. Setting the range at 50% to 90% would ensure that you would get good planning and organizing skills without severely restricting the number of potentially successful applicants. Keep in mind that you will be looking at a number of Hogan scales. You have to balance the success range and number of scales you consider, or you will screen out everybody; or worse, bring in candidates who will underperform. The process of setting ranges without empirical data often becomes more of an art than a science.

These six steps represent a nonempirical approach to relating our inventories to competencies. We offer empirical approaches that range from validity generalization methods to full criterion studies. We always advocate moving toward empirical approaches, and you should only rely upon this process as a starting point or one to be used only when collecting data is not possible.

We will present two examples of this process using commercially available competency models. The first example relies upon the Leadership Architect[©]

structure developed by Lominger International. This example focuses on a Vice President and General Manager of Operations position. The second example relies upon the executive competency structure created by Development Dimensions International (DDI). This example focuses on a Vice President of Sales and Marketing position.

The competency structures offered by these two companies have many differences, but they have been applied very successfully in describing the requirements of a job. In addition, they are well-supported with collateral materials and are considered by many professionals to be two of the most thoroughly researched structures that are commercially available.

Example 1 – Lominger's Leadership Architect© Structure

Step 1 – Job Description

An international pharmaceutical company has an opening for a Vice President and General Manager of Operations. The company (which we will call Xtra Pharmaceuticals) has recently undergone considerable change. Several new products have been launched, and the company's global presence is increasingly a factor in filling high-level positions. The Vice President position became available because the incumbent decided to take early retirement. There were no internal candidates ready for the position, so the company decided to do an external search.

Company Facts

- The company is rapidly growing, with a workforce of 15,000 employees.
- Two cancer drugs launched by the company have sold well in the global marketplace.
- The company has several new drugs in the pipeline, adding to growth expectations.
- The company has lost market share due to increased competition.
- The company has just come through a period in which there were new product delays.
- Although revenue growth has been on target, costs remain high.
- The company expects to do some restructuring over the coming year to contain costs.

Company Cultural Characteristics

- Precise, process-oriented company
- Long history of successful performance
- Innovative in its product development
- Highly regulated environment that can slow product launches
- Competition driving need to be faster and more adaptable to regulatory changes

Position

- Title of the position is Vice President and General Manager of Operations
- 12 direct reports (8 Regional Directors of Operations, a Finance Director, an HR Director, a Quality Manager, and a Special Projects Manager)
- 9,000 employees associated with Operations
- 22 manufacturing and distribution facilities
- P&L responsibility
- Business plan responsibility

Key Challenges

- A need to address cost issues in the face of aging facilities and global labor competition
- Resistance to change, given the company's prior track record of success
- An aging workforce, particularly at the leadership level
- Fast-moving competition that is able to adapt to regulatory changes

Step 2 – Competency Structure

The next step involves the identification of competencies that will be important to success in the job of Vice President and General Manager of Operations. We will be looking for competencies that will ensure solid business skills to facilitate success in coping with the complexities of a business this size (Business Skills Domain), strong leadership capabilities that will allow for success in leading change (Leadership Skills Domain), effective interpersonal skills that will facilitate communication running a global business (Interpersonal Skills Domain), and a strong results orientation with the ability to innovate under stressful conditions in a highly process-oriented environment (Intrapersonal Skills Domain).

There are 67 competencies associated with the Leadership Architect© structure. Lominger International offers a very rigorous process for selecting competencies for a position that involves the use of subject matter experts to complete a sorting process to identify key competencies. In this example, we have selected 11 competencies that would likely be related to success in positions similar to our fictitious Vice President and General Manager of Operations:

- Drive for Results
- Delegation
- Motivating Others
- Business Acumen
- Strategic Agility
- Decision Quality
- Managing Vision and Purpose
- Interpersonal Savvy
- Ethics and Values
- Composure
- Intellectual Horsepower

It is important to point out that the competencies we have selected are for illustration purposes only. We encourage our readers to consult with Lominger International* if they are planning to use Leadership Architect© competencies to profile a position.

Step 3 – Organizing Competencies by Domains

Competencies rarely fit perfectly into a particular domain. However, if you read the definition of the competency carefully, it will likely have a stronger fit in one domain than another. Furthermore, it is rare for well-defined competencies

---

* Leadership Architect© competencies have been reprinted with permission from Lominger International. For further information regarding Leadership Architect© or other Lominger products or services, contact Lominger International, a Korn/Ferry Company, 5051 Highway 7, Suite 100, Minneapolis, MN 55416.

to cross three domains. The Drive for Results competency provides a good example in this profile. Lominger International defines it as follows:

Can be counted on to exceed goals successfully; is constantly and consistently one of the top performers; very bottom-line oriented; steadfastly pushes self and others for results.

Drive for Results might be appropriately classified into the Intrapersonal Domain if viewed as a personal characteristic related to a person's conscientiousness in completing tasks. In this case, however, the definition includes "constantly and consistently one of the top performers," which has a strong element of competition or competing with others. It also includes "steadfastly pushes self and others for results," which clearly indicates leadership. Therefore, this competency seems to fit best with the Leadership Domain. Table 29 contains all the competencies classified into the four domains.

Step 4 – Selecting Competencies to Be Measured

We purposely chose competencies that could be measured by Hogan inventories for this example. However, we did include one competency, Intellectual Horsepower, that would be best measured using a cognitive assessment, or perhaps, through an assessment center exercise involving analysis. This is a common occurrence when profiling jobs with competencies. Many competencies do not lend themselves to being measured with personality inventories. It is important not to force-fit a measurement tool to a competency because it will only result in adding measurement error to the process.

Step 5 – Aligning Scales to Competencies

This is a key step in developing an accurate measurement system based on a competency profile. Chapter 10 provides much of the guidance to complete this step for our profile. In certain instances (such as Business Acumen), we selected a single scale, Learning Approach, from the HPI as the best measure. In other cases (such as Motivating Others), we selected a scale from each inventory (Ambition, Bold, and Recognition) to provide the best measure. Selecting scales in the absence of data requires reliance on the research-based tables in Chapter 10 and experience using the inventories. It is a balancing act between accurately measuring the competency and avoiding setting such a high bar that no one offers a solid profile for the position. This will come up again in Step 6 when setting ranges for the scales. In this step, it is best to keep things as simple as possible. The fewer scales used to measure a competency, the better. A selection process that screens everyone out is useless. Table 29 illustrates the alignment of scales to the Leadership Architect[c] competencies for this position.

Step 6 – Establishing Success Ranges

The final step involves establishing success ranges for each scale used in measuring the competencies. In this example, we are going to set up three fit levels—strong, moderate, and weak. Without data, setting the ranges is again more of an art than a science. The key is to set the ranges so that there is a strong probability of success without screening out everyone. It is also important to maintain consistency in the ranges. If Ambition is used as a scale for more than one competency, it is important to take the same range on Ambition for each competency. Sometimes that may not be possible. In those cases, it is important to avoid range conflict, for example, setting the range at 65% to 100% for one competency and 0% to 35% for another.

The Motivating Others competency has sufficient complexity to provide a useful illustration of establishing success ranges (see Table 28). Three scales were selected for this competency, one from each inventory (Ambition, Bold, and Recognition). Other scales might add value, but these were selected as particularly salient to the Motivating Others competency. Ambition was selected because of its assessment of the drive to be in a leadership role. Bold was selected because at moderate risk levels it indicates self-confidence, and recognition was selected because it can be a motivating force when used effectively by a leader. Note that we are using the scales from the Motives, Values, Preferences Inventory (MVPI) in these examples. The information available on the position and the culture of the company provides an appropriate backdrop for adding this inventory into the mix.

The question that remains is, "What success range should be established at the strong, moderate, and weak fit levels?" It is usually best to begin with the HPI scales because of their consistently high correlations with job performance. In this case, the only HPI scale is Ambition. Because of its importance to leadership roles and use with several competencies, it is best to set this range at a fairly high level for a strong fit and keep it at that level for a moderate fit (say, 60% to 100%). Next, we have the Bold scale. This is the only place it is used in the profile. Too high a score on Bold can indicate arrogance, so setting the strong fit level at 30% to 70% should be effective, while 20% to 80% should work for moderate fit. Scores outside the 20% to 80% range would indicate a weak fit. The final scale for this competency is Recognition. MVPI scales can play an excellent role in separating moderate fit candidates from strong fit candidates. In this case, an upper-middle range (35% to 75%) will help to indicate a leader who would attend to Recognition as a motivating force without overly driving his/her own recognition efforts. Furthermore, Recognition at this level would be consistent with the cultural factors portrayed in this case. The best a person can do with a score outside this fit range on Recognition would be a moderate fit.

The participant must score in all of the ranges of the scales associated with a competency in order to be classified into a fit category. The final fit score a person receives for a competency is based on the lowest fit category into which one or more of a person's scores fall. Table 28 summarizes fit ranges for the Motivating Others competency in this profile:

Table 28: Motivating Others Competency

Scale	Strong Fit	Moderate Fit	Weak Fit
Ambition	60% to 100%	60% to 100%	All other scores
Bold	30% to 70%	20% to 80%	All other scores
Recognition	35% to 75%	All other scores	

In this example, a person with 85% on Ambition, 40% on Bold, and 40% on Recognition would be considered a strong fit on Motivating Others. A person with 55% on Ambition, 60% on Bold, and 40% on Recognition would be considered a weak fit.

This process is simply extended to the remaining competencies associated with a position until a full selection profile is developed. The key point in developing the profile is to make sure the fit ranges are not so strict (or lenient) that the value of the profile is lost.

Table 29 pulls the six-step process together to illustrate the entire profile for the Vice President and General Manager of Operations position using the Leadership Architect© competency structure. The competencies have been organized by domains. The first column provides the name of the competency, and the second column provides a portion of the definition. The remaining columns illustrate the Hogan scales associated with each competency and the fit ranges associated with a strong, moderate, and weak fit profile. If the Hogan scale columns contain "N/A," it means the competency is important for success, but should be measured with another tool such as a structured interview. A structured interview process, such as Lominger International's Interview Architect®, not only helps assess competencies that do not correspond with the Hogan scales, it also helps provide more insight regarding why a particular scale score may have occurred and the implications for fit.

Table 29: Lominger International Leadership Architect© – Competency Model for VP and General Manager of Operations

Competency	Definition*	Hogan Scale	Strong Fit	Moderate Fit	Weak Fit
Business Skills Domain					
Business Acumen	Knows how businesses work; …	Learning Approach	65% to 95%	50% to 95%	All other scores
Strategic Agility	Sees ahead clearly; …	Inquisitive	60% to 90%	30% to 90%	All other scores
		Imaginative	35% to 70%	35% to 80%	All other scores
Decision Quality	Makes good decisions (without considering how much time it takes) based upon a mixture of analysis, wisdom, experience, and judgment; …	Ambition	60% to 100%	50% to 100%	All other scores
		Inquisitive	60% to 90%	30% to 90%	All other scores
		Cautious	35% to 70%	20% to 80%	All other scores
		Science	35% to 75%	All other scores	

* Complete competency definitions can be obtained from Lominger International.

Table 29 (continued): Lominger International Leadership Architect© – Competency Model for VP and General Manager of Operations

Competency	Definition*	Hogan Scale	Strong Fit	Moderate Fit	Weak Fit
Leadership Skills Domain					
Drive for Results	Can be counted on to exceed goals successfully; …	Ambition	60% to 100%	50% to 100%	All other scores
		Power	50% to 100%	30% to 100%	All other scores
		Commerce	30% to 100%	All other scores	
Delegation	Clearly and comfortably delegates both routine and important tasks and decisions; …	Ambition	60% to 100%	60% to 100%	All other scores
		Prudence	40% to 85%	25% to 85%	All other scores
		Diligent	< 60%	< 80%	All other scores
Motivating Others	Creates a climate in which people want to do their best; …	Ambition	60% to 100%	50% to 100%	All other scores
		Bold	40% to 70%	30% to 95%	All other scores
		Recognition	35% to 75%	All other scores	

* Complete competency definitions can be obtained from Lominger International.

Table 29 (continued): Lominger International Leadership Architect© – Competency Model for VP and General Manager of Operations

Competency	Definition*	Hogan Scale	Strong Fit	Moderate Fit	Weak Fit
Interpersonal Skills Domain					
Managing Vision and Purpose	Communicates a compelling and inspired vision or sense of core purpose; …	Sociability	50% to 85%	30% to 95%	All other scores
		Inquisitive	60% to 90%	30% to 95%	All other scores
		Colorful	35% to 70%	35% to 90%	All other scores
Interpersonal Savvy	Relates well to all kinds of people, up, down, and sideways, inside and outside the organization; …	Sociability	50% to 85%	30% to 90%	All other scores
		Inter. Sens.	50% to 90%	30% to 90%	All other scores
		Mischievous	35% to 70%	35% to 80%	All other scores
Intrapersonal Skills Domain					
Ethics and Values	Adheres to an appropriate (for the setting) and effective set of core values and beliefs during both good and bad times; …	Prudence	40% to 85%	25% to 85%	All other scores
		Tradition	35% to 75%	All other scores	
Composure	Is cool under pressure; …	Adjustment	50% to 95%	30% to 100%	All other scores
		Excitable	<50%	<80%	All other scores
Intellectual Horsepower	Is bright and intelligent; …	N/A	N/A	N/A	N/A

* Complete competency definitions can be obtained from Lominger International.

COMPETENCY INTERPRETATION USING THE LEADERSHIP ARCHITECT© PROFILE

In the previous section, we developed a scoring matrix for the position of Vice President and General Manager of Operations using Leadership Architect© competencies mapped to Hogan inventory scales. The scoring matrix outlined three fit levels: strong, moderate, and weak fit. The notion that this is a profile, not an overall fit recommendation, is important to highlight. It would be unlikely (nor should it be expected) that a candidate would be a strong fit across all of the competencies. Rather, the matrix will allow Hogan inventories to be scored according to the competencies to determine the strengths and weaknesses of a candidate and to compare candidates to identify the person that has the best fit for the position.

To illustrate this, consider the following candidate, Pat Smith, who received the following scores on the three Hogan inventories (see Table 30).

Table 30: Hogan Inventory Assessment Results for Pat Smith

HPI				
Scale	Score	Low (0%–35%)	Average (36%–64%)	High (65%–100%)
Adjustment	92			
Ambition	100			
Sociability	97			
Inter. Sensitivity	62			
Prudence	38			
Inquisitive	30			
Learning Approach	86			

HDS				
Scale	Score	No Risk (0%–39%)	Low Risk (40%–69%)	Mod. Risk (70%–89%)	High Risk (90%–100%)
Excitable	39				
Skeptical	69				
Cautious	33				
Reserved	59				
Leisurely	77				
Bold	94				
Mischievous	96				
Colorful	100				
Imaginative	69				
Diligent	28				
Dutiful	21				

MVPI				
Scale	Score	Low (0%–35%)	Average (36%–64%)	High (65%–100%)
Recognition	91			
Power	98			
Hedonism	73			
Altruistic	53			
Affiliation	97			
Tradition	97			
Security	2			
Commerce	32			
Aesthetics	18			
Science	50			

The following competency profile (see Table 31) for Pat Smith will result from these scores on the Hogan inventories, reconfigured using the scoring matrix in Table 29.

Table 31: Competency Assessment Results for Pat Smith

S = Strong Fit	M = Moderate Fit	W = Weak Fit

Competency	Competency Description*	Rating
Business Skills Domain		
Business Acumen	Knows how businesses work; ...	S
Strategic Agility	Sees ahead clearly; can anticipate future consequences and trends accurately; ...	M
Decision Quality	Makes good decisions (without considering how much time it takes) based upon a mixture of analysis, wisdom, experience, and judgment; ...	M
Leadership Skills Domain		
Drive for Results	Can be counted on to exceed goals successfully; ...	S
Delegation	Clearly and comfortably delegates both routine and important tasks and decisions; ...	M
Motivating Others	Creates a climate in which people want to do their best; ...	M
Interpersonal Skills Domain		
Managing Vision and Purpose	Communicates a compelling and inspired vision or sense of core purpose; ...	W
Interpersonal Savvy	Relates well to all kinds of people up, down, and sideways, inside and outside the organization; ...	W
Intrapersonal Skills Domain		
Ethics and Values	Adheres to an appropriate (for the setting) and effective set of core values and beliefs during both good and bad times; ...	M
Composure	Is cool under pressure; does not become defensive or irritated when times are tough; ...	S
Intellectual Horsepower	Is bright and intelligent; ...	N/A

* Complete competency definitions can be obtained from Lominger International.

This competency profile suggests that Pat would be a moderate to strong fit on competencies associated with the Business, Leadership, and Intrapersonal Skills domains. However, the Interpersonal Skills domain looks rather weak. Overall, Pat would probably be, at best, a moderate fit for the position of Vice President and General Manager of Operations.

This conclusion is quite consistent with the conclusion that would be drawn if Pat's Hogan inventories were interpreted directly. The strongest elements of Pat's profile include a very calm demeanor (Adjustment – 92%), a competitive, driven nature (Ambition – 100%), and a desire to be in charge or in control (Power – 98%). Some of the more salient weaknesses in Pat's profile stem from what might be described as "too much of a good thing" with respect to interpersonal skills. Pat's Sociability score (97%) and Colorful score (100%) suggest a person that would be constantly seeking attention and may be less than inspiring because of his/her self-focus. In addition, Pat would likely exhibit poor listening skills and may diminish trust based on a high Mischievous score (96%).

The important point to be made in this discussion is that Pat would probably not be the top choice for the Vice President and General Manager of Operations position. This conclusion would likely be drawn whether the assessment profile were based on Lominger International competencies or directly interpreted from the results of the Hogan inventories. Both approaches show moderate to weak results in key areas necessary for successful performance of the job.

We can now move to our second example using DDI's executive competency structure. DDI's approach, while different from Lominger International's, has the same fundamental goal of providing a systematic, behavioral way to describe what is necessary to be successful in a particular job. We will follow the same steps for the DDI competencies that we used to map the Leadership Architect© competencies to Hogan inventories.

Example 2 – Development Dimensions International's Executive Competencies

Step 1 – Job Description

An international food and beverage distributor has an opening for a Vice President of Sales and Marketing. The company, which we will call A&L Distributors, plans to launch a new line of food products that is expected to have global appeal in the wellness food market space. The wellness food market space has grown dramatically over the past 10 years, and A&L believes this new line of food products will be a significant revenue producer. The Vice

President position is new, but the company has significant experience hiring for positions of this type. They would prefer to hire an external candidate with a proven track record in the wellness market space and experience building a start-up business.

Company Facts

- The company is rapidly growing and has a workforce of 10,000 employees.
- The company has launched many new products domestically and internationally.
- The wellness market space is new to the company.
- The competition within this market is growing, and the winners have been aggressive.
- The company has spent considerable money developing this new product line.
- The company recognizes that a considerable investment will be needed for the launch.

Company Cultural Characteristics

- Sales-oriented, high-recognition culture
- Long history of pay for performance
- Diversity is a central theme as a result of the company's globalization efforts
- Fast-paced environment that expects results
- Competition that forces business flexibility for results to be achieved

Position

- Title of the position is Vice President of Sales and Marketing
- Leader of a new team composed primarily of sales and marketing personnel
- Anticipated initial organization of 200 employees worldwide
- Locations and offices to be determined
- P&L responsibility
- Business plan responsibility

Key Challenges

- Building a strong sales and marketing team
- Launching a new product line in a competitive market
- Little company experience in the wellness market
- Fast-moving, aggressive competition

Step 2 – Competency Structure

We will be looking for competencies that will ensure solid business development skills and the ability to open a new market (Business Skills Domain), strong leadership capabilities that will allow for success in building a new team (Leadership Skills Domain), effective interpersonal skills that will facilitate communication in a sales-oriented environment (Interpersonal Skills Domain), and a strong results orientation with the "can do" attitude needed in a start-up business (Intrapersonal Skills Domain).

DDI has a broad range of competencies that can be used to address virtually any type of job. The company also offers a very rigorous approach to identifying competencies for a position that can range from the use of one of their trained consultants to a software solution that can be brought in house. In this example, we have selected 11 competencies that would likely be related to success in positions similar to our fictitious Vice President of Sales and Marketing:

- Passion for Results
- Sharing Responsibility
- Coaching and Developing Others
- Entrepreneurship
- Driving Execution
- Operational Decision Making
- Strategic Influence
- Compelling Communication
- Executive Presence
- Positive Disposition
- Courage

It is important to point out that the competencies that have been selected are for illustration purposes only. We encourage our readers to consult with DDI[†] if they are planning to use their competencies to profile a position.

Step 3 – Organizing Competencies by Domains

DDI competencies are similar to other competencies in that they rarely fit perfectly into a particular domain. However, DDI does use a domain structure similar to the one employed by Hogan Assessment Systems (HAS). This simplifies the process of organizing their competencies and helps to ensure a more straightforward mapping to our inventories.

The Positive Disposition competency provides a good example in this profile. DDI defines it as follows:

> *Demonstrating a positive attitude in the face of difficult or challenging situations; providing an uplifting (albeit realistic) outlook on what the future holds and the opportunities it might present.*

DDI classifies this competency into a domain they call "Executive Dispositions." This domain is very similar to our Intrapersonal Skills Domain, and we would agree that Positive Disposition fits best into this domain. Table 33 contains all the competencies for this profile, with their definitions classified into the four Hogan domains.

Step 4 – Selecting Competencies to Be Measured

Again, we purposely chose competencies that could be measured by Hogan inventories for this example. We believe that our inventories can contribute to measuring these competencies in a significant way.

Step 5 – Aligning Scales to Competencies

This step is identical to that used for the Leadership Architect[©] competencies. It is a bit easier because of DDI's adherence to a similar domain structure as that used in the Hogan Performance Model. However, keeping it simple and using as few scales as possible to measure a competency will still pay dividends

---

[†] This competency structure has been reprinted with permission from Development Dimensions International. For further information regarding this competency structure or other products or services offered by Development Dimensions International, contact Development Dimensions International at their world headquarters, 1225 Washington Pike, Bridgeville, PA, 15017-2838.

in the long run. Table 33 illustrates the alignment of scales to the DDI competencies for this position.

Step 6 – Establishing Success Ranges

The final step is also the same as that used in the Leadership Architect[©] example. The Strategic Influence competency will provide a good example from the DDI competencies for establishing success ranges (see Table 32). Four scales were selected for this competency—Interpersonal Sensitivity, Ambition, Bold, and Science. Interpersonal Sensitivity was selected because of its role in building relationships. Ambition was selected because of its assessment of the drive needed to advance shared interests and business goals. Bold was chosen because, at moderate risk levels, it indicates the self-confidence needed to influence others. Science was chosen because of its relationship to using data as part of a rational decision-making strategy.

As in the previous example, the question that remains is, "What success range should be established at the strong, moderate, and weak fit levels?" In this case, there are two HPI scales involved, Interpersonal Sensitivity and Ambition. We should probably begin with Ambition again because of its importance to leadership roles and its use with several competencies. The range should be set at a fairly high level for strong fit and kept at that level for moderate fit (60% to 100%). Next, we have the Interpersonal Sensitivity scale. The midrange (35% to 65%) is probably best for this scale—too high, and the person will be looking to get along with everyone and avoiding conflict; too low, and the person will be argumentative, sometimes failing to build relationships. At the moderate level, this range can be expanded to 25% to 85%. The Bold scale should be set to select for a person with self-confidence without the derailing behaviors. Too high a score on Bold can indicate arrogance, so at the strong fit level, 30% to 70% should be effective, and 20% to 80% should work for a moderate fit. Scores outside the 20% to 80% range would indicate a weak fit. The final scale for this competency is Science. MVPI scales can again play an excellent role in separating moderate fit candidates from strong fit candidates within a given company (or culture). In this case, an upper-middle range (35% to 75%) will help to ensure the leader will use data without succumbing to "analysis paralysis" or relying too heavily upon intuition when trying to influence others. The best a person can do with a score outside this range would be a moderate fit.

As in the previous example, the participant must score in all of the ranges of the scales associated with a competency in order to be classified into a fit category. The final fit score a person receives for a competency is based on the lowest fit category into which one or more of a person's scores fall. The following (see Table 32) summarizes fit ranges for the Strategic Influence competency in this profile:

Table 32: Strategic Influence Competency

Scale	Strong Fit	Moderate Fit	Weak Fit
Inter. Sens.	35% to 65%	25% to 85%	All other scores
Ambition	60% to 100%	60% to 100%	All other scores
Bold	30% to 70%	20% to 80%	All other scores
Science	35% to 75%	All other scores	

In this example, a person with 60% on Interpersonal Sensitivity, 85% on Ambition, 40% on Bold, and 40% on Science would be a strong fit on Strategic Influence. A person with 90% on Interpersonal Sensitivity, 55% on Ambition, 60% on Bold, and 40% on Science would be a weak fit.

Table 33 illustrates the entire profile for the Vice President of Sales and Marketing position using the DDI competency structure.

Table 33: Development Dimensions International – Competency Model for Vice President of Sales and Marketing

Competency	Definition	Hogan Scale	Strong Fit	Moderate Fit	Weak Fit
Business Skills Domain					
Entrepreneurship	Using one's understanding of key market drivers to create/seize business and customer focus opportunities and/or expand into new markets, products, or services.	Learning App.	40% to 90%	20% to 90%	
		Ambition	60% to 100%	50% to 100%	All other scores
		Prudence	35% to 70%	20% to 70%	All other scores
		Commerce	30% to 100%	All other scores	
Driving Execution	Translating strategic priorities into operational reality; aligning communication, accountabilities, resources, culture, and processes to ensure that strategic priorities yield consistent, sustainable results.	Inquisitive	60% to 90%	30% to 90%	All other scores
		Prudence	35% to 70%	20% to 70%	All other scores
		Diligent	< 60%	< 80%	All other scores
Operational Decision Making	Securing and comparing information from multiple sources to identifying business issues; committing to an action after weighing alternative solutions against important decision criteria.	Ambition	60% to 100%	50% to 100%	All other scores
		Inquisitive	60% to 90%	30% to 90%	All other scores
		Cautious	< 70%	< 80%	All other scores
		Science	35% to 75%	All other scores	

Table 33 (continued): Development Dimensions International – Competency Model for Vice President of Sales and Marketing

Competency	Definition	Hogan Scale	Strong Fit	Moderate Fit	Weak Fit
Leadership Skills Domain					
Passion for Results	Setting high standards for personal and group accomplishment; tenaciously working to meet or exceed challenging goals; measuring progress and deriving satisfaction from goal achievement and continuous improvement.	Ambition	60% to 100%	50% to 100%	All other scores
		Power	50% to 90%	30% to 100%	All other scores
		Commerce	30% to 100%	All other scores	
Sharing Responsibility	Delegating tasks and accountability to encourage ownership of higher level issues, enable individuals to stretch their capabilities, and manage one's own workload.	Ambition	60% to 100%	60% to 100%	All other scores
		Prudence	35% to 70%	20% to 70%	All other scores
		Diligent	< 60%	< 80%	All other scores
Coaching and Developing Others	Providing feedback, instruction, and development guidance to help others excel in their current or future job accountabilities; planning and supporting the development of individual skills and abilities.	Ambition	60% to 100%	50% to 100%	All other scores
		Inter. Sens.	35% to 65%	25% to 85%	All other scores
		Learning App.	40% to 90%	20% to 90%	
		Altruistic	> 25%	All other scores	

Table 33 (continued): Development Dimensions International – Competency Model for Vice President of Sales and Marketing

Competency	Definition	Hogan Scale	Strong Fit	Moderate Fit	Weak Fit
Interpersonal Skills Domain					
Strategic Influence	Creating and executing influence strategies that persuade key stakeholders (e.g., internal or external partners, customers, or senior management) to take action that will advance shared interests and business goals.	Inter. Sens.	35% to 65%	25% to 85%	All other scores
		Ambition	60% to 100%	50% to 100%	All other scores
		Bold	35% to 70%	35% to 95%	All other scores
		Science	35% to 75%	All other scores	
Compelling Communication	Clearly and succinctly conveying information and ideas to individuals and groups in a variety of situations; communicating in a focused and compelling way that drives others' thoughts and actions.	Sociability	50% to 85%	30% to 95%	All other scores
		Inquisitive	60% to 90%	30% to 90%	All other scores
		Colorful	35% to 75%	35% to 90%	All other scores
Executive Presence	Championing the organization's vision and values in an authentic manner; demonstrating a poised and confident demeanor that reassures others and commands respect.	Sociability	50% to 85%	30% to 95%	All other scores
		Inter. Sens.	35% to 65%	25% to 85%	All other scores
		Mischievous	35% to 70%	35% to 90%	All other scores
Intrapersonal Skills Domain					
Positive Disposition	Demonstrating a positive attitude in the face of difficult or challenging situations; providing an uplifting (albeit realistic) outlook on what the future holds and the opportunities it might present.	Adjustment	50% to 95%	30% to 100%	All other scores
		Excitable	<50%	<80%	All other scores
Courage	Proactively confronts difficult issues; makes valiant choices and takes bold action even in the face of opposition.	Adjustment	50% to 95%	30% to 100%	All other scores
		Ambition	60% to 100%	50% to 100%	All other scores
		Bold	35% to 70%	35% to 95%	All other scores

COMPETENCY INTERPRETATION USING THE DDI COMPETENCY PROFILE

In the previous section, we developed a scoring matrix for the position of Vice President of Sales and Marketing using DDI competencies mapped to Hogan inventory scales. As an example of using this matrix, consider the candidate, Kelly Conners, who received the following scores on the three Hogan inventories (see Table 34).

Table 34: Hogan Inventory Assessment Results for Kelly Conners

HPI

Scale	Score	Low (0%–35%)	Average (36%–64%)	High (65%–100%)
Adjustment	92			
Ambition	100			
Sociability	90			
Inter. Sensitivity	62			
Prudence	23			
Inquisitive	88			
Learning Approach	86			

HDS

Scale	Score	No Risk (0%–39%)	Low Risk (40%–69%)	Mod. Risk (70%–89%)	High Risk (90%–100%)
Excitable	15				
Skeptical	42				
Cautious	11				
Reserved	74				
Leisurely	34				
Bold	91				
Mischievous	90				
Colorful	74				
Imaginative	86				
Diligent	57				
Dutiful	6				

MVPI

Scale	Score	Low (0%–35%)	Average (36%–64%)	High (65%–100%)
Recognition	75			
Power	100			
Hedonism	99			
Altruistic	93			
Affiliation	87			
Tradition	78			
Security	37			
Commerce	70			
Aesthetics	92			
Science	98			

The following competency profile (see Table 35) for Kelly Conners will result from these scores on the Hogan inventories, reconfigured using the scoring matrix in Table 33.

Table 35: Assessment Profile for Kelly Conners

S = Strong Fit	M = Moderate Fit	W = Weak Fit

Competencies	Competency Description	Rating
Business Skills Domain		
Entrepreneurship	Using one's understanding of key market drivers to create/seize business and customer focus opportunities and/or expand into new markets, products, or services.	M
Driving Execution	Translating strategic priorities into operational reality; aligning communication, accountabilities, resources, culture, and processes to ensure that strategic priorities yield consistent, sustainable results.	M
Operational Decision Making	Securing and comparing information from multiple sources to identifying business issues; committing to an action after weighing alternative solutions against important decision criteria.	M
Leadership Skills Domain		
Passion for Results	Setting high standards for personal and group accomplishment; tenaciously working to meet or exceed challenging goals; measuring progress and deriving satisfaction from goal achievement and continuous improvement.	M
Sharing Responsibility	Delegating tasks and accountability to encourage ownership of higher level issues, enable individuals to stretch their capabilities, and manage one's workload.	M
Coaching and Developing Others	Providing feedback, instruction, and development guidance to help others excel in their current or future job accountabilities; planning and supporting the development of individual skills and abilities.	S

Table 35 (continued): Assessment Profile for Kelly Conners

Interpersonal Skills Domain		
Strategic Influence	Creating and executing influence strategies that persuade key stakeholders (e.g., internal or external partners, customers, or senior management) to take action that will advance shared interests and business goals.	M
Compelling Communication	Clearly and succinctly conveying information and ideas to individuals and groups in a variety of situations; communicating in a focused and compelling way that drives others' thoughts and actions.	M
Executive Presence	Championing the organization's vision and values in an authentic manner; demonstrating a poised and confident demeanor that reassures others and commands respect.	M
Intrapersonal Skills Domain		
Positive Disposition	Demonstrating a positive attitude in the face of difficult or challenging situations; providing an uplifting (albeit realistic) outlook on what the future holds and the opportunities it might present.	S
Courage	Proactively confronts difficult issues; makes valiant choices and takes bold action even in the face of opposition.	M

This competency profile suggests that Kelly would be a moderate to strong fit on competencies associated with all four domains. Overall, Kelly would probably be a moderate to strong fit for the position of Vice President of Sales and Marketing.

This conclusion is consistent with the conclusion that would be drawn if Kelly's Hogan inventories were interpreted directly. The strongest elements of Kelly's profile include a very calm demeanor (Adjustment – 92%); a competitive, driven nature (Ambition – 100%); and a desire to be in charge or in control (Power – 100%). Kelly seems to have very good interpersonal skills, including high Sociability (90%) and average Interpersonal Sensitivity (62%). Kelly is also high on Inquisitive (88%) and Imaginative (86%), suggesting he will be able to handle the strategic thinking and creative marketing aspects of the job. Finally, it appears that Kelly will be effective at business development, with high Ambition (100%), moderately low Prudence (23%), and high Commerce (70%). Kelly will need to be challenged with a lot of variety and a fast environment and could probably benefit from a strong support person to keep things organized.

The overall conclusion that can be drawn on the basis of the DDI competency profile or the results of the Hogan inventories interpreted directly is that Kelly is a fairly strong candidate for the position of Vice President of Sales and Marketing.

DDI APPROACH

DDI is an avid user of Hogan inventories, particularly at the executive level. However, their approach combines high quality behavioral data with inventory results to gain a very high fidelity and business relevant picture of a person's fit for a position. In validation research, this approach of combining high quality behavioral data with inventory data has been known to produce some of the highest validity coefficients. We can illustrate this approach using an assessment coverage matrix that includes Hogan inventory data, Targeted Selection[©] (DDI's behavioral interviewing process), and business simulations that are often associated with this approach known as the Assessment Center Method. Our example will build off of Table 35.

In our example, we will use three people to assess the performance of Kelly Conners. They are called assessors. Each assessor will take responsibility for at least one component of the assessment process. In addition, we will already have the results of Kelly Conners' performance on the inventories. The goal is to have at least two behavioral measurement points for each competency, Hogan inventory data to supplement the behavioral measures, and at least two people that can comment on Kelly's performance on a competency. Table 36 illustrates this pattern of coverage.

To obtain the ratings in the coverage matrix, Kelly would complete the Hogan inventories, participate in a Targeted Selection[©] interview, and complete various business simulations that would be rated by one or more of the assessors. The Hogan inventories would provide supplemental information relevant to the behavioral ratings obtained for each competency as well as explain or challenge other patterns or trends at the domain level. The Targeted Selection[©] interview would yield a rating on each of the competencies. The Business Analysis Exercise would yield ratings on Entrepreneurship, Driving Execution, and Courage. The Decision Challenge Exercise (a series of e-mails, voicemails, and general correspondence that together present a variety of operational decision challenges) would measure Driving Execution, Operational Decision Making, Passion for Results, Sharing Responsibility, and Courage. A Direct Report Meeting (played by a trained role-player) would measure Coaching and Developing Others and Strategic Influence. Finally, the Business Presentation would yield ratings on Strategic Influence and Executive Presence. Both Compelling Communication and Positive Disposition would be measured across all of the business simulations involving interpersonal interaction (i.e., Direct Report Meeting, Business Presentation, and Targeted Selection Interview).

Once Kelly completed all the components of the assessment process, the assessors would get together and complete the assessment coverage matrix during a process called Data Integration. Data Integration is one of the most valuable aspects of the Assessment Center Method. It allows for ratings across multiple methods to be openly discussed among multiple assessors. The goal is for the assessors to arrive at a consensus rating for each one of the competencies. Furthermore, the assessors could produce a single overall rating for Kelly's fit for the position using this same process of discussion and consensus. Because Hogan inventories are used as complementary insights to behavioral competency ratings, DDI assessors would bring in personality interpretation at the end of integration, after arriving at consensus ratings.

Obviously, this process is quite thorough and can produce outstanding results. It combines the best of all available assessment techniques into an overall assessment process. However, there is a trade off in terms of time and cost using the Assessment Center Method. DDI has found this multi-method approach to be particularly relevant at executive levels, where job complexity and the high rate of business change make it valuable to have a more nuanced set of observations, so that organizations can plan for emerging challenges and avoid the huge risks associated with putting the wrong leader into a major assignment.

If you would like to learn more about this approach, we recommend the text *Assessment Centers and Managerial Performance* by Thornton and Byham (1982).

Table 36: Assessment Coverage Matrix for Kelly Conners*

Competencies	Hogan Inventories	Interview	Business Analysis	Decision Challenge	Direct Report	Business Presentation	Consensus Rating
Business Skills Domain							
Entrepreneurship	M	X	X				X
Driving Execution	M	X	X	X			X
Operational Decision Making	M	X		X			X
Leadership Skills Domain							
Passion for Results	M	X		X			X
Sharing Responsibility	M	X		X			X
Coaching and Developing Others	S	X			X		X
Interpersonal Skills Domain							
Strategic Influence	M	X			X	X	X
Compelling Communication	M	X					X
Executive Presence	M	X				X	X
Intrapersonal Skills Domain							
Positive Disposition	S	X					X
Courage	M	X	X	X			X

* The Hogan Inventory ratings are from Table 35. The X's represent rating points that would be obtained if Kelly completed the additional components of the assessment center.

SUMMARY

The examples from Lominger International and Development Dimensions International illustrate the flexibility of the Hogan inventories in developing competency-based profiles. While these examples were selection-oriented, the six-step process is virtually identical when creating a competency profile for development. The keys to success when using our inventories to evaluate a competency profile are to keep the number of scales per competency to a minimum and to avoid setting ranges that allow too few (or too many) people to do well. It is an art that has its roots in science. You should use as much available data as possible at the outset to pick scales and set ranges. You should also continue to work toward empirical support for a profile once it is in use. The six-step process is a starting point on the road to building an empirically supported profile.

PART 3

LEVERAGING ASSESSMENT RESULTS

CHAPTER 12

DELIVERING FEEDBACK

Be careful what you pretend to be because you are what you pretend to be.

– Kurt Vonnegut

Delivering feedback can be one of the most rewarding ways to use Hogan inventories. When feedback sessions are done well, the person receiving the feedback invariably finds the experience valuable and a real difference maker in terms of raising self-awareness. Giving feedback is also one of the most challenging experiences a person can take on in terms of building skills using our inventories. It is one thing to look at a profile and draw some conclusions about a person's strengths and weaknesses. It is something very different (and much more challenging) to sit across the table from a person and explain their assessment results in a meaningful and helpful way. The purpose of this chapter is not to teach a person how to give feedback; only experience can do that. Rather, this chapter will focus on best practices for delivering feedback and provide some tips from experienced professionals regarding the ways they have been successful in giving feedback.

FEEDBACK VERSUS DEVELOPMENT FEEDBACK

This is actually a very important distinction when delivering assessment results to a participant based on Hogan inventories. Feedback (using Hogan inventories) simply involves telling a participant about their behavioral tendencies based on their inventory scores. For example, a participant who scores very low on the Adjustment scale will tend to be emotional, self-critical, and worry a lot. These behavioral tendencies may negatively or positively impact performance. Great salespeople often have low Adjustment scores. Great air traffic controllers rarely have low Adjustment scores. The key to moving from feedback to development feedback is context, and context is derived from job requirements.

It is safe to say that the more knowledge a feedback provider has of the participant's job requirements (or future job requirements), the more prepared he/she will be to give development feedback. Furthermore, judging whether aspects of a profile can be leveraged as a strength or need to be addressed as an opportunity for development begins with a clear understanding of job requirements. Keep in mind that job knowledge is like a funnel of information. At the top end of the funnel, the knowledge is general, but can still provide context for delivering effective development feedback. Job knowledge at the bottom end of the funnel can be quite specific and may even include knowledge of cultural requirements or other organizational specifics.

For example, if a feedback provider knows that the participant is interested in moving into a leadership role, then that knowledge provides some context for interpreting results in light of the participant becoming a leader. Knowing that the sought after position is the leader of a sales team in which there is a lot of pressure to drive the achievement of sales goals adds more context that is useful for the interpretation of results. If you add in that the organization places a premium on recognition as a means of rewarding strong performance, the context for development feedback becomes even richer.

Each step down the funnel of job requirement information improves the chances of the feedback provider offering effective development feedback. We recognize that it is not always possible to gather a lot of job knowledge information prior to a feedback session. In fact, many times such information can only be gathered when you are beginning a session and establishing rapport with a participant. The point is that effective development feedback requires some context in the form of job requirements. The remainder of this chapter will deal with "development" feedback and what a feedback provider can do to enhance the effectiveness of a session of this type.

APPROACHES TO GIVING FEEDBACK

There are probably as many ways to give feedback as there are interpretive combinations across our three inventories. There is no absolute right way. In fact, it is probably best to develop a personal approach that builds on some basic success factors. There are at least four approaches to providing feedback that have been advocated by Hogan consultants.

- **Job Requirements Approach** – This approach can be very effective if the person giving feedback is very familiar with the requirements of the job. This approach begins with outlining the key job requirements that will truly make a difference in performance. Once the requirements have been outlined, we would advocate organizing them by the four domains associated with the Hogan Performance Model. Organizing requirements in this fashion simply adds some structure to how the feedback will be delivered. Next, a person's scores on our inventories can be associated with the various requirements of the job to determine areas of strength and potential areas for development. Using this approach, feedback would proceed through the various job requirements, outlining scale results as they pertain to the person's ability to perform each requirement.

- **Competency Approach** – This approach is somewhat similar to the job requirements approach. As the name implies, this approach is based on a competency model. It can be very effective if a sound competency model exists for the job or in situations where the organization would prefer that feedback center on competencies, rather than Hogan inventory scales. This approach begins with a clear understanding of the competency model and the way Hogan scales relate to the various competencies. Chapter 10 can be quite helpful in determining these relationships. We would also advocate organizing the competencies by the four domains when using this model. Feedback using this model would proceed through the various competencies, outlining scale results as they pertain to the person's ability to perform each competency.

- **Values-based Model** – This intriguing approach has been advocated by Hogan consultants when confronted with a potentially difficult feedback session, such as one involving a person with very low Adjustment. This model represents Hogan inventories as "what you want," as measured by the Motives, Values, Preferences Inventory (MVPI); "what can get you there," as measured by the Hogan Personality Inventory (HPI); and "what can get in your way," as measured by the Hogan Development Survey (HDS). Using this approach, feedback begins with the MVPI, continues with the HPI, and concludes with the HDS. The reason that it can be helpful in difficult feedback situations is that it begins with MVPI results. MVPI results rarely cause people to be defensive or worrisome, so a feedback session will usually get off to a very positive start with solid rapport developing early in the discussion.

- **Comprehensive Model** – This is probably the most common model used to provide feedback on Hogan inventories. It simply involves systematically covering the results of each inventory (scale by scale) and finishing up by providing themes or configural observations regarding the overall results. The comprehensive approach usually begins with the HPI, followed by the HDS, and concludes with the MVPI. The key to success when using this approach is being able to pull the results together into concise themes that will enhance a person's self-awareness and provide a foundation for development. Failure to provide these themes, or at least an effective summary of the results, can result in confusing a person with massive amounts of information from three inventories that contain 28 separate scales. However, when this approach is used effectively, it can provide a person with a deep level of self-insight that can be valuable to their development and job performance.

SUCCESS FACTORS

Regardless of the approach that is used, we have identified 10 success factors that can help ensure a good feedback session.

1. Preparing for the Session

There are some very clear steps to follow that will help ensure you are prepared to conduct a feedback session, and they are based on the results found in the HPI. First, determine whether you are interpreting an invalid or "Fake Good" profile. Look for a message on a report based on the HPI that says the profile is valid and interpretable. If it is, then determine whether you have a "Fake Good" profile. If the total number of items endorsed on the Moralistic, Mastery, and Virtuous Homogenous Item Composites (HICs) is equal to or greater than 13, then you are likely to have a "Fake Good" profile. In this case, the scale, HIC, and configural interpretations for the HPI profile are questionable, as are the results from any other Hogan inventory. Participants with a "Fake Good" profile likely (a) take a big picture approach and dislike details, (b) do not listen or take feedback well, (c) are ascendant, (d) have a high level of social skills and do well in interviews, and (e) may overestimate their own abilities and contributions to success.

Second, determine how anxious the participant will be during the feedback session. Review the results of the No Hostility HIC in Interpersonal Sensitivity and the Not Anxious HIC in Adjustment. Combined scores of two or less indicate that the participant could get angry and demonstrate a range of emotions during the feedback session.

Third, determine whether the participant will accept their results. Participants with very high Adjustment scores often discount feedback. You can also review the Not Autonomous HIC score in the Prudence scale. Participants with scores of 1 or less may discount feedback from others, including their HPI results.

Obviously, this preparation is only possible when HPI results are available. Once you have completed these steps, you are ready to begin a review of all the inventory results for the participant. The review can proceed according to any number of approaches, including those already outlined. The key to preparation at this point is to take good notes as you review results and organize the notes so you can present information in a manner that ensures the participant hears the key points you observed in the results.

2. Building Rapport

There are at least three areas that need to be covered when building rapport with a participant. First, always provide an introduction to yourself, your background, and your role in the feedback process. This does not have to be elaborate. A few sentences to put the participant at ease should do the trick.

Second, it is important to cover the purpose of the feedback session and how the data will be used. The participant will realize that he/she has completed the assessments, but it is amazing how many times the purpose of taking the assessments was never discussed (e.g., my manager told me to go online and take the assessments). The issue of confidentiality should also be covered at this point. This can be a tricky issue because confidentiality should have been covered when the participant was asked to take the assessments. If confidentiality has been covered, then your role is to remain consistent with established policy. If confidentiality has not been addressed or was left to you as the feedback provider, then the session should be treated as fully confidential. Fully confidential means that nothing addressed during the feedback session should be discussed with anyone other than the participant.

Finally, you should get some information about the participant. Ask the participant to provide an overview of his/her background (including his/her current role) and any development targets that are being worked on or suggested by his/her manager. This may be your only opportunity to gather information about job requirements; and, as pointed out in the beginning of this chapter, job requirements set the stage for effective development feedback. It is also important to be a bit careful with time, or you may end up using half the session for this part of the discussion. The total time to discuss all three of these points is usually around 15 minutes.

3. Outlining the Process

Once you have established rapport with the participant, you are ready to outline the process. The process outline will depend on the feedback approach you intend to follow. In general, though, the process will include a description of the inventories, a discussion of the results from each inventory, key configural observations, and a summary that includes pulling the results of the inventories together with any other data and targeting some development recommendations. There are many variations to the way the process unfolds, but it is almost always the case that these elements will be covered at some point during the feedback session.

4. Describing the Inventories

You will likely need to describe what the inventories measure at some point early in the discussion, usually when you are outlining the process. Again, it is possible to spend too much time doing this, so we offer the following capsule descriptions of the inventories that hit a few high points:

- **Hogan Personality Inventory** – The Hogan Personality Inventory, or HPI, provides insight about the "bright side" of personality. It assesses how you will be seen by others on a day-to-day basis. If I were to ask someone what you were like, there is a good chance he/she would describe you in a way that is consistent with what is being measured by the HPI.

- **Hogan Development Survey** – The Hogan Development Survey, or HDS, measures performance risks or tendencies that can interfere with your performance on the job. The HDS has often been described as a measure of the "dark side" of personality or a measure of derailing behaviors. Unlike the HPI, performance risks or tendencies measured by the HDS only emerge when your guard is down, such as when you are under a lot of stress, very comfortable with those around you, or when you are tired. However, when you exhibit these performance risks or tendencies (particularly the negative behaviors associated with elevated scores), they are quite noticeable and memorable for those around you.

- **Motives, Values, Preferences Inventory** – The Motives, Values, Preferences Inventory, or MVPI, provides insight regarding your interests or what you value most in a job, career, or organization. These interests or values will energize you to the extent that you will enjoy a job, career, or organization when they are satisfied; or they will potentially cause you to leave a job, career, or organization when they are not. In other words, the MVPI provides a measure of fit—fit with a job, fit with a career, and fit with an organization.

You can conclude this section by describing the inventories as systematic measures of the "bright side," "dark side," and "inside" of personality that will provide useful insights regarding performance strengths; opportunities for development; and fit with respect to a job, career, or organization. They will help you understand what you want (MVPI), what can be leveraged to get you there (HPI), and what you may have to overcome to be successful (HDS).

5. Giving Feedback on the Hogan Personality Inventory

Most feedback sessions cover all the primary scales of the HPI. Although style can enter into the order in which the scales are covered, it is usually best to follow the order in which they appear in the report that is being used. Providing behavioral implications at the high and low ends of each scale is a useful starting point. It is also useful to seek some input from the participant regarding his/her perspective of his/her scale score and associated behaviors. It is not typical to walk through the HIC or subscale scores. These are usually reserved for points in the discussion when they provide useful insights for interpretation. Summarizing a participant's overall profile can be a useful way to move on to other inventories or to transition into other parts of the feedback session. If, for instance, a participant were taking the assessment as part of a leadership development program, an effective summary would cover the leadership themes identified in the HPI results.

6. Giving Feedback on the Hogan Development Survey

HDS feedback is different from HPI feedback in that it is more important to cover performance risks falling into the "High Risk" range than it is to walk through all the scale scores. It is useful to point out that HDS score combinations and even low HDS scores can be valuable from an interpretation standpoint, but if possible, it is important to make sure that each score falling in the "High Risk" range gets covered in some way during the session. The only possible exception to this is when multiple "High Risk" scores suggest an underlying theme that goes beyond individual scale interpretation. This can happen in a variety of ways. For example, a person could be elevated across the scales associated with the "Moving Away" cluster (Excitable, Skeptical, Cautious, Reserved, and Leisurely). Interpreting the entire cluster will usually be more helpful in cases like this as opposed to going scale by scale.

An important aspect of HDS interpretation is determining if the negative behaviors associated with a scale elevation are being exhibited by the participant on the job. If they are being exhibited, you will want to determine the performance implications. If they are not being exhibited (or, at least, that is what the participant is telling you), you will want to determine how the negative behaviors are being controlled. It has been our experience that when the participant cannot point to actions used to control the negative behaviors, he/she may be unaware of his/her impact or simply in denial regarding performance implications.

The key here is not trying to convince a participant that he/she is elevated on an HDS scale or scales. Rather, your goal is to address elevations by figuring out how the negative behaviors are being dealt with (or not dealt with) and their impact on performance. This may be a subtle distinction, but we often encounter participants that have worked hard to control the negative behaviors. We have also encountered situations in which the negative behaviors are accepted in particular organizations and have little negative impact on performance. In cases such as these, the elevations are simply noted and may not draw a lot of development focus. These cases can be contrasted with participants that are unaware of the performance impact, in denial regarding the impact, or unable to put controls in place to minimize the impact. These participants can benefit greatly from development feedback on elevated scales and feedback regarding clear actions for minimizing the performance implications of the negative behaviors.

7. Motives, Values, Preferences Inventory Feedback

The MVPI is another inventory for which interpreting the top three or four scores is usually the best approach. These scores represent important interests or values for the participant, whereas low scores typically suggest indifference. The top three or four scores have two important implications that should be covered in feedback. First, those scores represent rewards or motivators the participant is looking to get out of a job or organization. This is usually a fruitful, nonthreatening area to explore with the participant because you are in essence asking what the participant enjoys most about a job or organization. Second, it is often the case that the participant will inject his/her top interests or values into the job or organization. This is particularly true for participants in leadership positions. Both of these areas are important to cover in a feedback session, and as it turns out, they tend to be the least threatening areas and ones that the participant will usually enjoy discussing.

8. Configural Interpretation

Participants usually find configural interpretations to be among the most useful insights to be gained from the feedback process. Less is usually better, meaning that a participant can be overwhelmed by a multitude of scale configurations. Configural interpretation requires the highest level of understanding about our inventories and only comes with experience. However, there are two aspects of feedback worth discussing when considering which configurations to share with a participant. First are instances where scale results conflict with one another. This could occur within an inventory or, more likely, across inventories. It is often the case that these apparent conflicts are not conflicts at all. Skilled configural interpretation can change these apparent conflicts into useful and insightful results for the participant that could not be gained by simply reading a report.

The second area of configural interpretation that participants find useful is pulling a number of scale results together to highlight a particular strength or development opportunity. Again, an assessment report by itself or even in combination with other data may not bring a configuration of this type into full light. However, a skilled feedback provider can use these configurations to build a clear picture of a strength or development opportunity.

9. Summarizing Results

Perhaps the best way to summarize results is to go back to the themes that typically come through in the participant's overall profile. As we pointed out earlier, a useful way to begin the summary is by characterizing the inventories as what the participant wants in a job or career (MVPI), what the participant can leverage to get there (HPI), and what the participant might have to overcome to be successful (HDS). The summary should also include a clear description of strengths and development opportunities. More than three of each will likely be overkill because the participant will already have heard more feedback in this one session than at any other point in his/her career. Providing three overall strengths and three overall opportunities for development will lead directly into a development planning discussion and will provide the foundation for the participant to go back through his/her assessment reports in a systematic way to identify subtleties that may have been missed when reviewing reports prior to feedback.

10. Development Planning

Most feedback sessions conclude with a focus on development planning or at least some tips on how to make the most of the results. Feedback sessions that do not include something in the way of development planning will leave the participant with the view that the session was interesting—but, so what? In fact, when we have evaluated feedback sessions, the development-planning component consistently comes up as an area in which participants want more, rather than less.

Too often, development planning is all about fixing something. We believe that development planning is as much about leveraging strengths as it is about addressing development opportunities. This view is particularly important when you consider the fact that there is no such thing as a bad personality profile when using our inventories. A person can be successful in a wide variety of ways in virtually any job, and usually success can be traced to optimizing strengths and minimizing the negative impact of weaknesses. Therefore, when helping a participant create a development plan, you should first consider the job (or target job) and the organization. From there, it is a simple step to move on to what strengths should be leveraged or what opportunities should be addressed.

If at all possible, the feedback provider should consider the participant's potential development plan in advance of the session. This may have to be done in broad terms if little is known about the job or the participant's organization. Two to three development targets with associated development actions that are prepared in advance of the session can significantly enhance this part of the discussion. They will help to involve the participant in discussing development at the very least. The effectiveness of this part of the discussion will ultimately depend on the accuracy of the interpretation, the buy-in of the participant, the soundness of the development actions, and the degree to which the participant is committed to improving his/her performance.

THOUGHTS FROM THE EXPERTS

We began this chapter by noting that there are probably as many ways to give feedback as there are interpretive combinations across the Hogan inventories. We thought it would be useful to have some of our experts provide tips on how they give feedback. These folks have conducted literally hundreds of feedback sessions. They have each developed their own "success formula." Their comments illustrate the diversity in feedback approaches and the richness that can be achieved in providing feedback using Hogan inventories. Running throughout their comments, you will see aspects of all 10 of the feedback success factors just described.

Douglas Klippel, Senior Consultant

While each session is a bit different, I have found that the Comprehensive Approach works well with virtually all participants.

I normally begin by asking the participant if he/she has completed similar assessments before, and I inquire as to which ones he/she has taken, and if he/she saw similarities or differences in his/her Hogan reports. I find that this "icebreaker" usually gets the participant to acknowledge that he/she found some of the information in the reports to be accurate, which establishes a positive tone for the meeting. I also acknowledge any "differences" that the participant chooses to mention, and I assure him/her that we will talk about these issues in more detail as we work through the reports.

Before going into the reports themselves, I remind the participant about the importance of remaining open and receptive to feedback, and point out that for many of us, it is a natural tendency to downplay or discount feedback that is inconsistent with how we see ourselves. I encourage the participant to see the Hogan reports as a sort of mirror and not to discount any of the feedback straight out of hand. I also try to remind him/her that part of being human involves having things that we do well, and things that we need to improve upon.

I always present the reports from our Leadership Forecast Series in the following order—the Potential Report (HPI), followed by the Challenge Report (HDS), and then the Values Report (MVPI). I have the participant turn to the overview graph in the front of the Potential Report first, where I explain what a percentile score is, and I describe the normative group his/her scores were compared against. I try to make sure the participant understands that high scores are not necessarily good on any scale and that none of the scores are necessarily bad. With this, I remind the participant not to give himself/herself too much credit for high scores, and not to beat himself/herself up for low scores, until we have gone completely through the reports. I then have the participant turn to the first scale page in the Potential Report (which is the Adjustment scale) and provide a brief scale overview, describe his/her score range, and touch on the strengths and potential weaknesses of his/her scale score. If I think it is warranted, I direct the participant to the "Coach's Report" (the final page of the Potential Report) to point out any interesting subscale (HIC) patterns that need to be investigated. I proceed in a similar fashion throughout the rest of the Potential Report.

I try to maintain an easygoing tone during the feedback, and I attempt to encourage questions as we go through the report. At all times, my approach is something like the following: "Your score is at the _____ percentile. This suggests that you have strengths in _____. Would you agree with that assessment? Also, your scores suggest that you may need to work on _____. Do you agree, and why or why not?" Maintaining this type of tone helps to make the participants less defensive and helps to encourage two-way communication.

After finishing the Potential Report, I summarize the key findings we discussed and then proceed to the Challenge Report. I have the participant turn to the overview sheet at the beginning of the report, and I explain the differences in the scoring scheme used for this report (with higher scores being more of a derailment concern). I point out that everybody has at least a few derailers. I go through the scales in descending order, taking extra care to point out any overlap (or interrelationships) with his/her scores on the Potential Report. I make sure the participant understands the Developmental Recommendations included at the end of the report, as well.

I always save the Values Report for last, as it is often the most personal assessment of the Leadership Forecast Series. I normally begin by turning to the overview graph at the beginning of the Values Report and cover the scales in descending order. I try to point out the organizational and career implications of high and low scores for the scales, but I give equal time to the personal implications of higher and lower scores. For example, low Power scores suggest that the person is comfortable letting others take the lead in a group, but may also suggest that the person may be overshadowed by others in his/her organizational peer group that have higher scores on this scale. In other words, I try to cover the Values Report from both a personal and corporate perspective.

Finally, when wrapping up, I try to step back and summarize any trends that have cut across the three inventories. I close the session by thanking the participant for his/her time and attention, and I make certain that the participant knows how to contact me if he/she has additional comments, questions, or concerns. I try to briefly summarize the key strengths of his/her profile, remind him/her that he/she can leverage these strengths as he/she moves forward in the future, and I wish the participant every success in his/her future endeavors.

James Killian, Consultant

I was exposed to a number of feedback styles when I was learning about Hogan inventories. There are a few ingredients to any feedback session that I have found to be necessary, including gaining knowledge of what the person does for a living, communicating what the assessments are actually measuring (and what they are not), and providing accurate feedback based on one's technical knowledge of the assessments themselves. All of these should be put in the context of a judgment-free environment that does not come off as a sales pitch for Hogan. I tell each candidate, "This is your time, and I want you to take something away from this session." Beyond that, I have found that so much of giving feedback depends on the person receiving feedback. The benefit is that you already know who they are because you have the assessments in front of you. Hence, I use the results and tailor my approach with every feedback session I conduct. For example, I will start with MVPI results when a person has very low Adjustment that may have depressed scores on other HPI scales. This approach often gets the person to admit, "Yeah, that's me, all right," and establishes buy-in early in the discussion. I then move to the HPI and ask, "Why are you so hard on yourself?" This has opened the door for all kinds of rich discussion and meaningful feedback. I have found that asking straightforward questions like this can open the door for you to draw some solid conclusions or even to make bold statements to the person receiving the feedback. I have also found that people who have an emotional response during their feedback session (a controlled response, of course) leave their session feeling empowered because they know three to five things they do well and they know three to five things to work on to improve their performance and advance their careers. I believe this is the real value of assessment feedback, and the approach I take leaves people without the question of what can they do with themselves now that they know all this great information.

Jamie Bomer, Consultant

When providing feedback to a participant, I foster a two-way conversation and partner with the participant to tell his/her "story." Nothing is more frustrating than a feedback provider who talks at the participant. After I have thoroughly described the purpose of the feedback session, I ask the participant about his/her job, goals, and objectives. I often ask the participant if he/she has recently participated in a 360 feedback process. If so, I ask the participant to tell me what statements regarding his/her behavior made the greatest impact (if appropriate, during the session, I use the statements to drive home specific points).

Throughout the session, I ask for questions and input. For example, in the event that there is a perceived contradiction in the results (e.g., high Cautious and high Mischievous), I will describe the behaviors associated with the scale scores and ask him/her about the way these behaviors manifest themselves at work. I avoid reading the reports to the participant. The feedback session provides me with opportunity to integrate results across the assessment tools and tailor the feedback session such that the participant will benefit from insights that he/she likely would not gain by reading the reports. When describing the behaviors associated with scale scores, I avoid "pigeonholing" the participant by using terms like always and never because this often puts him/her on the defense. For example, I often use statements like, "Individuals with similar scores tend to be described by others as _____. Is this consistent with how you think others likely would describe you?"

I consider the links between what the person wants out of life and how they go about getting it to be one of the most powerful and important discussions during the feedback session. For instance, discussing the perceived inconsistency between a participant's MVPI results and HPI results (e.g., high Power and low Ambition) often creates a "light bulb" moment.

Because of the comprehensiveness of the results and feedback, at the conclusion of the session, I (a) provide a summary of key points (e.g., highlight what to "start doing," "stop doing," and "keep doing" in relation to career goals) and (b) provide helpful suggestions for how the participant can increase effectiveness in his/her job.

Greg Barnett, Senior Consultant

I believe that a good feedback session occurs when you can create open dialogue and quickly build rapport with an individual. In a relatively short amount of time, you are going to be discussing some rather personal issues, so it is important for individuals to feel comfortable with the person providing feedback. In many cases, the first few minutes are spent talking about the weather, their family, their jobs, where they currently live, where they have lived in the past, and what their current job entails. Ideally, when they are talking about these topics, I am actively listening and conversing in a way that builds open and honest dialogue. I typically steer this rapport-building period to address the following topics:

1. Reaction to the assessments
2. Career aspirations
3. Personal strengths
4. Areas in need of development
5. Expectations for the feedback session

Responses to questions in these areas help me to frame the remainder of the feedback session. They also help me to understand the person's degree of self-awareness regarding his/her strengths and development needs. Ideally, this portion of the discussion will result in some specific strengths and development areas that I can link directly to assessment scores. When direct links can be made, it usually helps with buy-in regarding the accuracy of the tools and improves the dialogue. The final step before embarking on the path of feedback delivery is to assure confidentiality for the entire conversation. Some people like to do this as a first step, but I find that starting a session with the formality and seriousness of a "confidentiality statement" can be a barrier to developing good rapport and having a quality discussion.

Nicole Bourdeau, Consultant

Given tendencies highlighted by my own Hogan assessment results, prior to any feedback session, I always spend time reviewing the feedback recipient's reports in an effort to identify configural scoring patterns and, based on these patterns, general strengths and development opportunities. I also note tendencies and preferences that will help me tailor my approach to providing feedback. For example, an individual who scores high on the HPI Inquisitive, HDS Skeptical, and MVPI Science scales likely will benefit from a brief explanation regarding "how the inventories work" during the early stages of the feedback session.

From my perspective, feedback recipients derive the most benefit from feedback sessions that (a) are personally relevant and (b) help them answer the question, "What should I do with this information?" As such, after the feedback recipient and I discuss what we want to accomplish during the feedback session, I always segue the conversation away from Hogan in order to gain a good understanding of the feedback recipient's current job, goals, key objectives, challenges, career aspirations, etc. To initiate this conversation, I often ask questions like, (a) What are the primary objectives for which you are currently accountable? (b) What job-related competencies are most critical to your success (at the present point in time and in the future)? or (c) What is the most important outcome you produce (or contribute to)? In sum, I try to get the feedback recipient to answer the question, "Toward what are you developing?" I silently note important themes (e.g., this person's success and potential likely hinges on strong interpersonal skills) to reflect back upon as we review their results.

Prior to launching into a discussion regarding what particular scale scores (and patterns of scale scores) suggest, I always help the recipient understand (a) that the HPI, HDS, and MVPI (and corresponding reports) each yield a unique form of information and (b) how the inventories work together. Although I often briefly define the implications of the respondent's score on each scale, I place more emphasis on describing the relationships between the scales both within and across the inventories.

Throughout the feedback session, I make a concerted effort to facilitate dialogue with the feedback recipient (often by asking questions like "How might someone interpret _____?" or "How might _____ tendency impact your ability to _____ successfully?") and gauge the recipient's receptiveness to the feedback. Finally, to conclude the session, I always provide a summary of key points (e.g., highlight what to "start doing," "stop doing," and "keep doing" in relation to career goals) and encourage the participant to recognize that development often hinges on self-awareness and goal setting.

Audrey Wallace, Consultant

I begin each feedback session by stating the five things that will take place during the session. At the start of the feedback session, I ask the participant to tell me about his/her current position in the company and ask him/her to describe three challenges he/she is facing. Next, I explain the administrative details that will need to occur, such as why he/she took the assessments and who will have access to the results. During the third part of the feedback process, I provide an overview of the three assessments; MVPI (i.e., what you want out of life), HPI (i.e., what you are doing to get it) and HDS (i.e., what are you doing to hinder your performance). During the last two parts of the feedback process, I review the participant's results, help him/her understand interrelationships across the scales, and answer any questions he/she may have. At the end of the feedback process, to serve as a "take away," I tie in three actionable development opportunities by highlighting what the participant can start and stop doing in order to continue to enhance his/her performance.

Craig Haas, Consultant

I start the feedback session by breaking the ice with small talk. I remind the participant that our meeting and his/her assessment results are confidential, and I provide a quick outline of the session. I also like to ask the participant if there is anything additional that he/she would like to get from the session. I also ask the participant to give me a quick 60- to 90-second review of his/her career path.

After I have established rapport, I create a frame of reference for the participant by helping him/her understand what is being assessed and how the inventories tie to the reports. I then provide a few key facts to keep in mind as we go through the results.

1. There is no such thing as a perfect assessment. Everyone typically has high, moderate, and low scores, and there are positive and negative implications with each.

2. Typically, when people read over their reports, they find that they agree with about 75% of the interpretive text. However, if the participant is willing to verify the other approximately 25% of the interpretive text by speaking with at least five people who know him/her well, (e.g., coworkers, past coworkers, family, and friends), he/she will likely find that others will agree that an additional 15% to 20% of the interpretive text does, at times, describe the participant's behavioral tendencies.

3. There is likely to be 5% to 10% that does not in fact describe the participant, so he/she should try not to get caught up on one particular sentence that does not seem to fit.

4. I remind the participant that the session is intended to be a conversation in which he/she should ask questions, offer comments, and feel free to interrupt; however, I do reserve the right to redirect the conversation if we are getting far off track or running out of time.

Next, we get into talking about his/her actual results. I have found that frequently there are themes (strengths, opportunities for growth, and potential conflicts) across the battery of inventories that can be identified. I find it is helpful to talk about the big picture early on, so I spend about two minutes giving the participant the big picture review of the major themes in his/her assessment results (e.g., creative profile, risk-taking tendencies). I tend to ask the participant if these behaviors appear familiar, ring true, or resonate, and what, if anything, does not seem to fit. Based on his/her response to these questions, we start to dive into the scale combinations and individual scale level results. To do this, I typically use the bar graph and main scale scores displayed in the reports. I define the main scales in a brief sentence, explain how the pattern of scales is likely to play out for the participant in his/her work life, and discuss how these scale scores tie into the themes described earlier. If there are strong motivators or values (shown in his/her MVPI results) that are not being realized as reflected in his/her HPI or HDS results, we discuss possible reasons why the participant is not getting what he/she wants out of his/her work environment.

To wrap up the session, I again remind the participant of the key themes from his/her results in terms of his/her strengths and opportunities for growth. I provide some developmental tips to help maximize strengths and address one or two growth areas. I ask if there are any final questions for me. If not, then I typically recommend that the participant read through his/her reports a few times and find at least five people to help verify any results that he/she is unsure about or with which he/she disagrees. I also suggest that the participant take some time to create a developmental plan. Finally, I thank the participant for his/her time and offer to address any questions via e-mail after he/she has had an opportunity to read over his/her reports in more detail.

SUMMARY

In this chapter, we attempted to provide some guidance for giving effective development feedback using Hogan inventories. We tried to avoid being prescriptive in the approach we recommend for conducting the feedback process because we have observed many sound approaches that have produced outstanding results. We did provide 10 success factors that we think should be incorporated into an effective development feedback session. We also illustrated how experts have developed their own styles and have made use of the success factors to achieve results. The success of a development feedback session is ultimately determined by the participant in the way he/she embraces his/her results and leverages his/her results to improve performance. Structuring a development feedback session in a way that incorporates the success factors will help a feedback provider get one step closer to making a meaningful difference in a participant's future.

CHAPTER 13

DEVELOPMENT AND COACHING

No letters after your name are ever going to be a total guarantee of competence any more than they are a guarantee against fraud. Improving competence involves continuing professional development .... That is the really crucial thing, not just passing an examination.

– Colette Bowe

The notion of building a development plan around personality assessment data has long been a source of controversy. On the one hand, personality profiles are described as relatively stable over time and somewhat impervious to change. On the other hand, we have observed amazing results when people have executed development plans structured around insights gained from personality data. We believe that a correct position on this issue is related to the process we have observed people go through when they are making developmental changes. The process involves direct intervention at the behavioral level in the short term. In the long term, intervention at the behavioral level will impact a person's reputation that, in turn, could change one's personality profile. This perspective is illustrated in Figure 6.

Figure 6: Development Cycle

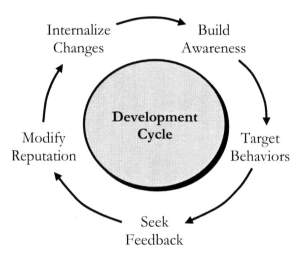

Building Awareness requires a person to fully understand "the what and the how" associated with a development need. Targeting Behaviors involves the identification of behaviors to be changed and the development techniques that will be brought to bear in making the change. Keep in mind that change comes in many forms. In this context, we view change in the broadest sense of altering the status quo. Seeking Feedback is necessary in order to calibrate progress. Reputation Modification will occur as others observe the changes. Finally, a person will begin to Internalize the Reputation Changes, allowing them to become a part of the person's identity. This is not a process that will occur overnight, and it also will not cause a person's assessment profile to change dramatically. However, it is clear that when people execute a well-designed development plan, positive behavior change can occur, and these changes over time can impact a personality assessment profile. The remainder of this chapter will focus on a six-step approach we recommend to create a well-designed development plan.

The domains of the Hogan Performance Model (Business, Leadership, Interpersonal, and Intrapersonal Skills), outlined in detail in Chapter 10, serve as the foundation for our approach to development. We use the domains to organize job description information, multi-rater data, Hogan inventory data, and job performance data. As part of the Hogan Leadership Forecast Series of reports, we have developed a Coaching Report that is structured around our six-step development planning process and the domain model. Figure 7 is a brief summary of the six-step development process as it appears in our Coaching Report.

Figure 7: Coaching Report Six-Step Development Process

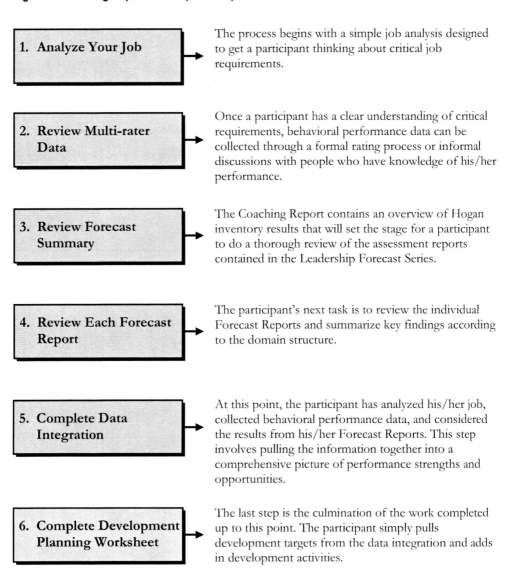

1. Analyze Your Job	The process begins with a simple job analysis designed to get a participant thinking about critical job requirements.
2. Review Multi-rater Data	Once a participant has a clear understanding of critical requirements, behavioral performance data can be collected through a formal rating process or informal discussions with people who have knowledge of his/her performance.
3. Review Forecast Summary	The Coaching Report contains an overview of Hogan inventory results that will set the stage for a participant to do a thorough review of the assessment reports contained in the Leadership Forecast Series.
4. Review Each Forecast Report	The participant's next task is to review the individual Forecast Reports and summarize key findings according to the domain structure.
5. Complete Data Integration	At this point, the participant has analyzed his/her job, collected behavioral performance data, and considered the results from his/her Forecast Reports. This step involves pulling the information together into a comprehensive picture of performance strengths and opportunities.
6. Complete Development Planning Worksheet	The last step is the culmination of the work completed up to this point. The participant simply pulls development targets from the data integration and adds in development activities.

To illustrate this process in action, we developed a full case study around a fictitious person named Terry Jones that works for a fictitious company named TransVirtual Corporation. The following summarizes a variety of data regarding Terry Jones, including a description of the situation, a description of the job for which Terry is being considered, a summary of 360 assessment results, and Hogan inventory results (see Table 37). These data provide a foundation for Terry Jones to build a development plan using the worksheets found in the Coaching Report.

TERRY JONES CASE STUDY

Situation

Terry Jones was hired as a Site Manager for a company named TransVirtual Corporation. TransVirtual Corporation is a world leader in providing in-home Virtual Experience Systems. These systems offer customers the leading edge in highly realistic, in-home virtual reality experiences.

Terry Jones was slated to be the successor to Pat Jacobson, Vice President of Operations. When Terry was hired, it was expected that there would be plenty of time for him to grow into the role because Pat was not planning to retire for another three years. Unfortunately, the timing did not work out. Pat informed Matt Cooper (Chief Operating Officer) that she would be retiring at the end of the year, which was only nine months away. Pat's announced retirement jeopardized the company's ability to achieve a number of key success factors:

- Growing the Operations Team sufficiently to handle the 30% growth target for all regions over the next 18 months.

- Creating operational synergies across the regions to reduce operating expenses by 10% without jeopardizing customer service or satisfaction.

- Developing more effective team relations within and across boundaries for all the regions as a means of improving region and company performance.

Despite Pat's retirement, Matt continued to believe that the success factors could be achieved. Matt also believed that there was a reasonable chance that Terry could be ready to take over for Pat at the end of the year. However, Matt was concerned about several issues related to Terry's performance and readiness to take over the position of Vice President of Operations. Matt decided that the best course of action was for Terry to put together and execute a formal development plan with the aid of an executive coach.

Matt summarized the situation with Terry as follows:

- Terry Jones is considered a high-potential employee that was hired approximately 10 months ago as the Site Manager at the Buffalo, New York, location.

- Terry was hired as a potential successor to Pat Jacobson, Vice President of Operations.

- The announcement of Pat Jacobson's impending retirement at the end of the year has forced the company to accelerate the consideration of Terry for the position.

- Some of Terry's weaknesses in the business skills area were recognized during the hiring process, but the company expected Terry to grow in this area given the demands of the Site Manager position.

- Terry recently completed a 360 assessment as part of TransVirtual's normal 360 assessment cycle for managers. The 360 assessment is usually the precursor to the creation of a formal development plan.

Terry was provided with the following data and was asked to build a development plan:

Job Description – Vice President of Operations

The Vice President of Operations is required to develop strategies, policies and procedures, and manage all five regional operations (1,750 employees) with an operating budget of $90,000,000 in order for the organization to achieve its objectives and fulfill the corporate mission and values. The accountabilities for the position include the following:

1. Provide a vision, a mission, and strategic direction for all regional operations.
2. Manage all personnel associated with day-to-day functioning of the Imagine Rooms, including all hardware system repairs.
3. Develop and manage all budgetary aspects of regional operations.
4. Implement cost control methods and procedures to meet company parameters and ensure bottom-line performance.
5. Manage the implementation of all hardware changes, upgrades, and/or improvements.
6. Ensure support and implementation of all company programs and change initiatives.
7. Promote TransVirtual values and support teamwork among all business units of the company.

8. Participate in community outreach efforts to help ensure a positive company image.

9. Ensure HR plans and policies are enforced fairly in all regional operations.

10. Oversee selection, appraisal, promotion, training, and discipline of personnel.

11. Ensure excellent customer service levels.

Summary of Terry Jones' 360 Assessment Results

Strengths – The following items from the 360 assessment were identified as strengths because they received the highest overall scores from each respondent group:

- Customer Focus: Item 55, this person takes initiative to promote customer service in his/her work area.

- Leisurely: Item 66, this person is typically on time for meetings.

- Measurement: Item 8, this person uses measurable results to organize his/her work.

- Business Results: Item 61, this person gets the job done on time.

- Leadership: Item 25, this person is always trying to improve processes at work.

Opportunities – The following items from the 360 assessment were identified as development opportunities because they received the lowest overall scores from each respondent group.

- Colorful: Item 21, this person seems genuinely modest.

- Bold: Item 19, this person has a genuine sense of humility.

- Colorful: Item 45, this person is willing to share the spotlight.

- Excitable: Item 14, this person expresses emotions in a mature and socially appropriate manner.

- Bold: Item 43, this person consistently shares credit.

Table 37: Hogan Inventory Assessment Results for Terry Jones

HPI

Scale	Score	Low (0%–35%)	Average (36%–64%)	High (65%–100%)
Adjustment	55			
Ambition	87			
Sociability	93			
Inter. Sensitivity	39			
Prudence	50			
Inquisitive	39			
Learning Approach	69			

HDS

Scale	Score	No Risk (0%–39%)	Low Risk (40%–69%)	Mod. Risk (70%–89%)	High Risk (90%–100%)
Excitable	68				
Skeptical	43				
Cautious	29				
Reserved	42				
Leisurely	19				
Bold	80				
Mischievous	50				
Colorful	80				
Imaginative	29				
Diligent	18				
Dutiful	59				

MVPI

Scale	Score	Low (0%–35%)	Average (36%–64%)	High (65%–100%)
Recognition	8			
Power	54			
Hedonism	14			
Altruistic	14			
Affiliation	46			
Tradition	73			
Security	16			
Commerce	64			
Aesthetics	20			
Science	55			

Once a person (in this case, our fictitious participant, Terry Jones) has these data, he/she can work his/her way through the six-step process in the Coaching Report to build a development plan. An individual can use the Coaching Report to build a development plan on his/her own. However, a professional coach or manager can be a valuable asset in working through the Coaching Report to develop an effective plan that, if executed, will produce significant, positive results. Involving a professional coach or manager will also ensure that a source for feedback will be readily available as the plan is executed.

The following section takes you through each step of the Leadership Forecast Coaching Report (Figures 8–14) and provides a completed worksheet for each step based on the profile of Terry Jones (Tables 38–43). Note that Table 40 (Leadership Forecast Series for Terry Jones) covers the actual performance summary that would appear in a Coaching Report based on Terry's inventory scores. The only portion of the Coaching Report that has been omitted is the introduction section, which outlines the Hogan Performance Model covered in Chapter 10. Keep in mind that this is just an example, but it was derived from the case study information outlined for Terry Jones.

Figure 8: Coaching Report Process Checklist

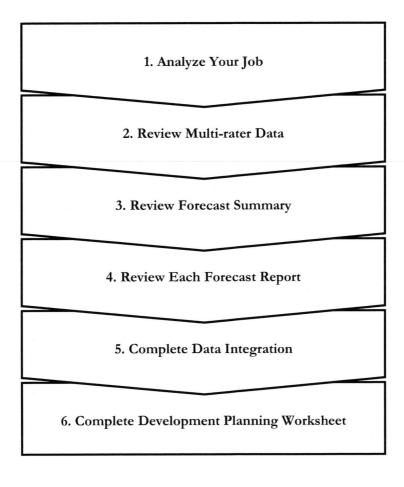

Figure 9: Process Checklist with Instructions (Analyze Your Job)

Process Steps	Instructions
1. Analyze Your Job	The starting point in building your development plan is to identify the key requirements of your job that are responsible for successful performance. Spend a few minutes thinking about the truly important requirements for success. You may want to ask your manager just to make sure you fully understand the requirements that will lead to success.
2. Review Multi-rater Data	
3. Review Forecast Summary	In the space below, write down the competencies that are critical to success, grouping them according to the Competency Domains. Once you have listed them, describe in your own words what you think is the most important job requirement for each domain.
4. Review Each Forecast Report	
5. Complete Data Integration	
6. Complete Development Planning Worksheet	

Table 38: Job Analysis Worksheet for Terry Jones

Domains	Competencies	Describe the most important requirement
Business	• Strategic Vision • Business Acumen • Process Improvement • Decision Making	• Knowing the business to accomplish growth objectives
Leadership	• Managing Performance • Delegating • Empowering Others • Leading Change • Talent Advocate	• Empowering others so they can accomplish the objectives
Interpersonal	• Building Relationships • Teamwork • Service Orientation	• Building team relations within and across boundaries • Increasing synergy • Influencing the organization
Intrapersonal	• Composure • Value Diversity • Trust • Openness and Flexibility	• Consistent and reliable reputation • Role model for organization • Empowering others

Figure 10: Process Checklist with Instructions (Review Multi-rater Data)

Process Steps	Instructions
1. Analyze Your Job **2. Review Multi-rater Data** **3. Review Forecast Summary** **4. Review Each Forecast Report** **5. Complete Data Integration** **6. Complete Development Planning Worksheet**	Multi-rater data can be very important to better understand "what" you do and "how" you do it on the job. If you have multi-rater data such as a 360 assessment, you can use this section to summarize the results. If you do not have 360 data, but do have feedback from your manager or others in your organization regarding your job performance, you may want to use this section to summarize that information. **Skip this section if you do not have any feedback regarding your job performance.** Review your multi-rater data and think about what the results reveal about your strengths and opportunities for development in each of the competency domains. Note your strengths and opportunities in the space provided and write down the specific multi-rater item (or statement) that was most important in leading you to your conclusions.

Table 39: Multi-rater Data Worksheet for Terry Jones

Domains	Strengths/Opportunities	Multi-rater Items
Business	*Strengths:* Business Acumen *Opportunities:*	Embraces culture

Leadership	*Strengths:*
	    Managing Performance
	
	Opportunities:
	    Motivating Others
		Measurement by-the-numbers
		
		Focus on morale and sharing credit

Interpersonal	*Strengths:*
	    Building Relationships
	
	Opportunities:
	    Teamwork
	    Building Relationships
		Customer focus
		
		Derailers (Colorful and Bold)
		Respect and sharing credit

Intrapersonal	*Strengths:*
	    Professionalism
	    Flexibility
	
	Opportunities:
	    Stress Tolerance
	    Professionalism
		Derailer (Leisurely)
		Business results
		
		Derailer (Excitable)
		Ethics and integrity

Figure 11: Process Checklist with Instructions (Review Forecast Summary)

Process Checklist	Instructions
1. Analyze Your Job	This section summarizes your results from the Leadership Forecast Potential Report, Challenge Report, and Values Report. The summary will prepare you to do a more detailed review of the individual Leadership Forecast Reports. This section is organized in four parts: (1) Performance Strengths, (2) Values and Drivers, (3) Challenges, and (4) Career Development. At the end of this section, there is a table containing your individual scale scores for each of the Leadership Forecast Reports.
2. Review Multi-rater Data	
3. Review Forecast Summary	
4. Review Each Forecast Report	
5. Complete Data Integration	
6. Complete Development Planning Worksheet	

Table 40: Leadership Forecast Series for Terry Jones

Performance Strengths

Personal Impact

You are active, hardworking, competitive, and eager to get ahead. You like leadership positions and enjoy being in charge. You are willing to take initiative in a group, and with the appropriate interpersonal skills, you will be able to assume leadership roles on team projects. These tendencies are particularly important in jobs that require directing others, persuasiveness, and working without supervision. Others will see you as energetic, talkative, and socially active. You should meet the public well and create a strong, even vivid, impression on others. You seem well-suited for work that involves interacting with strangers. You should perform well in front of groups and like public speaking. This is particularly important for jobs in which one must constantly deal with strangers in a positive way (e.g., sales, training, marketing, and customer service).

Interpersonal Skills

You are a pleasant and tolerant person, but one who will take a stand when necessary. You are reasonably planful and careful about procedures, but also able to be flexible enough to change directions when necessary.

Working and Learning Style

You are typically calm and able to handle pressure, but at the same time willing to admit faults and errors and listen to feedback. You are open-minded and curious, but you also take a practical approach to problem solving. You are bright, knowledgeable, and up-to-date concerning current issues and technology. You also seem self-disciplined, achievement-oriented, and productive and should enjoy pursuing tasks to completion. You will value training for yourself and others, will seek opportunities to grow and develop, and will want to apply the latest relevant knowledge to the work setting. These characteristics are important for most jobs.

Values and Drivers

Achievement Motivation

You prefer to put business before pleasure, you avoid distractions and activities that waste time and money, and you believe in maintaining a professional appearance and conduct at work. You seem appropriately interested in advancing your career, but you also pay attention to the demands of your career, family, and social life. Although you appreciate positive comments on your performance, you are reluctant to engage in self-promotion and prefer to wait for others to notice your accomplishments.

Social Interests

You seem equally happy working by yourself or as part of a team. You enjoy meeting new people, but you also like having time to yourself. You like people, but you do not need constant interaction. You focus on your work and take a practical, matter-of-fact interest in the needs and complaints of staff. You prefer to make staff decisions based on rational business considerations rather than people's wishes and fantasies, and as a result, you want meetings to start on time and follow sensible agendas. You typically follow established procedures and change things only when necessary—because you do not like to fix things that are not broken. You also believe that there are differences between right and wrong, and that they should be observed and respected.

Entrepreneurial Values

You seem to have a sensible attitude toward money; although you appreciate its value, you are not preoccupied by compensation issues. You judge yourself in part by income potential, but you also take pride in family, friends, and leisure time activities. You seem unconcerned about job security and are willing to take chances to advance your career. You do not need a lot of direction in your work, and you do not mind unexpected changes in work assignments.

Decision Making Style

You seem more concerned with how well things work than how they look or feel. You prefer no-frills, pragmatic, cost-effective solutions to the problems that come up in business and life—you make decisions based on functionality rather than appearance. You seem willing to make decisions based on data and research as well as your own personal experience. You are comfortable with technology, but you are not interested in technological innovations for their own sake—you understand the use of technology without being addicted to it.

Challenges

Reactions to Others

You seem to be an energetic and enthusiastic person, but one who tends to be easily annoyed or disappointed with other people's performance. As a result, at times you may seem somewhat irritable, critical, and willing to give up on people or projects. Because you appear unusually trusting of others, they may wonder if you are, in fact, as trusting as you seem. You seem active, confident, and open to challenges and are able to make decisions in a timely manner. You seem polite and considerate, which might be a problem if you work in an environment that rewards toughness. You seem coachable and responsive, which could be a problem if you need more feedback than others want to provide.

Personal Performance Expectations

You seem confident and assertive, you generally expect your projects to succeed, and you do not worry about failure or rejection. However, others may see you as demanding, overly competitive, resistant to feedback, and tending to blame your mistakes on others. You seem frank, straightforward, and understated. You expect others will find you engaging, and they often do. Over time, however, others may also see you as impulsive, disorganized, and not always delivering on promised work products. Whatever your talent may be for public speaking, you do not necessarily think others will find your performances entertaining.

Reactions to Authority

You seem willing to let others do their work, but you may not give them needed feedback. You seem willing to make your own decisions and may need to work harder at keeping others informed about what you have decided.

Career Development

When Strengths Become Weaknesses – Development Feedback for Mr. Jones

You should solicit feedback about your performance from coworkers and pay attention to the negative feedback—not just dismiss it. Make sure you understand the importance of contributing appropriately to team efforts. You are keenly interested in career advancement. Work to stay alert and look for opportunities to make these interests known. You need to remember not to intimidate younger or more junior team members, to practice letting others be in charge, and to be patient with others who are less motivated to succeed. You are so extraverted and enthusiastic that you may need to remember to listen carefully to what others are saying and not interrupt them—especially when dealing with younger or more junior colleagues and with clients. You should also make a point to share credit with others for successes achieved. You should anticipate others' expectations during interactions and respect their needs. You should be positive and remember that you can gain others' trust by being rewarding and honest in interactions with them. Remember to be patient when others make mistakes—typically, others do not make errors on purpose. You should stay open to change and be flexible in uncertain situations. When making decisions, you should remember that you may never have all of the relevant information, but should still decide promptly. Make an effort to prioritize work, keeping in mind that not every task requires equal time or attention. There is a big picture for every organization—it is the strategy and vision for the business. Make sure you understand it, are able to talk about it, and can determine how your activities contribute to this larger picture. You value being well-informed and will proactively seek training opportunities. Realize that you may become frustrated when they are not available. Moreover, you will enjoy setting your own performance goals because you are very achievement-oriented.

Dealing With Derailment Tendencies

First, lower your expectations for receiving special treatment and give credit to others. This will help in the process of building and maintaining the team you need to achieve your goals.

Second, because you may have trouble accepting negative feedback, make sure you listen to feedback from friends and family. You should try to realize that they know you well enough to be able to provide useful advice. In addition, they are not in competition with you, so the feedback is usually well meaning.

Third, because you are a very influential and energetic resource, you can intimidate others without intending to do so. Try to become aware of, and curtail, this tendency.

Fourth, try not to compete with your staff and peers. You should recognize that the real competition is outside the organization.

Finally, remember your strengths—you have the confidence and energy to make things happen. Difficulties and adversity will only make you more determined. Very little of importance in the world will get done without your kind of determination and drive.

Figure 12: Process Checklist with Instructions (Review Each Forecast Report)

Process Steps	Instructions
1. Analyze Your Job **2. Review Multi-rater Data** **3. Review Forecast Summary** **4. Review Each Forecast Report** **5. Complete Data Integration** **6. Complete Development Planning Worksheet**	The Leadership Forecast Reports are designed to help you better understand "why" you do what you do. There are three reports in the series—the Potential, Challenge, and Values Reports. Use this section to record strengths and opportunities as identified in the Leadership Forecast Reports. In the previous step, you reviewed a summary of the three Leadership Forecast Reports. You are now ready to complete an in-depth review of the individual reports. We suggest you read all three reports before completing this section. Once you have read the reports, you should go back, and beginning with the Potential Report, review and record strengths and opportunities for development in each of the competency domains. Do the same for the Challenge and Values Reports. **Keep in mind that it is not necessary to put something in every box. Only record the strengths and opportunities that are pertinent to your job success.**

285

Table 41: Leadership Forecast Report Worksheet for Terry Jones

Domains	Potential Report	Challenge Report	Values Report
Business	*Strengths:* Learning Approach Prudence (moderate) *Opportunities:* Inquisitive	*Strengths:* Cautious *Opportunities:* Excitable	*Strengths:* Commerce Science *Opportunities:*
Leadership	*Strengths:* Ambition Sociability *Opportunities:*	*Strengths:* Bold Colorful *Opportunities:*	*Strengths:* Power Commerce *Opportunities:* Hedonism Recognition
Interpersonal	*Strengths:* Adjustment *Opportunities:* Sociability	*Strengths:* Dutiful *Opportunities:* Bold Colorful	*Strengths:* Affiliation *Opportunities:* Altruistic
Intrapersonal	*Strengths:* Adjustment Prudence *Opportunities:*	*Strengths:* *Opportunities:* Bold Colorful Excitable	*Strengths:* Tradition *Opportunities:*

Figure 13: Process Checklist with Instructions (Complete Data Integration)

1. Analyze Your Job	You have now completed an analysis of your job, reviewed your 360 results, and reviewed your assessment results. You have all the data you need to identify some high-impact development targets.
2. Review Multi-rater Data	
3. Review Forecast Summary	First, use your overall impression of the data to identify any behaviors that you believe need to change to improve your job performance. Record those behaviors in the right-hand column under the appropriate domain. It is not necessary to list something in every box. Record only those behaviors that indicate a clear need for attention.
4. Review Each Forecast Report	
5. Complete Data Integration	Second, in the middle column, record the actual 360 items (or statements) that suggested a need for improvement.
6. Complete Development Planning Worksheet	Finally, in the left-hand column, record the Leadership Forecast Report results that help you understand "why" you exhibit these behaviors. Keep in mind, the best development targets are those that will significantly improve your job performance, for which you have clear data supporting the need for change, and for which you have acquired some insight as to the reasons for exhibiting the behavior.

287

Table 42: Data Integration Worksheet for Terry Jones

Domains	Using the assessment data from Step 4, describe the results that indicate "why you do what you do"	Using the 360 data (or statements) from Step 2, list items that led you to select behaviors needing improvement	Describe behaviors that need to change in order to improve your performance
Business	• Drive and business knowledge • Lacks vision (Imaginative) • Numbers focused • Risk tolerance	• Embraces culture (focused on results, not people) • Vision and strategy • Results driven	• Articulate a strategic vision • Leverage business knowledge • Mentor/coach (internal) • Compensating competencies (Creativity)
Leadership	• Overly competitive with subordinates • Poor communication • Push for results by setting high expectations	• Poor communication • Motivated by the numbers vs. motivated by people • Authoritarian	• "Fireside chats" • Stop competing with peers • Start collaborating (learn skills to do so) • Shift focus to balance people with the results • Empower others to lead (get out of the way)
Interpersonal	• Poor listening skills • Competing with others • Attention seeking • Disempowering to others	• Lack of respect and sharing credit with others • Trust • Low humility and modesty	• Practice active listening skills • Reflective listening • Seeking behavior—ask, don't tell • No "I" in team (make me look good via your work) • Creative ways to recognize team members
Intrapersonal	• Detail-oriented • Tradition (like doing it my way) • Mood swings • Not an organizational citizen	• Not believable or consistent • Big stories (embellished and distorted) • Volatile and moody	• More than one way to solve problems • Stress management • Follow rules ("walk the talk") • Be a positive example • Build professional credibility

Figure 14: Process Checklist with Instructions (Complete Development Planning Worksheet)

1. Analyze Your Job

2. Review Multi-rater Data

3. Review Forecast Summary

4. Review Each Forecast Report

5. Complete Data Integration

6. Complete Development Planning Worksheet

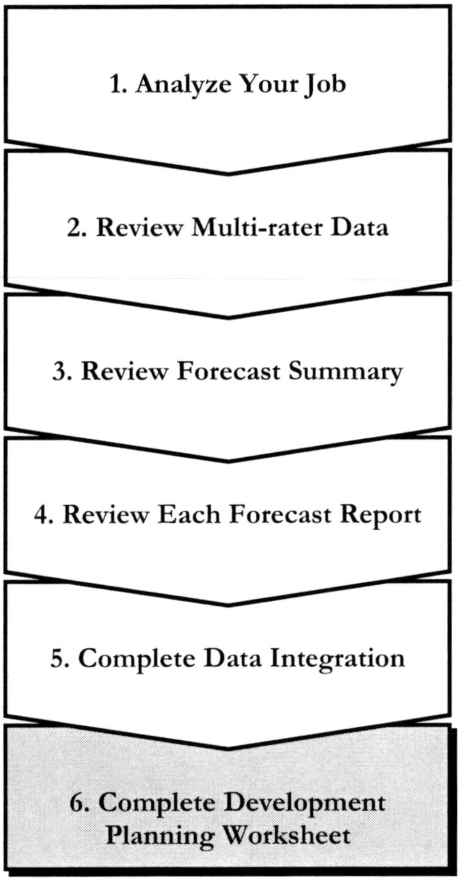

Based on the information you recorded on the Data Integration worksheet, you should identify one or two development goals and record them in the first column of the form.

A good development goal is one that is stated in behavioral terms and can be measured over time to ensure progress. Development action items can be listed in the second column, and progress toward achieving the goal can be recorded in the subsequent columns over time. If you need suggestions for development actions, the Internet provides a rich source of information. An inverted pyramid approach is recommended to complete a successful Internet search. Begin with a specific development question, perhaps even the goal you have selected. Work backward, using less-specific search questions until you locate information that you find useful. This approach often reduces search time on the Internet and improves the probability of finding information directly related to your development goal.

Table 43: Development Planning Worksheet for Terry Jones

Goal	Development Actions	Anticipated impact on critical success factors for the job
Participative leadership style to promote team spirit	• I will spend more time listening and integrating others' ideas in the decision-making process. • I will recognize others' contributions to decisions. • I will not provide my own solutions until I have heard the input of others. • I will provide a rationale behind my decisions to promote a clearer understanding. • I will utilize task force assignments to make the decision-making process more participative. • I will identify a trusted source for structured feedback on a weekly basis.	• Build better team relationships • Increase 360 ratings ("reputation") • Increase retention
Balance task focus with fun and praise	• I will implement a structured recognition program and keep it "fresh" so that it stays current and responsive. • I will enlist a resource to plan a team event quarterly to encourage recognition in an enjoyable manner. • I will conduct occasional meetings without a strong focus on the "numbers." • I will be aware of and use more "stage presence" in my communications with the team.	• Less stress • More commitment
Composure	• I will increase my self-awareness and monitor my behavior to diminish the "drama" present in my behavior. • I will solicit honest and open feedback from others with explicit or implicit retribution. • I will practice positive stress management techniques. • I will share the limelight with team members and consciously recognize their contribution.	• Decrease number of outbursts • Consistent presentation • Fewer embellishments and distortions

Development Strategies

The Coaching Report provides a nice framework to systematically process data that can then be used to create an effective development plan. We have observed that most individuals use a limited number of development strategies when deciding how to make improvements. Most of these strategies involve traditional methods of improving performance such as a training course or simple statements about new behaviors to be employed. Change is hard, and change that will result in altering one's reputation is even harder. We believe that a well-structured development goal and the use of creative development strategies can significantly improve the chances for successful change.

In terms of writing development goals, we advocate writing what are called S.M.A.R.T. goals. These goals are:

  S – Specific, significant, stretching
  M – Measurable, meaningful, motivational
  A – Agreed upon, attainable, achievable, acceptable, action-oriented
  R – Realistic, relevant, reasonable, rewarding, results-oriented
  T – Time-based, timely, tangible, and can be tracked

The following (see Figure 15) illustrates an example of a S.M.A.R.T. goal that was developed in the context of the Coaching Report.

Figure 15: S.M.A.R.T. Goal Example

Hogan Inventory Results	360 Assessment Results	Change Need
Low Interpersonal Sensitivity score that manifests itself in being overly challenging in public situations	1. Argumentative 2. Has to be right 3. Blunt	Needs to be more measured in his comments in meetings and group settings and be more willing to see others' perspectives

S.M.A.R.T. Goal

Terry will eliminate argumentative, blunt "tell" behaviors in meeting and group situations by substituting "seek" and "clarifying" behaviors that will raise his awareness of the positions of others and change his reputation (as measured by 360 results) to be viewed more as an interpersonally sensitive team member that strives for "win-win" solutions.

291

Goals written in this fashion clearly spell out what is needed, and they tend to point to a development strategy that has a high probability of success.

We have also examined a wide range of development plans that were created in response to a combination of personality data (as measured by Hogan inventories) and behavioral data (often measured with a 360 assessment). In addition to well-defined goals, these plans contained clearly written development strategies, and the strategies tended to match the goals. We identified five categories into which most of these development strategies could be classified. Table 44 outlines the five strategies with a description of when they are most effective and an example of their use.

Table 44: Development Strategies

Strategy	Description	Effectiveness	Example
Strategy 1 – Develop through education or training	The use of formal programs, classes, or workshops to build skills or develop behaviors that will close an existing learning gap.	Most effective with competencies or behaviors associated with the Business Domain and skill areas of the Leadership Domain. Effectiveness increases when the underlying potential for performance is high.	Improving an individual's ability to make high-quality decisions based on a rational decision-making process that incorporates generating and evaluating alternatives, and selecting a course of action with the highest probability of success.
Strategy 2 – Leverage an area of strength	The use of an existing, but heretofore unused or underused (leveraged) strength to overcome or substitute for a weakness.	Most effective when an area of strength exists in a lower order domain such as the Intrapersonal Domain that can be leveraged to offset a weakness in a higher order domain such as the Interpersonal Domain. Effectiveness increases when the strength is systematically (or overtly) incorporated to offset a weakness.	Improving an individual's ability to make an effective public speech (Interpersonal Domain) by engaging and winning over an audience using stories and anecdotes that have their foundation in a good sense of humor (Intrapersonal Domain).
Strategy 3 – Compensate with alternative behaviors	The overt use of positive behavior(s) to rebuild or rebalance a reputation that was marked by a clear absence of the behavior(s) or the existence of counterproductive behavior(s).	Most effective when positive behavior(s) can be identified, incorporated into an ongoing behavioral repertoire, and easily observed by others when it is demonstrated. Effectiveness increases when a physical reminder or awareness builder is used to ensure frequent and appropriate use of the positive behavior(s).	Improving an individual's reputation as an interested, involved team player by incorporating nonthreatening "seek" behaviors into team meetings and interactions. Changing an individual's wristwatch from the left to right hand prior to meetings or interactions as a physical reminder to use the positive behavior(s).

Table 44 (continued): Development Strategies

Strategy	Description	Effectiveness	Example
Strategy 4 – Support the weakness with resources	Utilizing a strength of another employee or team member to fill a gap or weakness that is unlikely to be ameliorated through developing, leveraging, or compensating strategies.	Most effective when behaviorally a weakness is clear, the personality results support the existence of the weakness, and the individual has struggled to little or no avail to successfully address it. Effectiveness increases when the target behavior can be isolated and supported by another individual without diminishing that individual's overall effectiveness in his/her role.	An individual that is quite disorganized with a low score on Prudence employs an administrative support person to provide a degree of structure and order in the performance of day-to-day responsibilities.
Strategy 5 – Redesign the job or assignment	Changing a job or position by removing a key role or responsibility and assigning it elsewhere in the organization.	Most effective when performance of a role or responsibility is ineffective and it is clear that allowing the individual to struggle will diminish his/her effectiveness and potentially hurt the overall organization. Effectiveness increases when the gap created by removing the role or responsibility from the position can be backfilled by expanding a role or responsibility that is valued by the organization.	An individual that is very effective at sales, but does a poor job at managing others, has the managerial role of the position assigned to another person in the organization, and the gap created is backfilled by expanding the individual's account responsibilities.

Coaching

We believe firmly that an individual can create an effective development plan independent of a professional coach, or even a manager, for that matter. However, we have observed that when a professional coach is involved, the individual can benefit in a number of significant ways. First, a professional coach can really help with assessment and performance data reduction and interpretation. Second, a coach can be of benefit in creating a well-targeted development plan that includes S.M.A.R.T. goals and clearly outlined development strategies. Finally, and perhaps most importantly, a coach can provide valuable ongoing feedback to the individual in terms of progress against goals and future adjustments to the plan.

A growing concern is determining if someone has the proper qualifications to be a coach and would be likely to provide good support during the course of an individual's effort to make developmental changes. We have identified 10 standards that can be used to evaluate a potential coach. These standards will apply to varying degrees depending on the nature of the coaching engagement, but they should provide sufficient guidance for anyone to consider the basic viability of someone being considered for virtually any type of coaching engagement.

1. Certification in Assessment Technology – Coaches using assessment tools should be able to clearly demonstrate that they possess the qualifications necessary to use those tools.

2. Certification in Coaching Best Practices – No two coaches provide coaching services in exactly the same way. However, there are proven best practices. A coach should be able to demonstrate their awareness of those practices.

3. Mentor or Consortium Support – Coaches are constantly being presented with new and challenging coaching situations. Coaches should have confidential resources available to discuss challenges they may not have encountered in the past.

4. Candidate Team – The most successful coaching engagements rely on a strong team model that includes the candidate, the coach, the manager, and human resources.

5. Coaching Contract – All coaching engagements should include a written contract describing the roles and responsibilities of the entire candidate team.

6. Defined Protocol – Coaching engagements should not be made up as you go. The engagement should begin with a defined protocol that provides a basic outline of how the engagement will progress.

7. Communication Plan – The effective involvement of a candidate team means that a clear communication plan is outlined, and it has fully described how confidential information will be handled.

8. Coaching Agenda – Regularly scheduled meetings should follow a written agenda. This helps to avoid having sessions turn into unproductive discussions.

9. Re-energizing Mechanism – Almost all coaching engagements run out of steam after a few successes or setbacks. A re-energizing mechanism should be established at the outset of the engagement to ensure long-term success.

10. Engagement Closeout – One of the most difficult things about coaching engagements is ending them. Closing out a coaching engagement does not mean that the coach and the candidate never talk again. It simply means that a mechanism should be in place to summarize the engagement at its formal conclusion.

SUMMARY

In this chapter, we provided some basic guidance on building a development plan that includes personality data. We approached the process on the basis of using the Leadership Forecast Series, including the Coaching Report. We consider this series of reports to be our flagship for people interested in their own development. We also believe that the six-step process outlined in the Coaching Report will result in an effective development plan. Change is difficult. It can only happen if an individual is motivated to change and has the proper tools to guide change. The information in this chapter in conjunction with our Leadership Forecast Series of Reports will provide the proper guidance, and if followed with some degree of diligence, it will result in positive behavioral (and reputation) change.

CHAPTER 14

RESOURCES AND SUPPORT

Polls estimate that if companies could get 3.7% more work out of each employee, the equivalent of 18 more minutes of work for each eight hour shift, the gross domestic product of the U.S. would swell by $355 billion, twice the total GDP of Greece.

– The Gallup Organization

We think it is important to begin a chapter on resources and support by recognizing the contributions of our partners in building the Hogan brand. We have a substantial network of domestic and international partners. Our domestic partners are well-versed in all our assessments and have made significant contributions to our assessments through the development of their own practices. Internationally, our partner network has expanded significantly over the past three years. We now have virtual global coverage through our international partners and they, like our domestic partners, continue to add to the knowledge base that is the Hogan brand. If you would like more information on our domestic or international partners, you can contact us at 800-756-0632.

The remainder of this chapter covers the resources and support available within Hogan Assessment Systems (HAS). We developed this chapter on the basis of the wide range of inquiries we receive on a daily basis. The information provides a good starting point for identifying specific resources or the right place to go for support when using Hogan inventories.

HOGAN BUSINESS MODEL

One of the biggest challenges in working with a consulting firm is figuring out where to go to get resources and support. We have worked very hard to keep the structure of HAS simple and have tried to ensure that our consultants and support services are easy to access. In this chapter, we will outline our business model and provide an extensive resource list based on common questions we have received from our customers over the years.

Our integrated business model is unique in the industry and is largely responsible for our success and our ability to be very responsive to our customers. It is based on the notion that we provide our customers with information in the form of reports that are derived from our inventories and supported through our service organization. Figure 16 illustrates our business model.

Figure 16: Hogan Business Model

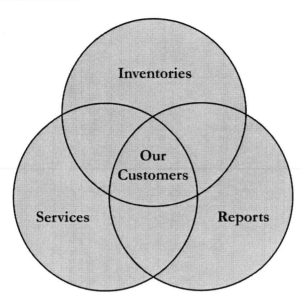

Inventories

Assessment inventories, or tests, are the core of our business. We offer four inventories: the Hogan Personality Inventory (HPI); the Hogan Development Survey (HDS); the Motives, Values, Preferences Inventory (MVPI); and the Hogan Business Reasoning Inventory (HBRI). We supplement these inventories with a variety of customized reports that can be configured to meet virtually any employee selection or development need.

Reports

Reports are the lenses through which our customers view assessment results. Our reports vary in terms of scope and complexity, depending on their intended purpose. We frequently develop customized reports that are configured for each customer's specific business needs.

Services

We offer our customers five basic services: Consulting, Research, Technology, Support, and Coaching. Each of these services is based on our inventories to meet the needs of businesses.

HOGAN CONTACT INFORMATION

Services offered by the company:

- Consulting – Our consulting team understands the fundamentals of assessment as well as the practical requirements of employee selection and development. They provide customers with expert design and implementation support.

- Research – Our research team plays a central role in applying our assessments by ensuring that every system we implement is supported by validity data. They also play a major role in the development and validation of all our new products.

- Technology – Our assessment platform is one of the most secure, reliable, and flexible in the world. Utilizing cutting-edge technology and a team of technology specialists, we have the capability of customizing the platform to meet the business needs of our customers.

- Support – Our assessment platform is managed by our Customer Service Team. The team is dedicated to ensuring high-quality assessment services, and customer support is available 24 hours a day, seven days a week. We also have a team dedicated to handling administrative issues that include invoicing, packaging, and shipping materials.

- Coaching – We offer coaching services that help users understand the results of our assessment inventories. These services range from individual feedback to APA-accredited workshops.

Who to contact for help:

- HAS is devoted to providing customers with exceptional service; however, we realize that it is sometimes difficult to pinpoint who should be contacted regarding a particular issue. First, it is important to point out that you can always contact your Hogan consultant as a starting point. If you do not have a consultant, you can call 800-756-0632 and ask for one to be assigned to you. In addition, Table 45 lists some common service questions and who to contact within the company for an answer.

Table 45: Common Service Questions and Who Should Be Contacted

Service Area	Sample Question/Issues	Contact	Contact Information
Online account	• I am having difficulty accessing my online account. • I need user IDs. • My client is having difficulty accessing the online system.	Customer Service Team	800-756-0632 - or - support@ hoganassessments.com
Assessment use	• How do I get an online account? • How do I get training? • I have an implementation-related question. • I do not know which report option to use. • I have never helped a client implement for candidate screening purposes, and I need guidance. • I need resources (e.g., report templates or marketing materials). • I have a question regarding an individual's assessment profile.	Consultant	Tulsa, OK Office 918-749-0632 Jacksonville, FL Office 904-992-0302
Partners	• I would like to become a Hogan distributor.	Consultant	800-756-0632
Research	• What data are available regarding adverse impact?	Research	800-756-0632
Systems	• I am having trouble with my customized Hogan Web site.	Technology	800-756-0632
Finance	• I have a question regarding my invoice.	Accounting	800-756-0632
Shipping/ materials	• Can you track the reports that were shipped to me?	Administration	800-756-0632

HOGAN ONLINE ASSESSMENT PLATFORM

Establishing an online account:

- In order to use Hogan assessment tools, you must have an online account. You can establish an account by contacting a Hogan consultant or the Customer Service Team. You will be required to complete a User Qualification Form and provide some basic information regarding your assessment needs. You also can establish an account by attending a Hogan Assessment Certification Workshop.

Accessing your Hogan online account:

- In order to access your Hogan online account, you will need to follow these directions:
  1. Direct your Internet browser to www2.hoganassessments.com or www.assessmentlink.com/halo
  2. Enter your User ID
  3. Enter your Password

Generating User IDs and Passwords from your account that will enable participants to complete Hogan assessments online:

- Contact the Customer Service Team if you want help generating User IDs and Passwords. Alternatively, you can participate in a Hogan online training session (45 minutes). This session will provide you with the training necessary to autonomously generate User IDs and Passwords for your clients.

Enabling participants to access the Hogan assessment platform (in order to complete the assessments):

- In order to complete the Hogan assessments online, each participant will need (a) a unique User ID and Password and (b) instructions for accessing the Hogan online assessment platform. Be sure to note that the participant login site differs from the administrative site you access for your Hogan online account.
  - Participant Access – In order to complete the assessment(s), participants should direct their Internet browser to **www.gotohogan.com**

o Online Account Access – In order to access your online account, you will need to direct your Internet browser to **www2.hoganassessments.com** or **www.assessmentlink.com/halo**

Completing Hogan assessments in non-English languages:

- The HPI, HDS, and MVPI can be administered in numerous non-English languages. Contact your Hogan consultant or the Customer Service Team for assistance with administration in non-English languages.

HOGAN ONLINE REPORTS

Based on the HPI, HDS, and MVPI, numerous different automated report options can be generated, each geared toward unique applications (see Table 46). Your Hogan consultant can help you determine which report option(s) likely will best help you satisfy your various assessment needs. Should your online account not provide you with the option of using any of the reports in Table 46, please contact the Customer Service Team at 800-756-0632.

Table 46: Hogan Report Options

Report	Purpose		Assessment Options			Description
	S	D	HPI	HDS	MVPI	
Data File	X	X	X	X	X	Data Files can be generated for each of our three main assessment tools. These brief, one-page reports provide scale scores in tabular format (the HPI data file contains subscale and occupation scale scores). Data Files do not present results in graphical or descriptive format or provide a selection recommendation.
Suitability Report [a]	X*		X	X	X	The Suitability Report compares a candidate's scores on the HPI, HDS, and/or MVPI to research-based and validated cutoff scores in order to present a selection recommendation.
BASIS Report [a]	X*		X	X	X	BASIS combines personality assessment data with the flexibility of behav oral interviewing. BASIS provides critical narrative information for making selection decisions and incorporates this information into a behavioral interviewing system. The BASIS report can be generated with or without a selection recommendation or interview guide.
Candidate Potential Reports	X*		X			As a result of the sheer quantity and quality of research conducted, we have developed off-the-shelf selection systems for several job families. Organizations can use the HPI with minimal implementation expense to evaluate applicants in terms of very general job fit categories.
Effective Coaching Report for the Manager (Management Builder Report) [b]	X	X	X			The Management Builder Report (a) uses HPI results to highlight general job-related strengths and development needs and (b) provides tips for best managing the person assessed; as such, it can be used to make informed selection decisions and facilitate new-hire on-boarding.
Career Builder Report [b]		X	X			The Career Builder Report uses HPI results to identify general job-relatec strengths and development needs, and provides detailed tips for development to the respondent.
Career Compass Report		X			X	The Career Compass Report uses MVPI results to outline the occupational significance of a person's core values and provides descriptive information to facilitate career planning processes.

* Indicates that prior validation research must be conducted prior to using the specified reports.

[a] Suitability and BASIS per report costs depend upon the number of inventories employed (e.g., one, two, or three inventories).

[b] The Career Builder Report and Effective Coaching Report for the Manager can also be used for an on-boarding process.

[c] The Leadership Coaching Report is complimentary if ordered in conjunction with the Leadership Forecast Series of Reports.

Table 46 (continued): Hogan Report Options

Report	Purpose		Assessment Options			Description
	S	**D**	**HPI**	**HDS**	**MVPI**	
Leadership Forecast Series of Reports						The Leadership Forecast Reports provide an in-depth evaluation of leadership competencies in terms of HPI, HDS, and MVPI results. These reports are highly informational and geared toward leadership or high-potential individual contributor positions. They are typically used for development or coaching purposes.
• Leadership Potential Report	X	X	X			The Potential Report explores day-to-day leadership style under normal conditions and provides comprehensive tips for development.
• Leadership Challenge Report	X	X		X		The Challenge Report explores behaviors that can inhibit leadership effectiveness in times of stress, novel or ambiguous situations, or heavy workloads and provides comprehensive tips for development.
• Leadership Values Report	X	X			X	The Values Report explores the motives, values, and goals that identify the best working environment for an individual. The Values Report also provides information regarding an individual's fit within his/her career, team, and organization, and can indicate the kind of environment a leader will create for his/her employees.
• Leadership Coaching Report [c]		X	X	X	X	The Coaching Report helps individuals integrate information from the HPI, HDS, and MVPI assessments and is designed to lead them through the development planning process. It is typically used in conjunction with the Leadership Forecast Series of Reports.
Personality Executive Summary Report	X	X	X	X	X	The Personality Executive Summary Report integrates results across the HPI, HDS, and MVPI, and provides a comprehensive, valid, and in-depth summary of a candidate's performance strengths, challenges, and values.
Group Report		X	X	X	X	The Group Report can be used to summarize (a) group/team strengths and development opportunities and (b) the cultural environment within the group, as indicated by results on the HPI, HDS, and/or MVPI.

* Indicates that prior validation research must be conducted prior to using the specified reports.

[a] Suitability and BASIS per report costs depend upon the number of inventories employed (e.g., one, two, or three inventories).

[b] The Career Builder Report and Effective Coaching Report for the Manager can also be used for an on-boarding process.

[c] The Leadership Coaching Report is complimentary if ordered in conjunction with the Leadership Forecast Series of Reports.

305

SAMPLE PARTICIPANT INVITATION LETTERS

The following are sample letters that can be used to invite participants to take Hogan assessments. These letters are designed for specific purposes, ranging from selection situations to team-building events. They all require a proper account to be set up with HAS, with User IDs and Passwords generated off the account.

Generic instruction sheet (bulleted list):

Using at least a minimum version of Microsoft Internet Explorer 4.0 or Netscape Navigator 6.2, access the assessment site by typing http://www.gotohogan.com.

1. Enter the User ID (e.g., BB123456).

2. Enter the Password (e.g., EXAMPLE).

3. Click "Logon."

4. Enter your information and click "Submit." You are ready to take assessments.

5. Click "Start Assessment."

6. Answer the assessment questionnaire by selecting the appropriate responses.

7. Click "Next" to continue. If you would like to view the previous screen, click "Previous." You can stop the assessment at any time to interrupt administration. All information submitted prior to stopping the assessment will be retained. To resume the assessment process, log back into the system using your User ID and newly created personal password.

8. Click "Submit" to complete the assessment.

9. Please select the next assessment and continue in the same fashion as before, and then continue with the same process until you have completed all of the assessments.

Please contact Hogan Assessment Systems' Customer Service Team at 1-800-756-0632 between 8:00 a.m. and 5:00 p.m. CST if you experience technical difficulties.

A letter-format instruction sheet oriented toward selection-based applications:

Month XX, Year

FirstName LastName
Address
Address

Dear XXXX,

As a component of the application process for the JOB TITLE position at
COMPANY NAME, you are respectfully being asked to complete three assessments:
the Hogan Personality Inventory (HPI), the Hogan Development Survey (HDS), and
the Motives, Values, Preferences Inventory (MVPI). Your assessment results will
automatically be sent via e-mail to COMPANY NAME/HIRING MANAGER once
you complete the three inventories, and will be maintained in Hogan Assessment
System's secure database. The results of the assessment process will provide key
decision makers with important information regarding your characteristic leadership
style and values; when combined with additional pertinent data (e.g., résumé, relevant
background, and experience), your assessment results will (a) allow COMPANY
NAME to make a valid and objective selection decision, and (b) ensure that the
ultimate selection decision maximizes job and satisfaction fit for yourself, COMPANY
NAME, and all other candidates under consideration.

The brief instructions below will allow you to complete the HPI, HDS, and MVPI
online via Hogan Assessment Systems' secure assessment platform. You will simply
need to:

1. Use Microsoft Internet Explorer 4.0 or Netscape Navigator 6.2 to access the
   Hogan assessment platform: http://www.gotohogan.com
2. Enter your User ID and Password and click "Logon"

User ID	Password
BB123456	EXAMPLE

Once you have submitted your User ID and Password, please refer to the assessment
site for the remainder of the instructions. We recommend that you allow approximately
one hour to complete all three assessments. Please contact Hogan Assessment Systems'
Customer Service Team at 1-800-756-0632 between 8:00 a.m. and 5:00 p.m. CST if you
experience technical difficulties. Please direct any other questions regarding the JOB
TITLE assessment process to NAME at COMPANY at PHONE NUMBER.

307

A letter-format instruction sheet oriented toward development-based applications:

Month XX, Year

FirstName LastName
Address
Address

Dear XXXX,

As a component of the coaching process at COMPANY NAME, you are respectfully being asked to complete three assessments: the Hogan Personality Inventory (HPI; a measure of day-to-day interaction style), Hogan Development Survey (HDS; a measure of characteristics that can inhibit job performance), and the Motives, Values, Preferences Inventory (MVPI; a measure of values and drivers), the results of which will provide you and YOUR COACH with the information you will need to capitalize on performance strengths, strategically target development needs, and devise an action plan for bringing about behavioral change. Your assessment results will automatically be sent via e-mail to NAME once you complete the three inventories, and will be maintained in Hogan Assessment Systems' secure database.

The brief instructions below will allow you to complete the HPI, HDS, and MVPI online via Hogan Assessment Systems' secure assessment platform. You will simply need to:

1. Use Microsoft Internet Explorer 4.0 or Netscape Navigator 6.2 to access the Hogan assessment platform: http://www.gotohogan.com
2. Enter your User ID and Password and click "Logon"

User ID	Password
BB123456	EXAMPLE

Once you have submitted your User ID and Password, please refer to the assessment site for the remainder of the instructions. We recommend that you allow approximately one hour to complete all three assessments. Please contact Hogan Assessment Systems' Customer Service Team at 1-800-756-0632 between 8:00 a.m. and 5:00 p.m. CST if you experience technical difficulties. Please direct any other questions regarding the assessment process to NAME at COMPANY at PHONE NUMBER.

A letter-format instruction sheet oriented toward team-based applications:

Month XX, Year

FirstName LastName
Address
Address

Dear XXXX,

As a component of the COMPANY NAME Executive Team-Building Retreat that will occur on DATES, you are respectfully being asked to complete three assessments: the Hogan Personality Inventory (HPI; a measure of day-to-day interaction style), the Hogan Development Survey (HDS; a measure of characteristics that can inhibit job performance), and the Motives, Values, Preferences Inventory (MVPI; a measure of values and drivers). The Hogan assessments will form the basis for a team-building session during the retreat that will focus on (a) capitalizing on team strengths, uncovering potential barriers to team success, and identifying the team's predominant values and (b) how this information relates to the Executive Team's ability to accomplish its strategic goals.

In order to ensure that the team-building component of the retreat is maximally successful, prior to the retreat, Hogan Assessment Systems would like to provide you with individualized feedback on your assessment results. The individualized feedback you will receive will serve as a foundation for using the assessment results in an aggregate fashion during the retreat.

The HPI, HDS, and MVPI can be completed online, with a time commitment of approximately one hour. The instructions on the following page contain all of the information you will need to log on to the Hogan online system and complete the assessment process. Once you have completed the assessments, you will be contacted by NAME regarding scheduling a date and time for your individualized feedback session (which will require approximately 1 to 1.5 hours of your time). Given that the retreat is rapidly approaching, I recommend that you complete the assessment process at your earliest convenience to allow for the greatest degree of flexibility with respect to scheduling your feedback session.

Please do not hesitate to contact me should you have any questions regarding the Hogan assessment process or the upcoming retreat. Have a wonderful week!

A sample prefeedback letter:

Month XX, Year

FirstName LastName
Address
Address

Dear XXXX,

As a component of your coaching and development process, you were provided the opportunity to complete the Hogan Personality Inventory (HPI; a measure of day-to-day interaction style), the Hogan Development Survey (HDS; a measure of characteristics that can inhibit job performance), and the Motives, Values, Preferences Inventory (MVPI; a measure of values and drivers). I have attached copies of your assessment results, which were scored in terms of our Leadership Forecast Series of Reports. The Leadership Forecast Series is composed of four reports:

- Leadership Forecast Potential Report (based on HPI results)

- Leadership Forecast Challenge Report (based on HDS results)

- Leadership Forecast Values Report (based on MVPI results)

- Leadership Forecast Coaching Report (integrates HPI, HDS, & MVPI results)

Although your first impulse may be to review all of the reports prior to your feedback session, I want to suggest you wait until *after* you have received feedback to formulate a final impression regarding the results. I make this suggestion for a couple of reasons:

- There are 28 main scales and 42 subscales across all three assessments, which is a lot of information.

- The potential interactions between the scales are numerous, leaving open the opportunity for misinterpretation. Many of the scales are psychological in nature and therefore easy to misinterpret. For example, the Leadership Forecast Challenge Report provides insight regarding behaviors that arise only under certain situations, not day-to-day reaction style, as described by the Leadership Forecast Potential Report.

For a quick overview of your assessment results, I recommend focusing on pages 11–14 of the Leadership Coaching Report, which integrates your results across the assessments. When glancing at the Leadership Forecast Potential, Challenge, and Values Reports you will see that you have high, average, and low scores on all three assessments. That is perfectly normal and what we see in almost all participants. High scores are not always better and low scores are not always worse. Realize these are assessments of your personality characteristics, not a test of "good" and "bad."

To prepare for your feedback session, you will need to print page 20 of the Leadership Forecast Potential Report and page 5 of both the Leadership Forecast Challenge and Values Reports. NAME, I look forward to talking with you on DAY at TIME (I will expect your call at (PHONE NUMBER). In the meantime, please don't hesitate to let me know if you have any questions regarding the assessments or the feedback process.

HOGAN MARKETING MATERIALS

There are many occasions when it would be helpful to have materials to explain Hogan inventories and our approach to personality assessment. The following section includes descriptions and locations of some of our marketing materials available to the public. We also have included some descriptive information regarding the positioning of Hogan inventories to internal or external customers.

1. Location of Hogan marketing materials:

   The HAS Web site, www.hoganassessments.com, will provide you and your clients with a considerable amount of information regarding Hogan assessments and related applications, services, reports, and, in general, personality as it relates to work. The Hogan Web site will provide you with access to key Hogan marketing materials, including brochures and sample reports.

2. Positioning Hogan tools against other assessment tools:

   We have found that, by presenting the information below and appealing to potential clients' sensibilities, a clear case for the use of the Hogan tools emerges. Our rationale is as follows:

   a. Assessment tools are used to predict job performance. If an assessment is not directly related to job performance or does not otherwise facilitate understanding regarding how a person will perform, use of the assessment tool will waste time and money. The HPI, HDS, and MVPI are the result of 44 cumulative years of development, refinement, and validation; across more than 400 validation studies conducted to date, research results demonstrate that (a) the Hogan assessments predict performance in jobs ranging from entry level to CEO and (b) the Hogan tools predict performance in a demographics-blind manner (i.e., mean scale scores do not vary significantly by gender, age, or race).

   b. If you think about performance, 100% is available for "capture" (can be measured). Assessments should try to measure as much of this job performance "pie" as possible.

   c. Hogan thinks about job performance in terms of four very broad, yet simple, categories:
      - Technical (what a person knows, what they have done, their cognitive abilities, their competence). Technical competence is typically measured via résumé screens, interviews, and cognitive ability measures.

- Job Fit Positive (how a person reacts in routine situations or their day-to-day interaction style). Job Fit Positive pertains to how a person approaches others and their job on a day-to-day basis and is measured by the HPI. We sometimes call this the "bright side" of personality.
- Job Fit Negative (how a person reacts under stressful conditions and conditions of uncertainty). These characteristics show up under times of stress and inhibit a person's ability to (a) achieve work through other people and (b) get ahead in the workplace. Job Fit Negative is measured by the HDS. We sometimes call this the "dark side" of personality.
- Satisfaction Fit (how well a person will fit into a job/work group/department/company and their predominant motivators and values). An individual's motivations and preferences facilitate an understanding of how satisfied they will be in certain situations and, as leaders, the type of work environment they will create. Satisfaction Fit is measured by the MVPI. We sometimes call this the "inside" of personality.

d. At least 95% of assessment tools available to measure personality directly compete with the HPI. We believe that our research, ROI numbers, and worldwide approach exceed that of the competition.

e. There are few (if any) assessments of derailment characteristics (HDS) or satisfaction/motivators/values (MVPI) available, and even if they exist, the research associated with the tools is weak compared to ours.

Given the above, here is some information regarding the "sales" process. If you think about the performance "pie," your selling point is less about competing against someone else (and their assessment tools) and more about helping the client (a) to agree that accurate measurement of performance entails measurement of all four pieces of the performance "pie" and (b) to look at competing instruments and determine whether Hogan or the competition measures performance better (more accurately and reliably) and more completely.

The Hogan approach is as follows. First, determine which piece of the "pie" the _____ (insert assessment) measures. Second, show that Hogan offers an assessment that provides similar insight (HPI). Third, demonstrate that the HPI has a much firmer research background and record of success. Fourth, highlight the other pieces of the pie that are not measured. Fifth, point out that Hogan offers reports that pull all of our assessments and the "pie" together (e.g., the Leadership Forecast Coaching Report). For example, we frequently make statements similar to the following: "The HPI and _____ measure the same thing, and though we believe we measure it better and more accurately and reliably, they are in the same assessment arena. We also offer the HDS and MVPI, which measure two different aspects of personality untouched by the _____. So, even if you want to purchase the _____, your assessment process will not be complete without the HDS and MVPI. And, if you use all three assessments, you can combine reporting and ease of use."

EVALUATING AN ASSESSMENT PROVIDER

Currently, in excess of 2,500 assessment publishers exist within the United States alone. Organizations seeking partners to provide assessment tools face a challenge when evaluating these numerous assessment publishers, given that (a) no barriers exist with respect to entry into the test publication industry (i.e., anyone can create an assessment and start selling it), (b) few industry guidelines exist (i.e., there are few standards available and publicized to aid organizations with respect to evaluating various assessments), and (c) there is no policing of the industry (i.e., assessment vendors face no ramifications for low-quality assessments). Hogan Assessment Systems has taken a leadership role with respect to helping consumers of assessment tools evaluate the quality of the assessment tools they are investigating. The following table (see Table 47) highlights key questions that consumers of assessment tools should ask potential assessment providers. The aforementioned document also can be found online by directing your Internet browser to the following site: http://www.hoganassessments.com/about_hogan/checklist.aspx.

Table 47: Key Questions to Ask Your Test Vendor

Question	Hogan Response
1. What are the assessments designed to do relative to the needs/goals of the customer?	HAS assessments are designed to do three things: (1) Evaluate the basic employability of an applicant (is the person honest, will the person come to work, will the person be accident prone, can the person provide competent customer service); (2) Determine if the person fits the job (extraverts are needed for sales positions, introverts are needed for long-distance truck drivers); (3) Provide a solid basis for coaching or development.
2. Is the provider a member of the American Psychological Association (APA), Society of Industrial/Organizational Psychology (SIOP), or another professional organization that mandates ethical and statistical guidelines for creating assessments?	Drs. Joyce and Robert Hogan are Fellows of Division 5 (Measurement and Assessment), Division 8 (Personality and Social Psychology), and Division 14 (Industrial and Organizational Psychology) of the American Psychological Association.
3. Have the tests been reviewed in Buros' Mental Measurement Yearbook?	All of the tests offered by HAS have been reviewed (positively) in Buros.
4. Is each test supported by a test manual that is organized according to the Uniform Guidelines on Employee Selection Procedures?	The test manuals for HAS assessments are exemplary; they contain full information on the development and validation of the inventories.
5. Does the provider supply technical reports containing competent validity studies (as defined by the Uniform Guidelines) using the tests in real organizations?	HAS has a library of technical reports containing competent validity studies, prepared according to the Uniform Guidelines, describing research conducted with adults in real organizations.
6. Can the provider produce a summary of validation results for jobs similar to the one under consideration?	HAS can provide a summary for validation results for virtually every job in the U.S. economy.
7. What standardized validation process is followed before the provider implements a selection test in an organization?	HAS scrupulously follows the procedures outlined in the Uniform Guidelines, as can be determined by reading any of our technical reports.

Table 47 (continued): Key Questions to Ask Your Test Vendor

Question	Hogan Response
8. How are cutoff scores established for selection purposes?	Before cutoff scores can be established, it is necessary to demonstrate that the assessment is a valid predictor of performance in the job under question. Once validity has been established, cutoff scores are defined, using bivariate plots that maximize the number of true negatives and true positives for each score distribution.
9. What process does the provider use to systematically evaluate the performance of the tests it recommends?	HAS encourages organizations to revalidate selection procedures on a periodic basis. The revalidation involves demonstrating that the test (and cut scores) continues to remain valid for the job under consideration.
10. Does the provider maintain a research archive that can be accessed to confirm the results of individual validity studies?	HAS maintains an extensive research archive, searchable by outside researchers, that can be used to confirm the results of previous validity studies.
11. What is the provider's policy for supporting customers in the event of a legal challenge to the use of a test?	HAS will provide any customer with supporting documentation should the validity research, on the basis of which a selection process rests, be challenged.
12. Has the provider been involved in any legal challenges of a test, and if so, what was the outcome?	HAS selection procedures and validation research have never been challenged successfully.

Table 47 (continued): Key Questions to Ask Your Test Vendor

Question	Hogan Response
13. What was the most recent date of your product's validity and reliability studies?	HAS is, first and foremost, a research based organization; as such, all Hogan tools are updated regularly on the basis of (a) rigorously conducted research and (b) the resulting continual growth of our research archive of matched assessment data and job performance indicators. All Hogan research, recommended implementation strategies (e.g., cutoff scores), and technical documents conform both to guidelines and best practices defined in the Principles for the Validation and Use of Personnel Selection Procedures and the Uniform Guidelines. The 3rd edition of the HPI Technical Manual will be released in 2007.
14. What were the final scores from these studies? (.50, .60, .80, etc.)	Meta-analyses of HPI scales indicate that the estimated true validities for six of the seven HPI scales for predicting job performance are as follows: Adjustment (.43), Ambition (.35), Interpersonal Sensitivity (.34), Prudence (.36), Inquisitive (.34), and Learning Approach (.25). The HPI internal factor structure supports seven scales. The average alpha for all scales is .80, and test-retest reliabilities range from .74 to .86. Research indicates the average alpha for all of the MVPI scales is .77, and test-retest reliabilities range from .64 to .88.

SUMMARY

This chapter offered a variety of information that can be helpful when using Hogan tools. Under most circumstances, you can call our main number at 800-756-0632 and be directed to the right person to help you with any information that we covered. We also strongly encourage anyone wishing to work with Hogan tools to have a consultant assigned to them for support. It does not cost anything, and our consultants are dedicated to helping customers make effective use of Hogan tools and resources.

BIBLIOGRAPHY

Allport, G. W. (1961). *Pattern and growth in personality*. New York: Holt, Rinehart, and Winston.

Allport, G. W., Vernon, P. E., & Lindzey, G. (1960). *Study of values* (3rd ed.). Boston: Houghton-Mifflin.

American Psychiatric Association. (1987). *Diagnostic and statistical manual of mental disorders* (3rd ed., rev.). Washington, DC: American Psychiatric Association.

American Psychiatric Association. (1994). *Diagnostic and statistical manual of mental disorders* (4th ed.). Washington, DC: American Psychiatric Association.

Americans with Disabilities Act of 1990 102(b)(7), 42 U.S.C.A. 12112.

Bentz, V. J. (1985, August). *A view from the top: A thirty year perspective of research devoted to discovery, description, and prediction of executive behavior.* Paper presented at the 93rd Annual Convention of the American Psychological Association, Los Angeles.

Browne, J. (2002). *Charles Darwin: The power of place*. New York: Knopf.

Butcher, J. N., Dahlstrom, W. G., Graham, J. R., Tellegen, A., & Kaemmer, B. (1989). *Minnesota Multiphasic Personality Inventory (MMPI-2): Manual for administration and scoring*. Minneapolis: University of Minnesota Press.

Digman, J. M. (1990). Personality structure: Emergence of the Five Factor model. *Annual Review of Psychology*, 41, 417–440.

Goldberg, L. R. (1992). The development of markers for the Big Five factor structure. *Psychological Assessment*, 4, 26–42.

Gough, H. G. (1975). *Manual for the California Psychological Inventory* (rev. ed.). Palo Alto, CA: Consulting Psychologists Press.

Gregory, S. (1992, May). *Noncognitive measures for Army technical training placement.* Paper presented at the Seventh Annual Meeting of the Society for Industrial-Organizational Psychology, Inc. Montreal, Canada.

Hase, H. D., & Goldberg, L. R. (1967). Comparative validities of different strategies of constructing personality inventory scales. Psychological Bulletin, 67, 231–248.

Hathaway, S. R., & McKinley, J. C. (1943). *Manual for the Minnesota Multiphasic Personality Inventory*. New York: Psychological Corporation.

Hazucha, J. F. (1991). *Success, jeopardy, and performance: Contrasting managerial outcomes and their predictors.* Unpublished doctoral dissertation, University of Minnesota, Minneapolis.

Hogan, J., & Hogan, R. (1991). *Levels of analysis in big five theory: The structure of self-description.* Paper presented at the Sixth Annual Conference of the Society for Industrial and Organizational Psychology. St. Louis, MO.

Hogan, J., & Holland, B. (2003). Using theory to evaluate personality and job-performance relations: A socioanalytic perspective. *Journal of Applied Psychology*, 88, 100–112.

Hogan, R., Hogan, J., & Roberts, B. W. (1996). Personality measurement and employment decisions: Questions and answers. *American Psychologist*, 51, 469–477.

Hogan, R., & Warrenfeltz, R. (2003). Educating the modern manager. *Academy of Management Learning and Education*, 2: 74–84.

Holland, J. L. (1966). *The psychology of vocational choice: A theory of personality types and model environments.* Waltham, MA: Ginn.

Holland, J. L. (1985). *Making vocational choices: A theory of vocational personalities and work environments* (2nd ed.). Englewood Cliffs, NJ: Prentice-Hall.

Holland, J. L. (1987). *1987 manual supplement for the Self-Directed Search.* Odessa, FL: Psychological Assessment Resources.

Horney, K. (1950). *Neurosis and human growth.* New York: Norton.

Hough, L. M. (1992). The "Big-Five" personality variables—construct confusion: Description versus prediction. *Human Performance*, 5, 139–156.

Jenkyns, R. (2003) Victorian selection (a review of Janet Browne's Charles Darwin). *The New Republic*, 4, 597, 31–34.

John, O. P. (1990). The "Big-Five" factor taxonomy: Dimensions of personality in the natural language and in questionnaires. In L. A. Pervin (Ed.), *Handbook of personality theory and research* (pp. 66–100). New York: Guilford.

Jones, W. H. (1988). *User's manual for PROFILE.* Unpublished report.

Kamp, J. D., & Hough, L. M. (1986). Utility of personality assessment: A review and integration of the literature. In. L. M. Hough (Ed.), *Utility of temperament, biodata and interest assessment for predicting job performance: A review and integration of the literature* (ARI Research Note No. 88–02, pp. 1–90). Alexandria: U.S. Army Research Institute for the Behavioral and Social Sciences.

Leary, T. (1957). *Interpersonal diagnosis of personality.* New York: Ronald Press.

Lombardo, M. M., Ruderman, M. N., & McCauley, C. D. (1988). Explanations of success and derailment in upper-level management positions. *Journal of Business and Psychology*, 2, 199–216.

McAdams, D. (1993). *The stories we live by: Personal myths and the making of the self.* New York: William Morrow.

McCall, M. W., Jr., & Lombardo, M. M. (1983). *Off the track: Why and how successful executives get derailed* (Tech. Rep. No. 21). Greensboro, NC: Center for Creative Leadership.

McCrae, R. R., & Costa, P. T., Jr. (1987). Validity of the five-factor model of personality across instruments and observers. *Journal of Personality and Social Psychology*, 52, 81–90.

McGovern, J., Lindemann, M., Vergara, M., Murphy, S., Barker, L., & Warrenfeltz, R. (2001). Maximizing the impact of executive coaching: Behavioral change, organizational outcomes, and return on investment. *The Manchester Review*, 6, 3–11.

Millikin-Davies, M. A. (1992). *An exploration of flawed first-line supervision.* Unpublished doctoral dissertation, University of Tulsa, Tulsa.

Murray, H. A. (1938). *Explorations in personality: A clinical and experimental study of fifty men of college age.* New York: The Oxford University Press.

Norman, W. T. (1963). Toward an adequate taxonomy of personality attributes: Replicated factor structure in peer nomination personality ratings. *Journal of Abnormal and Social Psychology*, 66, 574–583.

Novacek, J., and Lazarus, R. S. (1990). The structure of personal commitments. *Journal of Personality*, 58, 693–715.

Spranger, E. (1928). *Types of men: The psychology and ethics of personality.* Halle: Max Niemeyer Verlag.

Schmitt, N. (2004). Beyond the big five: Increases in understanding and practical utility. *Human Performance*, 17, 347–357.

Thornton, G. C. III, & Byham, W. C. (1982). *Assessment centers and managerial performance*. New York: Academic Press.

Thurstone, L. L. (1934). The vectors of mind. *Psychological Review*, 41, 1–32.

Tupes, E. C., & Christal, R. E. (1961). *Recurrent personality factors based on trait ratings* (Tech. Rep. No. ASD-TR-61-97). Lackland Air Force Base, TX: Aeronautical Systems Division, Personnel Laboratory.

Wiggins, J. S. (1979). A psychological taxonomy of trait-descriptive terms: The interpersonal domain. *Journal of Personality and Social Psychology*, 37, 395–412.

Wiggins, J. S. (1996). *The Five-Factor Model of personality*. New York: Guilford.

Wiggins, J. S., & Pincus, A. L. (1992). Personality structure and assessment. *Annual Review of Psychology*, 43, 473–504.

Zonderman, A. B. (1980). *Inventory construction by the method of homogenous item composites*. Unpublished manuscript, The Johns Hopkins University, Baltimore.

INDEX

A

Accomplishment, 35, 52, 74, 78, 98–101, 103, 149, 152, 155, 158, 161, 168, 171, 174, 178, 204, 237, 241, 282

Actor's View, 14

Adjustment, 22, 25, 29–32, 40, 124, 127, 130, 132, 135, 137, 140, 144, 147, 150, 153, 156, 159, 163, 166, 168, 175–176, 178, 186, 195, 199–212, 217, 226, 228, 230, 238, 240, 242, 250, 252–253, 260–261, 273, 286, 295, 316

Adverse Impact, 12, 301

Aesthetics, 89, 97, 114–115, 142, 146, 149, 152, 155, 158, 161–162, 173–174, 182, 194, 228, 240, 273

Affiliation, 89–91, 97, 106–107, 142, 146, 149, 152, 155, 158, 161–163, 173–175, 179, 181, 183, 195, 228, 240, 273, 286

Agreeableness, 15–16, 20

Altruistic, 89–90, 97, 104–105, 142, 146, 149, 152, 155, 158, 161, 173–174, 179, 181, 186, 195, 228, 237, 240, 273, 286

Ambition, 22, 24–25, 29, 33, 34–35, 38, 89–90, 124–125, 127–128, 130, 132, 135, 137, 140, 144, 147, 150, 153, 156, 159, 162–163, 166–168, 175–179, 182, 194, 199–204, 206–210, 212, 221–225, 228, 230, 234–238, 240, 242, 262, 273, 286, 316

Arrogance, 57, 63, 130, 171, 178, 222, 234

Assessment Platform, 300, 302, 307–308

Assessment Profile, 230, 241–242, 268, 301

Assessment Results, 198, 228–229, 240, 247, 250, 263–265, 270, 272–273, 299, 307–310

Attributes, 54, 136, 166, 190–192, 196–197

Aversions, 92–93

Avoidant, 54, 57, 110

Avoids Trouble, 44, 167

B

Beliefs, 55, 58, 60, 92–93, 108, 172, 180, 226, 229

Bold, 36, 57, 63, 74, 132–135, 138, 141, 145, 148, 151, 154, 157, 160, 162, 166, 171, 178, 180, 182, 194, 199–212, 221–223, 225, 228, 234–235, 238, 240, 242, 261, 272–273, 279, 286

Bright Side, 20, 60, 134, 254–255, 312

Business Domain, 194, 199–201, 293

Business Skills, 192, 216, 219, 224, 229, 232, 236, 241, 271

C

California Psychological Inventory (CPI), 20–21

Calmness, 32, 64

Career-derailing Tendencies, 13

Caring, 41, 70, 90

No Social Anxiety, 35, 177

Norm Data, 27, 62, 95

Normal Personality, 13, 20–22, 53, 166

Not Anxious, 32, 253

Not Autonomous, 44, 169, 253

Not Spontaneous, 44, 167

O

Observer's View, 14

Occupational Preferences, 92–93

Online Account, 301–303

Openness to Experience, 20, 22

Organizational, 12, 16, 42, 44, 48, 55, 88, 94, 104, 116, 139, 143, 169, 172, 186, 195, 250, 260, 288, 314

P

Perfectionism, 58, 63

Performance Implications, 30–31, 33–34, 36–37, 39–40, 42–43, 45–46, 48–49, 64–85, 98, 100, 102, 104, 106, 108, 110, 112–114, 116–117, 122–123, 182, 256

Performance Risks, 52–53, 55, 59, 62

Personality Assessment, 12, 20–21, 53, 268, 304, 311

Personality Characteristics, 130, 167–168, 179–180, 191, 310

Personality Profiles, 268

Personality Psychology, 13

Personnel Decisions International, 59

Power, 22, 54, 74, 89–90, 97, 100–101, 122, 130, 134, 136, 139, 142, 146, 149, 152, 155, 158, 161–163, 173–174, 179–180, 182, 185, 194, 207, 225, 228, 230, 237, 240, 242, 260, 262, 273, 286

Predictor, 12, 15, 61, 198, 315

Preferred Associates, 92–93

PROFILE, 55, 57–58, 61

Prudence, 23, 25, 29, 36, 42–45, 124–130, 132, 134–137, 140, 144, 147, 150, 153, 156, 159, 162–163, 167–169, 175–178, 180, 184, 195, 199–200, 202–203, 205, 207–212, 217, 225–226, 228, 236–237, 240, 242, 253, 273, 286, 294, 316

R

Reading, 50, 113, 177, 257, 262, 314

Recognition, 22, 36, 75, 89–90, 97–99, 142, 146, 149, 152, 155, 158, 161, 173–174, 185, 195, 221–223, 225, 228, 231, 240, 251, 273, 286, 290

Report Options, 303–305

Reputation, 14–15, 22, 55, 172, 190, 268, 277, 290–291, 293, 296

Research Archive, 27, 95, 197, 315–316

Reserved, 36–37, 54, 57, 63, 70, 81, 98, 102, 125, 128, 132–135, 138, 141, 145, 148, 151, 154, 157, 160, 162, 171, 177, 181, 183, 186, 195, 203–209, 228, 240, 255–256, 273

V

W

About Hogan Assessment Systems

We are a premium test publishing company that uses a comprehensive suite of personality assessments to help companies select employees, develop leaders, and identify talent. We help organizations maximize their human resources through our vast library of research and scientifically based predictive power. We are the science of personality.

Our history is defined by the business applications of personality. This dates back to the 1930s when assessment centers were used to select individuals for dangerous wartime assignments. Rooted in this tradition, Dr. Robert Hogan developed the Hogan Personality Inventory in the 1970s—it was the first measure of normal personality designed specifically for business applications. He spent more than 15 years accumulating mountains of evidence demonstrating that this personality inventory would predict job performance. And he was right. The first commercial applications of the inventory began in the very early 1980s, and in 1987, Drs. Robert and Joyce Hogan founded Hogan Assessment Systems to make this science available to the business community. Today, we continue to build our position as the innovative leader in providing scientifically based personality assessment, development, and talent management solutions for business and industry.

Quick Facts

- Hogan Personality Inventory was introduced in 1980
- Hogan Assessment Systems was founded in 1987
- Owners – Dr. Robert Hogan, Dr. Joyce Hogan, Dr. Rodney Warrenfeltz
- Hogan Assessment Systems has local distributors in more than 30 countries
- We have provided assessment services to more than 1,500 companies worldwide
- Performance data are available for more than 400 jobs, ranging from janitor to CEO
- Millions of job applicants have completed the Hogan Personality Inventory

- Assessments are available via Internet platform 24/7
- Reports are available in more than 20 languages
- Assessments administered and scored online with results available in 60 seconds
- Nearly 60% of the Fortune 100 companies have trusted our inventories to help them produce positive business results

EXPERTISE

Employee selection, perhaps more than any other process in an organization, has the power to change a company's destiny. We design and implement selection systems aimed at improving bottom-line business results.

Employee development reports provide important insights to help employees develop to their full career potential. Our assessments help companies determine the right fit for each employee and provide feedback to develop each person into his/her most valuable role within the organization.

Talent management is now recognized by organizations as a key factor in their future growth. Our talent management expertise helps organizations identify talent, which we define in terms of personality, cognitive ability, and leadership potential.

OUR INVENTORIES

Hogan Personality Inventory (HPI) – The bright side of the personality—what we see when people are at their best.

Hogan Development Survey (HDS) – The dark side of the personality—what we see when people are stressed.

Motives, Values, Preferences Inventory (MVPI) – The inside of personality—reveals a person's core values, goals, and interests.

Hogan Business Reasoning Inventory (HBRI) – The reasoning aspect of cognitive ability—measures the reasoning skills necessary for success in a business environment.